A Legal History of the Civil War and Reconstruction

Although hundreds of thousands of people died fighting in the Civil War, perhaps the war's biggest casualty was the nation's legal order. *A Legal History of the Civil War and Reconstruction* explores the implications of this major change by bringing legal history into dialogue with the scholarship of other historical fields. Federal policy on slavery and race, particularly the three Reconstruction Amendments, are the best-known legal innovations of the era. Change, however, permeated all levels of the legal system, altering Americans' relationship to the law and allowing them to move popular conceptions of justice into the ambit of government policy. The results linked Americans to the nation through individual rights, which were extended to more people and, as a result of new claims, were reimagined to cover a wider array of issues. But rights had limits in what they could accomplish, particularly when it came to the collective goals that so many ordinary Americans advocated. Ultimately, Laura F. Edwards argues, this new nation of rights offered up promises that would prove difficult to sustain.

Laura F. Edwards is the Peabody Family Professor of History at Duke University. Her book *The People and Their Peace: Legal Culture and the Transformation of Inequality in the Post-Revolutionary South* was awarded the American Historical Association's 2009 Littleton-Griswold Prize for the best book in law and society and the Southern Historical Association's Charles Sydnor Prize for the best book in southern history.

New Histories of American Law

Series Editors

Michael Grossberg *Indiana University*
Christopher L. Tomlins *University of California-Irvine*

New Histories of American Law is a series of bold, synthetic, and concise inter-pretive books that will cover all the key topics in American legal history, written by leading scholars in the field and intended for student use in colleges and law schools.

Other Books in the Series

Elizabeth Dale, *Criminal Justice in the United States, 1789–1939*
Jack P. Greene, *The Constitutional Origins of the American Revolution*
Barbara Young Welke, *Law and the Borders of Belonging in the Long Nineteenth Century United States*

A Legal History of the Civil War and Reconstruction

A Nation of Rights

LAURA F. EDWARDS

Duke University

CAMBRIDGE
UNIVERSITY PRESS

CAMBRIDGE
UNIVERSITY PRESS

32 Avenue of the Americas, New York NY 10013-2473, USA

Cambridge University Press is part of the University of Cambridge.

It furthers the University's mission by disseminating knowledge in the pursuit of education, learning and research at the highest international levels of excellence.

www.cambridge.org
Information on this title: www.cambridge.org/9781107401341

First published 2015

A catalogue record for this publication is available from the British Library

Library of Congress Cataloguing in Publication data
Edwards, Laura F., author.
A legal history of the Civil War and Reconstruction : a nation of rights / Laura F. Edwards, Duke University.
pages   cm – (New histories of American law)
Includes bibliographical references and index.
ISBN 978-1-107-00879-3 (hardback) – ISBN 978-1-107-40134-1 (paperback)
1. Law – United States – History – 19th century.   2. Civil rights – History – 19th century.   3. African Americans – Legal status, laws, etc. – History – 19th century.   4. United States – History – Civil War, 1861–1865 – Law and legislation.   5. Reconstruction (U.S. history, 1865–1877)   I. Title.
KF366.E39   2015
349.7309′034–dc23   2014033240

ISBN 978-1-107-00879-3 Hardback
ISBN 978-1-107-40134-1 Paperback

For John,
Again.

Contents

Acknowledgments

When Chris Tomlins and Mike Grossberg invited me to write the chapter on the Civil War and Reconstruction for *The Cambridge History of Law in America*, I resisted. I had just published my first book on Reconstruction, was finishing my second book on women in the Civil War era, and wanted to leave the period behind and move on to a new project. I tried to say no. In fact, if memory serves (which, admittedly, it often does not), I said no twice. Chris and Mike, however, kept coming back, and I finally agreed to the project. At the time, I was unsure about that decision. Now I cannot thank them enough for their persistence or their faith in me. Handing over the chapter on the Civil War and Reconstruction, with its voluminous and contentious historiography, to a then-junior scholar whose work had focused more on gender than on legal history was a gamble that others would not have taken. In fact, I realize now that my initial hesitance was as much about my own doubts about this particular intellectual challenge as it was about my eagerness to move on to a new project that I thought – mistakenly – was unconnected to this one. I am now grateful that I took on *The Cambridge History of Law in America* essay. The essay and this book (which is based on that essay) have challenged me in ways I never anticipated and have changed the way I think about the nineteenth century more generally. I am even more grateful to Chris and Mike, whose encouragement and support saw me through.

I also owe a huge debt to the undergraduate students who have taken my U.S. legal history courses and my U.S. women's history courses. I worked through the ideas in this book through those courses over the past fifteen years. My students were, unknowingly, engaged in the process of revision with each comment they made and each question they asked. Their input has added immeasurably to this book.

Nancy MacLean, Lisa Levenstein, and Jacquelyn Hall read the first half of the manuscript at a critical moment, and their feedback was crucial in framing the book's analysis, setting its tone, and keeping its author on track. Greg Downs, Kate Masur, and Mike Ross generously read and commented on drafts of the entire manuscript, and their comments have strengthened the analysis enormously. The conference "The World the Civil War Made," organized by Kate and Greg with Bill Blair at Penn State University, provided a particularly important intellectual space for thinking through some of the big issues in the book toward the end of the writing process. I also benefited from feedback at a workshop at the University of Oregon Law School, the Third Biennial UnCivil Wars Conference at the University of Georgia, and a seminar at the History Department, University of Tennessee. The comments of two anonymous readers on the initial proposal were particularly engaged and thoughtful, and they helped me enormously in crafting this manuscript.

I may have resisted the project initially, but I had more fun writing this book than I have had writing any other book. The opportunity to read widely, explore connections among various strands of the scholarship, and put all those ideas together in narrative form was incredibly rewarding. That experience owes to the uninterrupted time made possible by a John Simon Guggenheim Postdoctoral Fellowship, and I thank the Guggenheim Foundation for seeing the promise in this project and providing the opportunity to realize its potential. I also thank Duke University for providing leave that allowed me to take a full year to write.

This book is dedicated to my husband, John McAllister, as are my last book and my first book. That is because he has been and always will be the center of my world.

Introduction

To read an American newspaper in 1860 was to trip constantly over invocations of the U.S. Constitution, usually stated with vigor and passion and infused with a sense of utter righteousness. "A Crime to Sustain the Law and the Constitution," screamed the *Weekly Wisconsin Patriot*, in an article defending the state's refusal to enforce the Fugitive Slave Act (1850) or to recognize the U.S. Supreme Court's ruling in *Dred Scott* (1857). The Fugitive Slave Act, which required local and state authorities to aid in the capture of escaped slaves, had never been popular in the free states (states that had abolished slavery). *Dred Scott* dramatically raised the stakes by allowing slaveholders not only to take slaves into free states and territories but also to keep them enslaved there indefinitely, in violation of those states' and territories' laws.[1] For the editors of the *Weekly Wisconsin Patriot* the Constitution justified their opposition to federal policies that – as they saw it – elevated the protection of slavery over state laws that had abolished property in slaves. But those on the other side of the argument also invoked the Constitution. So far as the *Augusta Chronicle* was concerned, the Fugitive Slave Act was completely constitutional. So was property in slaves. The problem was the "reckless band of disorganizers" in the

---

[1] "A Crime to Sustain the Law and the Constitution," 14 January 1860, *Weekly Wisconsin Patriot*, vol. 6, issue 43, p. 4, at America's Historical Newspapers, http://infoweb.newsbank.com.proxy.lib.duke.edu/iw-search/we/HistArchive?p_product=EANX&p_action=timeframes&p_theme=ahnp&p_nbid=R56P57J LMTQxNTY0OTY4OC4yNTI2NDQ6MT0xMz0xNTIuMy4xMDIuMjQy &p_clear_search=&s_search_type=timeframes&d_lastaction=&d_ETC=&s_category=none&d_refprod=EANX&s_browseRef. Fugitive Slave Act, 9 U.S. Statutes at Large 462 (1850). *Dred Scott v. Sandford* 60 U.S. 393 (1857).

North "working to force the common government in a position ... to override the Constitution."[2]

Therein lay the conflict that led to secession. Critics of slavery feared that federal policies would perpetuate the institution and even allow for its extension into free states. Proponents of slavery feared that federal policies would undermine the power of slave states to maintain slavery. Yet the similarities were as striking as the differences. Both sides held up the Constitution, and the legal order it established, as the ultimate authority, the one that trumped all others. References to the Constitution were so ubiquitous on both sides of the debate that a traveler with no knowledge of context might be excused for confusion as to the nature of the sectional crisis. All the arguments came back to the U.S Constitution. Everyone revered it and claimed it as their own.

The Civil War was as much about Americans' belief in their legal order as in their disagreements over it. At the outbreak of the conflict, secessionists advocated an extreme view of states' rights, while their opponents predicted the end of the Union should such a position prevail. Yet the polarized rhetoric overstated the differences between the two sections. Federalism – the relative balance of legal authority between states and the federal government that defined the rhetoric of states' rights – had not always divided the nation into opposing geographic sections. At the time of the nation's founding, political leaders from slaveholding states were among those who favored a stronger federal government. In 1832, during South Carolina's Nullification Crisis, most southern political leaders still rejected the extreme states' rights position of the radicals in that state. Even in subsequent decades, as states' rights became a lightning rod for sectional differences, the rhetoric did not accurately describe federalism's practical dynamics. Political leaders shifted back and forth, depending on the issue and their strategy for obtaining a desired outcome. Stances on the Fugitive Slave Act and

---

[2] "Our Country – The Constitution, The Union, and the Enforcement of the Laws," 13 May 1860, *Augusta Chronicle*, p. 2, at America's Historical Newspapers, http://infoweb.newsbank.com.proxy.lib.duke.edu/iw-search/we/HistArchive?p_product=EANX&p_action=timeframes&p_theme=ahnp&p_nbid=R56P57J LMTQxNTYoOTY4OC4yNTI2NDQ6MToxMzoxNTIuMy4xMDIuMjQy &p_clear_search=&s_search_type=timeframes&d_lastaction=&d_ETC=&s_category=none&d_refprod=EANX&s_browseRef.

the U.S. Supreme Court's decision in *Dred Scott* are representative. Many leaders in free states saw both as illegitimate encroachments on states' established purview over the legal status of those who lived within their borders. Yet leaders in slaveholding states viewed both as necessary support for property rights that they believed to be threatened by other states' laws. Tensions escalated during the 1850s and culminated in Abraham Lincoln's election in 1860. To many of slavery's proponents, particularly those in the Deep South where the economy depended on the institution, Lincoln's election was the beginning of the end. It signaled a fundamental shift in the balance of power that would leave slave states in the minority and result in federal policies that undermined those states' ability to maintain the institution of slavery. The only solution was to secede: to abandon the federal government that would undermine the authority of slave states.[3] At that point, faith in the Constitution and the rule of law it represented led the country past the breaking point. Secessionists sought to found a new nation based on the Constitution as they saw it. Political leaders remaining in the Union vowed to defend their vision of the Constitution. And the American people lined up to fight for the legal order they identified with that document.

But the legal order that generated the conflict numbered among the Civil War's casualties: both the Union and Confederate governments' Herculean efforts to sustain the military conflict forever altered what they sought to preserve. At war's end, many of the legal system's foundational assumptions had been intentionally dismantled or unintentionally eviscerated. Most notably, both the Union and the Confederacy extended the scope and authority of their federal governments, significantly weakening the traditional powers of states. If anything, the Confederacy outdid the Union in this regard, despite its stated attachment to states' rights.

The turmoil of war also created space for people to express popular conceptions of justice and to move them into the ambit of government policy. Most well known are the efforts of slaves, free blacks, and white abolitionists to realize emancipation and racial equality. But other Americans – in both the Union and the

---

[3] Donald E. Feherenbacher, *The Slaveholding Republic: An Account of the United States Government's Relationship to Slavery* (New York, 2001).

Confederacy – also seized the opportunity to pursue their own legal agendas. As a result, the Civil War stirred up existing, but previously suppressed conflicts about the legal status of individuals, their relationship to government, and the location of legal authority: Who was a citizen? What did that mean? How, and by whom, were these matters decided? Reconstruction was forced to address these questions while dealing with two urgent tasks: bringing the slave states of the Confederacy back into the Union and contending with the status of former slaves. While both of those tasks centered on emancipation, they necessarily involved broader, structural changes that institutionalized wartime policies and ultimately transformed the legal status of all Americans.

Before the Civil War, the nation formed an ambiguous part of people's identities as Americans. They spoke of "these United States" or the Union, referring to an entity that was less a coherent nation than it was a coalition of separate states. People expressed their legal relationships to government in similar terms, identifying themselves as citizens of their states or even their hometowns as often as they did as citizens of their country. By the end of the war, those rhetorical constructions had become more singular and definitive among those who identified with the Union: Americans were now citizens of *the* United States. That new construction was most clearly articulated by Lincoln in the Gettysburg Address, with its powerful image of a newly consecrated nation, one built on the past but remade in the crucible of war: "It is rather for us to be here dedicated to the great task remaining before us – that from these honored dead we take increased devotion to that cause for which they gave the last full measure of devotion – that we here highly resolve that these dead shall not have died in vain, that this nation under God shall have a new birth of freedom, and that government of the people, by the people, for the people shall not perish from the earth."[4] Legal change in the United States during the Civil

---

[4] Gettysburg Address, 9 November 1863, available at The Avalon Project: Documents in Law, History, and Diplomacy, http://avalon.law.yale.edu/19th_century/gettyb. asp. Priscilla Wald, *Constituting Americans: Cultural Anxiety and Narrative Form* (Durham, NC, 1995). Of course, people referred to "the United States" before the Civil War, just as they continued to refer to "these United States" after the Civil War. But, as Wald's work suggests, the shift was at the level of conceptualization:

War gave institutional form to these national aspirations, providing the federal government the legal authority necessary to connect the people to it in ways that had not been possible before. The heavy-handed policies of the Confederate federal government also brought people into a more direct relationship with that new nation. At first glance, the centralization of authority within the Confederate government might seem odd, given secessionists' emphasis on states' rights. But conducting a war to establish states' rights required a centralized, federal government. By the end of the war, the Confederate federal government had assumed far more authority than the U.S. federal government ever had, at least on paper. In practice, however, the continued commitment of some white southerners to states' rights undercut the central government's legitimacy and tied it up in controversy. The upheaval of war, which was fought primarily in the Confederacy, further undermined the credibility of government at all levels. It was not just the war, moreover, that produced conflicts over the legal order. Different people had long defined law in their own terms, and the dislocation of war provided opportunities for those differences to flourish. Even as the Confederate government continued to centralize, its legitimacy collapsed. In many places, people simply gave up on federal and even state government, a situation that resulted in a radical decentralization of legal authority that went far beyond what states' rights advocates ever imagined or desired. The end of the war may have led to the demise of both the Confederate government and the legal order that it tried to create. But the conflicts generated by that government and its policies defined the postwar years, as the region became part of a newly reimagined United States. Indeed, white southerners' skepticism of federal authority was as much a product of their experience with the Confederacy as it was of their experience with the U.S. government.

Confederate defeat put all Americans within the jurisdiction of one nation, the United States. The Republican Party's Reconstruction Amendments then solidified the connections between the nation and the American people that the Union had been building during

in many Americans' perception of their connection to United States as a unified, national entity.

the Civil War. These amendments abolished slavery and secured the people's civil and political rights through federal authority. They also allowed people to imagine the federal government as a more immediate presence in their lives: a legal ally in their efforts to give rights meaning and to use those rights to effect change in their own lives and in society at large. Legal change not only flowed from above, but also welled up from below, as ordinary Americans confronted questions about law in the course of the war and its aftermath. The result was conflict, because many Americans imagined rights in far more expansive ways than their political leaders or their courts did. Where they saw rights as a means to accomplish social and economic change, federal policy and the courts tended to define rights in highly individualized terms, as the bundle of privileges necessary for individuals to access the legal system in civil and criminal matters and to attend to their economic interests. Once individuals had these privileges, they could take care of themselves, without further alterations to social relations, the economy, or the legal order and without further assistance from the federal government. That view, which ultimately prevailed, disaggregated the American people into a nation of individuals, each one connected to the federal government through his or her own rights. It was a legal order at odds with both the rhetorical promises of the Republican Party and the aspirations of so many Americans. This legal order was also unstable and subject to change, precisely because of the American people's faith in it and their insistence on accessing it. In the wake of the Civil War and Reconstruction, their faith took new forms. Not only did many Americans embrace their new relationship to the federal government, but they also expected it to act on their vision of rights. Even those who rejected federal policies accepted the fact of federal power and tried to channel it toward their own interests.

HISTORIOGRAPHY

A Legal History of the Civil War and Reconstruction: A Nation of Rights tells the legal history of this era by developing two interrelated arguments that emphasize the depth and breadth of legal change. Debates about whether the period is best characterized by change or by continuity have defined the historiography of the Civil War and Reconstruction since its inception. This book argues that historians have tended to underestimate the extent of change because they have not brought legal history into dialogue with the scholarship of other historical fields.

The first group of professional historians to write about the era ensured that questions about change would dominate the historiography. This group – influenced by the Dunning School, after its intellectual mentor, William A. Dunning, a professor at Columbia University – was composed of white men who were raised in the bitter aftermath of the war and, not surprisingly, deemed Reconstruction an unmitigated failure. Although the work of Dunning School historians found little in the period to praise, the legal changes at the federal level – the Thirteenth, Fourteenth, and Fifteenth Amendments – received their harshest criticism. Open apologists for white supremacy, these historians argued that the amendments constituted an illegal usurpation of state authority by imposing the will of a radical minority and granting rights to African American men who were incapable of exercising them, thereby destroying the South and jeopardizing the nation's future. Inflammatory today because of its open racism, Dunning School scholarship reflected the politics of sectional reunion in the late nineteenth and early twentieth centuries, in which white northerners joined white southerners in distancing themselves from the more radical policy changes of the Civil War and Reconstruction, particularly emancipation and the granting of full civil and political equality to African Americans. In that context, the scholarship associated with the Dunning School characterized the war and, particularly, its aftermath, as an avoidable aberration, the result of radicals in the North who captured the national stage and imposed their wild schemes on an unsuspecting populace.

The Dunning School has had a remarkable and enduring influence on the historiography, including legal history. The aftershocks of World War II, when the scope of the Holocaust was revealed, brought down its overtly racist props. But its themes continued to define basic questions about legal change: Was the Civil War inevitable, within the existing constitutional framework? To what extent did postwar policies alter the legal order of the nation?

By mid-century, the New Deal, World War II, and the civil rights movement had cast a more favorable light on federal authority and, ultimately, the Civil War era. Reflecting that viewpoint, a new body of revisionist literature emphasized the accomplishments of federal policies, particularly during Reconstruction. If anything, revisionist scholarship faulted federal officials for not reaching far enough and, thus, falling short of their goals. The combination of judicial foot-dragging and political maneuvering in the 1870s turned back the clock nearly to where it had been before the war. Not only were white southerners allowed to regain control, but they were also allowed – even encouraged – to ignore new federal laws and to resurrect a racial system that closely resembled slavery. To make matters worse, federal courts then turned to the Fourteenth Amendment to buttress the position of corporations at the expense of labor, creating new inequalities from the very laws that were intended to promote greater equality. Other historians saw the glass half full, rather than half empty. To them, federal policy, particularly the Fourteenth Amendment, constituted a "second American revolution" that provided the constitutional basis to at last fulfill the promises of the first. Progress came slowly, culminating only eventually in the mid-twentieth century with the civil rights movement. But those changes never would have been realized at all had it not been for the policies of the Reconstruction era.

The tendency to see Reconstruction as an era that promised great legal change has spilled over into the scholarship on the Civil War. Recent scholarship has treated the war as if it were inevitable, a fight that had to be waged in order to clear the way for what came next. In this body of work, the conflict becomes the collision of two distinct social orders, each with different conceptions of individual rights, the role of law, and the reach of the state. Only one could survive. One branch of this scholarship has focused on the dynamics leading up to the war, with an eye toward explaining why those conflicts reached the point where the existing order could no longer contain them. The work has tended to point to inherent weaknesses, attributable to the Constitution, particularly the lack of authority at the federal level, which short-circuited the development of a strong, effective nation state. Those weaknesses not only contributed to the outbreak of the war but also presaged problems that the reconstructed nation would need to address afterward. Another branch of scholarship has looked to the war years more directly as a precursor to Reconstruction, examining wartime policies within the Union and the Confederacy to contextualize subsequent legal innovations and reactions to them. This work also has tended to emphasize change rather than continuity by showing how the war took the nation in new legal directions. The positive reinterpretation of federal power that has marked recent scholarship on Reconstruction extended to the war years as well, although measures such as the draft, martial law, and the suspension of *habeas corpus* have been harder to defend than efforts to secure African Americans' civil and political rights. But even those policies have emerged as a means of preserving, not undermining individual liberty.

Historians have not paid as much attention to the Confederacy's legal order, because they assume that defeat ended its historical significance. While treating Confederate laws and policies as fleeting products of a short-lived political experiment, the scholarship has focused on the extent to which the Confederacy lived up to its principles of states' rights as well as the effectiveness of its policies in waging war. All this literature emphasizes change – in fact, dramatic change. The exigencies of war ultimately swept away the Confederacy's legal order. What remained after the collapse of conditions on the home front and military defeat succumbed to the political changes of Reconstruction.

Yet even those legal historians who have emphasized change have missed its broad reach because of their emphasis on particular arenas of law. Much of the existing work within the field of legal history has focused on the federal level in the United States, exploring policy debates there, tracing the effects through the states and, from there, to people's lives. The lines of causation tend to flow from the top down, with the most significant changes emanating from the three branches of the national government. That focus, however, has limits. It misses much of the historical action, because many of the most profound changes in legal culture did not happen at the federal level. This perspective also tends to frame analytical questions primarily in terms of the intended objectives of U.S. policy: the expansion of federal authority and the extension of civil and political rights to African American men. That focus has a regional and temporal frame, foregrounding the South (where most African Americans lived) and defining the end of Reconstruction in 1877 (when the disputed presidential election resulted in the Compromise of 1877, which the historiography identifies, mistakenly, as the end of federal involvement in the former Confederate states and, by implication, of any effective support for the Reconstruction Amendments in those states).

The historiographical assessments of federal authority actually recapitulate the terms and limits of political debate at the time of the Civil War, with one side opposing federal authority as a perversion of the country's basic principles and the other advocating it as a means of achieving them. This overly simplistic conceptual frame fails historiographically for the same reasons it failed politically in the 1860s: the expansion of federal power led in multiple, contradictory directions in matters of political participation, civil rights, and even opportunities for economic advancement. The one clear outcome was the transformation of the people's relationship to the federal government and, consequently, to the nation's legal order.

Other strands of scholarship, both within and outside legal history, create a very different temporal and geographic range. There is a large body of scholarship in legal history tracing the implications of the Fourteenth Amendment beyond what the historiography has conventionally identified as the formal end of Reconstruction. Yet such work is not usually considered to be about Reconstruction, because its focus is later in the nineteenth century and because it deals with questions of gender, labor, and economic development outside of the South. Yet, as that scholarship suggests, the Reconstruction Amendments and other state and federal policies from this period actually had legal consequences across time and region. They altered the status of people whom federal lawmakers never intended to touch, not only all women, but also all men in all areas of the nation. Beyond that, Reconstruction-era policies profoundly transformed legal institutions and legal culture throughout the nation, not just for a brief decade in the states of the former Confederacy and not just at the federal level. As the work in legal history shows, Reconstruction fundamentally altered the dynamics of law and governance in ways that transformed the lives of all Americans.

Recent work outside legal history has underscored the broad reach of Reconstruction-era legal change as well. In this body of scholarship, the focus has been on legal dynamics that unfolded outside federal purview and in spite of lawmakers' stated aims. Although situated in women's, African American, and labor history and inspired by the approaches used in social, cultural, and economic history, this scholarship nevertheless engages questions that have been central to legal history. Even more important, such work highlights the legal component of issues not usually considered in that field. As it shows, the war opened up a series of questions about the location of legal authority and the daily operation of law throughout the nation.

Because these elements of the historiography do not fully engage legal history, however, they tend to misunderstand, or ignore, the particular legal dynamics they are uncovering and analyzing. While many historians use legal records for information about social relations, for instance, they do so without exploring the institutions that produced those records or the laws that guided legal decisions. Beyond that, many of these historians are uninterested in engaging questions about legal change, because they see legal history as a fundamentally different bailiwick than their own. This scholarship, nonetheless, speaks directly to issues of legal change, in ways that ultimately reshape the contours of legal history.

Synthesizing the work in these other fields with legal history fundamentally changes the narrative of both legal change and of people's relationship to the law during the Civil War and Reconstruction. Doing so expands the analysis beyond the usual areas of historiographical preoccupation, namely federal policy, slavery, and race. To be sure, secession and the Civil War forced the nation's leaders to confront slavery and racial inequality. That confrontation then altered basic elements of federal authority, most notably with three amendments to the U.S. Constitution. But, as the work outside the field of legal history shows, change neither began nor ended there. It extended much further than historians have previously acknowledged, permeating all levels of the nation's legal order and ultimately transforming the legal status of all U.S. citizens, connecting them to the nation through the promise that the federal government would secure their rights, while also opening up new questions and conflicts about the meaning of those rights.

The book is divided into six chapters, with three on the Civil War and three on Reconstruction. The first three chapters explore legal change during the war years and deal specifically with the legal implications of secession; the formation of two competing yet similarly structured federal governments; military mobilization; and a bloody war fought amidst a civilian population. As the first section argues, wartime policies in the United States and the Confederacy fundamentally remade the legal authority of the nation, not only by enhancing the power of the federal government, but also by reconfiguring Americans' relationship to the nation's governing institutions and the law.

Chapter 1, "The United States and Its Use of the People," focuses on the states that remained in the Union. The chapter traces the evolution of government policies as well as people's conceptions of and relationships to the legal order. During the war, President Abraham Lincoln and Congressional Republicans centralized legal authority at the federal level by solidifying the connections between the nation and its people. Wartime changes laid the foundation for a new legal order, one based on a nation of citizens who were equal in theory, but vastly unequal in practice. They also laid the foundation for future conflicts, by raising people's expectations of what the federal government could and should do, expectations at odds with the existing legal structure and the inequalities sanctioned in federal law.

Chapter 2, "The Confederacy and Its Legal Contradictions," turns to the broad swath of territory in that new nation. Secession was a rash, even radical act. Yet Confederates' legal vision was profoundly conservative: they made their new federal government in the image of the U.S. government and left governance at the state and local levels intact. Ultimately, however, Confederates' radical attempts to preserve a slave society destroyed not just the slave system, but also the legal order that maintained it. Confederate officials immediately started centralizing authority in the federal government, creating a legal order at odds with its stated governing principles. During the course of the Civil War, the Confederate federal government continued to assume authority, at least in theory, even as it continued to lose legitimacy among the people it purported to govern. The loss of legitimacy ultimately spread to all levels of government, an experience that had profound implications for the way all southerners viewed law and legal change in the postwar years.

Chapter 3, "Enslaved Americans, Emancipation, and the Future Legal Order," considers the implications of emancipation for the nation's emerging legal order. The chapter's reference to "enslaved Americans" is meant to capture the legal tensions created by slavery. Enslaved people lived in America and even saw themselves as Americans, but slavery made them legally different from other Americans and, in the eyes of many white people, not really Americans at all. To make enslaved people Americans required structural legal change. Yet slavery was so deeply embedded within the legal order of the nation that it was impossible to eradicate without fundamental alterations in the law. The various wartime policies designed to establish federal authority over slavery and even to abolish it were not sufficient. Slavery's end ultimately required changes to the U.S. Constitution, the implications of which extended beyond the institution of slavery. The Thirteenth Amendment, ratified after the end of the Civil War, not only abolished slavery, but also changed the people's relationship to the federal government by making questions about their individual rights a matter of federal jurisdiction for the first time.

The next three chapters explore the legal changes associated with Reconstruction and trace their implications over the course of the late nineteenth century. Reconstruction usually refers to federal efforts to abolish slavery and bring Confederate states back into the Union. As the chapters in this section show, those tasks ultimately unsettled the nation's entire legal order, with implications that reached deep into the lives of all Americans. Change flowed from the top down and from the bottom up, although in complicated ways that ultimately belie the metaphor that associates the federal government with the "top" and popular conceptions of law with the "bottom" and that draws a clear distinction between the two. Legal change at the federal level tied Americans more closely to the federal government and, hence, the nation through the rubric of individual rights. Federal policies, however, provided only a starting point, setting the conditions for even more profound change as Americans took the opportunity to act on their own ideas about the meaning of rights.

Chapter 4, "The Federal Government and the Reconstruction of the Legal Order," examines legal change at the federal level. The analysis emphasizes two kinds of Reconstruction-era legal change: its democratizing effects, which extended civil and political rights to African American men and encouraged white and black southerners, in particular, to participate actively in law and government; and its centralizing tendencies, which relocated the locus of rights and citizenship as well as augmented the authority of legal institutions at both the state and national levels in all parts of the country. While much of the chapter focuses on the South, the analysis also examines the relationship between federal policies there and in other parts of the country, with particular emphasis on Indian policy in the West. Federal policies toward Indians and enslaved African Americans were of a piece: both emphasized the preservation of particular kinds of property rights, namely those in land and other forms of productive property, with a preference for the rights of people who already owned those kinds of property. The existing historiography has explained the emphasis on property rights – and its problematic implications for Indians, African Americans, and other poor and marginalized Americans – in terms of the economic interests of the country's ruling elite. But such policies also owed to the existing rubric of individual rights, which was deeply embedded within the nation's legal order. It was that same rubric of individual rights, with its narrow focus on property rights and its affirmation of existing economic inequalities, that Republicans would employ to address the legal status of African Americans during Reconstruction.

Chapter 5, "The Possibilities of Rights," explores popular conceptions of Reconstruction-era legal change. It focuses particularly on the efforts of African Americans in the South to bring meaning to the civil and political rights promised to them in the Reconstruction Amendments and in their new state constitutions. It then connects the struggles of African Americans to those of white women and working people elsewhere in the nation, who also saw new possibilities for social change in the promise of rights and the enhanced authority of the federal government. These popular conceptions of rights, however, did not focus on narrow constructions of property rights. They also did not draw a sharp distinction between the individual and society. In fact, many Americans saw rights as a way both to empower individuals and to realize various visions of a just society.

Chapter 6, "The Power of Law and the Limits of Rights," takes the story of Reconstruction into the 1890s and considers the various conceptions and uses of the Reconstruction Amendments. The chapter begins with the collapse of Reconstruction. Conservative Democratic regimes in the South and the federal government's refusal to address structural inequalities in that region were characteristic of a national legal order that emerged in this period, one that individualized rights so as to completely abstract them from social context. The chapter then turns to the Fourteenth Amendment's application in the areas of women's rights, race relations, immigration, Indian policy, economic matters, labor relations, and federalism. The changes in Americans' legal status were profound. But the route from Reconstruction-era legal change to the various civil rights movements of the twentieth century was not as direct as much of the scholarship now posits. In fact, the changes in Americans' legal status during and after Reconstruction did not lead inevitably to the expansion of rights that came later. Those later changes in the twentieth century required concerted political action on the part of people who imagined rights differently. Even then, the notion of rights situated in the individual made it difficult to draw on them in the service of broad, social change – and still do.

The United States and Its Use of the People

It was an unlikely scene: on an early fall day in 1861, people crowded into the U.S. sub-treasurer's office in New York City to buy treasury notes. Describing the event, a *New York Herald* reporter rolled out a parade of characters worthy of Dickens. There was a "short, stout, broad-faced gentleman ... with a gold-headed cane, gold spectacles, and a general banking air about him"; an "old woman, poorly dressed, bent down by age, and looking like the keeper of an apple stand or corner grocery of peanuts and dirty candies"; a "veritable Bridget" ("How in the world could she know of the loan and of its advantages?"); a "former comptroller of the city, now totally blind, and led in by his daughter"; a "negro, colored man, an African, or whatever he prefers to be called"; a "lady sweeping her long trail past you, and displaying rich diamond rings"; a clerk "who subscribes thousands of dollars for his employers, and then, after a moment's hesitation, $100 for himself"; an elderly gentleman who "has not left his native town in New Jersey for five years, but has taken this long and fatiguing journey because he thinks his country needs his savings"; a lady from the backcountry who "wants to know how she is to invest her money to aid the country"; the "inevitable Irishman and German, who say exactly what they do not mean, but whose business the quick clerks dispatch before the inexplicit, episodical, and curiously intertangled story of the depositors is half finished"; and a clergy man "who says ten words about his business and fifty about his determination to sustain the government." Many insisted on seeing Mr. Cisco, the sub-treasurer, even though it was unnecessary and slowed the process to a snail's pace. But, as the reporter explained, everyone waited patiently. They "feel that by showing themselves personally to the Sub-Treasurer they are, in some sort, giving aid and comfort to the government of which he appears to them the representative." [1]

The reporter's point was as obvious as his characters were overdrawn. All these people – men and women, rich and poor, white and black, native-born and immigrant – made up the United States. Less obvious was the mechanism that drew them all together and into a direct relationship with the federal government, namely the economic policies of the Republican Party. Upon taking office, Treasury Secretary Salmon P. Chase faced a difficult truth: the United States could not cover current expenses, let alone the cost of a protracted war. Chase had little experience in finance, other than what he had obtained growing up in the school of hard knocks. His mother was widowed with ten children when Chase was nine years old. Chase, who was supporting himself by age sixteen, eventually left New England to make his home in Cincinnati, where he began his career defending fugitive slaves and ended up as one of the Republican Party's founders. Never, though, had Chase been asked to conjure money out of thin air, which was basically what was required of him as treasury secretary. He first turned to conventional funding sources, negotiating with the banks for loans. But he found them unforthcoming. Equally disappointing were his overtures to European powers, which were still smarting from the repudiation of Revolutionary-era debts and unwilling to consider a repetition of that experience. Desperate, Chase got creative: he turned to the American people. In the summer of 1861, he constructed a scheme that tapped the savings of ordinary Americans to fund the war: $25 million in three-year treasury notes that paid 7.3 percent interest and were quickly (and affectionately) dubbed seventy-thirties. The response was overwhelmingly positive, as the *Herald* article suggests. In fact, the notes proved so popular that the federal government issued more, at various terms, throughout the war.

---

[1] "Taking of the Popular Loan," 14 September 1861, *Scientific American*, vol. 5, no. 11, p. 171, available at American Periodical Series Online, http://search.proquest.com/docview/126564000?accountid=10598.

The seventy-thirties capture central elements of legal change in the United States during the Civil War. "Suppose," the *Milwaukee Daily Sentinel* mused, "that from Maine to California the bonds of the government formed the only basis of circulation, would not every man's immediate pecuniary interest make him wakeful of the slightest danger to the perpetuity and integrity of the government?"[2] The elision between war bonds and the bonds between the American people and the nation described the ambiguities of people's changing relationship to the national government. During the Civil War, Americans gave the nation their labor, their earnings, and their lives. All that might have become sacrifices necessary in the crisis of war, but of no lasting import in terms of fundamental change to the nation's legal order. Yet wartime policies did carry broader, more permanent meanings, precisely because Republican Party leaders framed them as something more than temporary wartime measures. They justified the expansion of the federal authority in terms of the national government's essential relationship to "the people." The rhetoric did not accurately reflect legal change: it ignored the limited reach of federal power, the conflicts of interest those policies generated, and the inequalities they affirmed. It, nonetheless, fueled expectations that the federal government would do – and should do – more for all the people than it had in the past. Americans began looking to the federal government, not just state or local governments, to protect, support, and further their interests. And those expectations did fundamentally alter the imagined legal landscape, clearing the way for a new legal order that was national in scope and composed of citizens who were equal in theory, but unequal in practice.

THE WAR EFFORT, FEDERAL EXPANSION, AND THE AMERICAN PEOPLE

Political tensions erupted in armed conflict with astonishing speed in the spring of 1861. States in the Deep South – South Carolina,

[2] "A Bond of Union," *Milwaukee Daily Sentinel*, 22 January 1863, issue 17, col. A, available at 19th Century U.S. Newspapers, http://infotrac.galegroup.com. proxy.lib.duke.edu/itw/infomark/891/644/19571475 1w16/purl=rc1_NCNP_0_GT3002871135&dyn=12!xrn_1_0_GT3002871135&hst_1?sw_aep=duke_perkins.

Georgia, Alabama, Mississippi, Louisiana, Texas, and Florida – left the United States after Lincoln's election, certain that it meant the end of slavery. In February 1861, secessionists formed the Confederate States of America. Just weeks later, on April 12, 1861, the South Carolina militia fired on Fort Sumter. The fort's token crew surrendered the next day. In response, on April 15, Lincoln ordered the states to raise militia units, totaling seventy-five thousand troops, to stop what he identified as a rebellion against the United States. Anticipating this scenario, some state leaders had been readying their militias and immediately dispatched troops to Washington, D.C. Lincoln then declared a blockade of all Confederate ports on April 19. But it was the call for troops that proved particularly decisive, because it forced the remaining slave states to choose between the Confederacy and the United States. Within two months, the Upper South states of Virginia, North Carolina, Tennessee, and Arkansas seceded.

The efforts of Confederate sympathizers in Maryland, Kentucky, and Missouri might have succeeded as well, if not for the proximity of federal soldiers. In March, Missouri voted to remain in the United States by an overwhelming majority. Days after Lincoln's call for troops, however, the pro-Confederate governor ignored that vote and ordered the state militia to seize federal arsenals. The plot was foiled when federal troops chased the governor to the southwestern corner of the state and martial law was declared. In Maryland, rioters attacked a Pennsylvania regiment traveling through Baltimore on its way to Washington, D.C. In the riot's aftermath, Confederates destroyed telegraph lines and railroad bridges, exposing the vulnerability of the nation's capital by cutting it off from the rest of the United States. Lincoln sent in militia units, which quelled the rebellion and occupied Baltimore. In the wake of events in Missouri and Maryland, Lincoln called for about forty-two thousand additional volunteers to augment federal forces. Armed conflict followed quickly. In July, Union forces were routed at the First Battle of Bull Run. The United States and the Confederacy were at war.

As Americans responded with a surge of patriotism, Lincoln made creative use of his presidential powers. Insisting on the sovereignty and indissolubility of the United States, Lincoln identified secession as a hostile, aggressive act that necessitated an immediate response. Based on that legal view, Lincoln took the country to war, calling up troops, declaring a naval blockade, and extending federal authority over the civilian population through martial law and the suspension of *habeas corpus*. He did all this, moreover, while Congress was out of session. Consistently elevating federal authority over that of state and local governments, Lincoln also set in motion a conceptual shift that fundamentally altered how Americans thought about the location of legal authority.

The use of martial law is a key example of the expansion of the federal government's legal authority. In the U.S. context, martial law was defined as temporary and limited, confined to a particular geographic area in immediate danger and lasting just as long as that threat persisted. Only in those circumstances could military authority replace civilian authorities – at least in theory. Throughout the Civil War, however, federal commanders deployed much more capacious interpretations of martial law. Its first controversial use came from John C. Fremont, who commanded federal troops in Missouri. After removing the state's secessionist governor, Fremont declared martial law in the entire state without obtaining Lincoln's permission. He then used those powers to abolish slavery and confiscate secessionists' property, also without Lincoln's permission.

It was not so much the declaration of martial law as what Fremont did with it that caused trouble. Fremont was an ambitious man with a taste for power. The Republican Party's first nominee for the presidency in 1856, he was disappointed not to receive the nod again in 1860. In 1864 he would challenge Lincoln's nomination, causing a split in the Republican Party. He was also a strong opponent of slavery, not just in the territories, but also in states where it already existed. No wonder that Lincoln did not take kindly to Fremont's efforts to supplant his authority and his political agenda, which promised to leave slavery alone so as to keep Border States in the Union. The showdown ended when Lincoln removed Fremont from command. While Fremont left, martial law stayed. Lincoln made that clear to Fremont's replacement, directing him to exercise martial law at his "discretion to secure the public safety and the authority of the United States."[3]

---

[3] Dennis K. Boman, *Lincoln and Citizens' Rights in Civil War Missouri: Balancing Freedom and Security* (Baton Rouge, LA, 2011).

While Lincoln did monitor military commanders' use of martial law to intervene in slavery, he allowed them considerable discretion in other areas. Federal commanders used martial law to silence political opposition in occupied territory. They also used martial law to keep the peace in places under their control. In some instances, military authorities ended up either overseeing or replacing civilian courts and adjudicating a wide range of offenses that usually fell within state or local jurisdiction. That situation obtained not just during the Civil War, but also afterward, during Reconstruction. In fact, the use of martial law was so broad and so varied that people then and historians later have had difficulty defining it.[4]

The suspension of *habeas corpus* paralleled the imposition of martial law. On April 27, 1861, as the uprising in Baltimore fed fears of Washington, D.C.'s strategic vulnerability, Lincoln authorized the suspension of *habeas corpus* on the railway corridor between the capitol city and Philadelphia. *Habeas corpus*, a legal action that allows detainees to challenge unlawful imprisonment, had a long history in English common law as a means of limiting the state's – particularly a monarch's – power. It was intended for instances in which people were imprisoned under questionable charges or without being charged at all. By filing writs of *habeas corpus*, prisoners forced state officials to name the legal charges, justify them, and proceed with the case, instead of detaining them indefinitely. *Habeas corpus* had acquired political resonance during the American Revolution as one of the fundamental English rights that had been denied the colonists. It was important enough to make it into the U.S. Constitution, which did not go so far as to affirm it as a positive right, but did prohibit Congress from denying it, except "in Cases of Rebellion or Invasion the public Safety may require it." Lincoln invoked that constitutional language in suspending *habeas corpus* in Maryland. "You are engaged in repressing an insurrection against the laws of the United States," Lincoln wrote in his order to Winfield Scott, the Commanding General of the Army of the United States. "At the point that resistance occurs," Scott and any of his officers should suspend the writ. The order provoked

---

[4] Gregory P. Downs, "The Ends of War: Fighting the Civil War after Appomattox," unpublished manuscript.

heated opposition because many thought only Congress had the power to suspend *habeas corpus* – and Congress was not in session when Lincoln issued his order, although he called legislators back in order to affirm it and his other war measures.[5]

Challenges to Lincoln's order arrived even before Congress could convene. Among the secessionist leaders who had been rounded up and jailed at Fort McHenry in Baltimore was John Merryman. Arrested on May 25, his lawyers petitioned the U.S. Circuit Court for a writ of *habeas corpus* on May 26. On May 27, Chief Justice Roger B. Taney, who heard the case in his capacity as a federal circuit court judge, granted the request, arguing that the power to suspend *habeas corpus* lay with Congress, not the president. While Taney's decision had support in the legal profession, it had no practical effect, because Lincoln flatly refused to support it. Cleaving to his view of secession, Lincoln maintained that the president could suspend *habeas corpus* to protect the Union. "It cannot be believed," Lincoln argued, that "the framers [of the Constitution] intended, that in every case, the danger should run its course, until Congress called together."[6] That was particularly true in this case, where the prisoners' actions could have prevented Congress from convening at all. Attorney General Edward Bates affirmed Lincoln's position, although he backed off Lincoln's broad rendering of the issue by casting it in terms of the president's ability to override writs of *habeas corpus* (rather than suspending the right altogether).[7]

Lincoln used established powers given to the federal government when he invoked martial law and suspended *habeas corpus*. In theory, he did not alter the nature of federal authority. In practice, however, his reliance on those powers extended the legal authority of the federal government into areas of law that had been controlled by states and localities. The first applications of such policies, in 1861, might be dismissed as temporary aberrations that

---

[5] Lincoln's Suspension of Habeas Corpus, 27 April 1861, in Christian G. Samito, ed., *Changes in Law and Society during the Civil War and Reconstruction: A Legal History Documentary Reader* (Carbondale, IL, 2009), p. 63.

[6] Lincoln's Message to Congress, 4 July 1861, in ibid., p. 68.

[7] Opinion of Attorney General Bates on the Suspension of Habeas Corpus, 10 Op. Att'y Gen., 74 (July 5, 1861), in ibid., pp. 72–9. Mark E. Neely, Jr., *The Fate of Liberty: Abraham Lincoln and Civil Liberties* (New York, 1991). Subsequent court decisions did not uphold Lincoln's interpretation.

addressed particularly volatile crises. In Missouri and Maryland, civil order had already deteriorated to the point of chaos. The secession of those states, moreover, could spell disaster for the rest of the United States. Yet the use of martial law in these and other occupied areas effectively substituted federal jurisdiction for state and local jurisdictions in civil and criminal law – a situation that continued in many areas during the Civil War and well into Reconstruction. And the use of federal powers did not stop there. During the war, Lincoln extended federal authority to people and places not in open rebellion against the United States. In 1862, one year after the onset of war, he began applying martial law to anyone who resisted the draft, discouraged others from enlisting, or was deemed disloyal to the Union war effort. He also suspended *habeas corpus* for all those arrested under that application of martial law. Historians remain divided on the implications for Americans' civil rights. The traditional interpretation is that Lincoln's administration went too far, using federal authority to muzzle individuals who were critical of the war, shut down dissident newspapers, and shape editorial policy. Other historians, however, argue that such a view is not grounded in the documentary evidence, but in an assumption, characteristic of early-twentieth-century scholarship, that Lincoln was a wartime dictator – a view largely abandoned in the historiography today. Even if Lincoln's policies did not limit individual rights to the extent one thought, it is nonetheless clear that the imposition of martial law and the suspension of *habeas corpus* significantly amplified federal authority, by bringing the federal government into legal matters that traditionally had been the responsibility of states and localities.[8]

Congress formally affirmed presidential purview over *habeas corpus* in 1863, despite vigorous political and judicial opposition. The Habeas Corpus Act extended not only presidential authority, but also the jurisdiction of the federal courts. Even the act's procedural safeguards for prisoners, which were meant to address

---

[8] Lincoln's Suspension of Habeas Corpus, 24 September 1862, in Samito, ed., *Changes in Law and Society*, p. 80. Habeas Corpus Act, 12 U.S. Statutes at Large 755 (1863). For the connection between politics and historiographical debates over the interpretation of martial law and the suspension of habeas corpus, see Neely, *The Fate of Liberty*, pp. 223–35.

concerns about civil rights and place limits on presidential authority, had the effect of institutionalizing the federal judiciary's expansion. Congress duplicated the pattern when, in the same year, it created the Court of Claims, which handled claims against the U.S. government that had formerly been settled in Congress. To be sure, this act addressed practical considerations. Claims on the federal government had multiplied exponentially as a result of the war, making it impossible for Congress to keep up. But here, again, Congress delegated its power in a way that institutionalized the extended jurisdiction of the federal courts.[9]

The Habeas Corpus Act highlighted a general change of direction, as Congressional Republicans followed down the path blazed by Lincoln and enhanced federal authority in ways that were, potentially, more substantive and more permanent. The Republican Party was inclined in this direction, given its vision of a nationally integrated economy and federal support for policies that opened up economic opportunities for a broad range of Americans. The exigencies of war forced the issue, exposing the gap between what was required of the government and what its current structure could support. To be sure, many Republicans went along with wartime policies because they saw them as temporary measures to address the immediate crisis, not because they favored centralization. Even so, wartime policies ultimately had that effect. They extended the federal government's reach in the lives of the American people in ways that would be impossible to negate or overturn at the end of the war.[10]

One of the first to struggle with the need for increased federal power was Treasury Secretary Salmon P. Chase, who found himself scrambling to pay for the conflict at the very beginning of the war. His solution, war bonds, was only the first of an ambitious plan to fund the war that, ultimately, ended up overhauling the nation's financial

[9] Habeas Corpus Act (1863). Harold M. Hyman, *A More Perfect Union: The Impact of the Civil War and Reconstruction on the Constitution* (New York, 1973), pp. 245–62. For the limitations, see Jonathan W. White, *Abraham Lincoln and Treason in the Civil War: The Trials of John Merryman* (Baton Rouge, LA, 2011).

[10] Richard Franklin Bensel, *Yankee Leviathan: The Origins of Central State Authority in American, 1859–1877* (New York, 1990).

structure and consolidating federal authority over it. Republican Party leaders rooted wartime changes in the financial system, at least rhetorically, in the labor power of the American people. The 1861 issue of treasury notes – or war bonds – was one of many such sales, by which the American people loaned their savings to the government to fund the war effort. To sell bonds, Chase relied on Philadelphia banker Jay Cooke, who set up a nationwide system to sell them on commission. Cooke advertised in local papers, educating the public on the terms, advantages, and availability of bonds. He also opened offices all over the country with locations and hours to accommodate working people. He even targeted women as customers. By the end of the war, the American people had funded a national debt of more than 2.5 billion dollars.[11]

But bonds, alone, were not sufficient to meet the war's expenses. To augment funding streams, Chase proposed the issue of paper currency – greenbacks – unredeemable in specie. Many in Congress balked, including Republicans who generally supported the Lincoln administration. The notion of currency – any currency – issued by the federal government was extremely controversial. In practical terms, the issuance of paper currency represented a significant increase in federal authority and a significant departure from the current system. At the outset of the Civil War, the federal government had virtually no institutional involvement in the nation's financial system. It did not issue its own currency or influence monetary issues through a national bank, which had been demolished with the demise of the Second National Bank in 1836. The existing financial system was thoroughly decentralized, operating through state-chartered banks that issued their own notes and decided what value to assign to other notes they received. A new federal currency meant the insinuation of federal authority into this system, an idea that many found problematic.

The whole concept of paper currency unredeemable in specie, however, also generated moral opposition that went well beyond practical discussions of government involvement in the financial system and that is difficult to grasp today. Such notes, opponents

---

[11] Heather Cox Richardson, *The Greatest Nation of the Earth: Republican Economic Policies During the Civil War* (Cambridge, MA, 1997); debt figure from p. 63.

argued, had absolutely no value. Flimsy and ephemeral, they were nothing more than an unfulfilled contract, the promise of future payment that, without backing, was entirely empty. Paper notes had to represent something of actual value. They had to be redeemable in something real. If not, then paper notes were just so much worthless paper. As such, they carried the entire country into dangerous economic waters. Printing notes was to make something of nothing, encouraging extravagance, indolence, and licentiousness. While an economy floated on paper might be sustainable in the short run, the bubble would ultimately burst and destroy the value of hardworking people's property in the process. In that sense, paper currency could result in chaos.

Proponents at the time countered with the logic of nineteenth-century political economy, which emphasized labor as the source of all value and, like Adam Smith, connected a nation's economic power to the productivity of its people. Paper currency, they argued, would reduce the nation's reliance on bankers and place its financial future in the hands of its people, who would always be able to create value by working. Maine Senator William Pitt Fessenden, who helped shepherd wartime financial measures through Congress, articulated that connection clearly. As he maintained, the best capital America could have was the labor of its people: "the power and the will to work; and the disposition, the desire, the anxiety, the policy to make that labor more productive by educating it; under which policy of educating labor and thus increasing the power of production, the country has grown up with such unexampled, unparalleled rapidity." The argument capitalized on the unpopularity of banks, the reputations of which had plummeted to new lows because of their well-publicized reluctance to fund the war. As one senator from Ohio put it, "We are all in favor of the citizens of the Republic becoming its *creditors*, rather than the *debtors* of the bankers and capitalists." But this conception was difficult, demanding that Americans make a leap of faith into an unfamiliar and uncomfortable level of abstraction.[12]

The problem, though, was not just the issuance of greenbacks. For those greenbacks to be a truly national currency, they had to

---

[12] Fessenden quote from ibid., pp. 79–80; Ohio Senator quotation from p. 74.

be legal tender, meaning that the federal government had to compel their acceptance for all debts. Unless that was the case, greenbacks were only one currency among many – one that, like any other currency, could be discounted or refused by the banks. Given the varied circumstances of different banks and the power that individual state banks held, the value of commonly denominated state notes varied widely. A ten-dollar note issued by one state bank might be valued at only five dollars in another state. The value of notes from one state bank might sink so low that other banks would refuse to accept them at all. To complicate matters, counterfeit notes flooded the system, making it even more difficult to determine the value of any given bank note. When greenbacks, which were not backed by gold, entered this system, their value began to fluctuate as well.[13]

That situation is captured in a short satirical article critical of greenbacks. It begins with a well-meaning passerby who sees that several young boys are using a treasury note to make a kite. The connection between the kite and paper currency would have been obvious to nineteenth-century readers. Kiting was a well-known method of fraud, in which a series of notes were floated to create the appearance of more credit than was actually the case. If the delicate balancing act collapsed, those who accepted the notes found that they were worthless. To the opponents of unredeemable paper currency, greenbacks were akin to kiting: they were, essentially, worthless notes floated by the federal government to make it seem like there were resources where there were none. Trying to discover the owner of the note, the passerby took possession of it and escorted the boys to their home. There he found that a woman associated with the household had found the note in the street and, not knowing what it was, "picked it up because there were pretty pictures upon it." Given that those "pretty pictures" were Republican officials, the satire was hard to miss. Eventually, the bond was returned to its owner, bringing it back down to earth, so to speak. Besides its political critique, this story underscores both the instability of the country's currency as well as its scarcity. The humor depended on the fact that the value of bank notes fluctuated

---

[13] Stephen Mihm, *A Nation of Counterfeiters: Capitalists, Con Men, and the Making of the United States* (Cambridge, MA, 2007).

so widely. In fact, it was difficult to determine the value of any given note in the nineteenth century. It was entirely possible that a note's best use might be as material for making actual kites.[14]

The kite also describes the federal government's financial position without a national currency that was also legal tender. It would be tossed about by prevailing economic winds as long as it did not control its currency and, therefore, the value of its debt. Banks could either discount greenbacks to the point where they were no longer viable or refuse to accept them altogether, which bankers threatened to do in retaliation for Chase's efforts to exert more control over the nation's finances. Congress addressed those concerns in 1862 with the Legal Tender Act, which required that greenbacks be accepted for all debts, private and public. That requirement fundamentally transformed the federal government's relationship to the financial system. It essentially restructured all existing debts, substituting greenbacks (that were not redeemable in gold) for payment of specie. All current and future economic transactions were tied to the circumstances of the United States – or, as many Republicans would have expressed it, the labor of its people.[15]

For opponents, the Legal Tender Act was tantamount to theft. It allowed debts that had been contracted in specie to be paid back in fluctuating paper currency of lesser value. Even wartime proponents of paper currency found that taint of immorality hard to shake. Most notable was the about-face of Salmon Chase. In 1870, when serving as Chief Justice of the U.S. Supreme Court, Chase wrote the majority opinion in *Hepburn v. Griswold*, which struck down the wartime Legal Tender Acts that he had pushed to pass. At issue was whether debts contracted in specie could be paid in paper notes. Ultimately, Chase thought not. His opinion brimmed with the kind of moralistic language that opponents of his financial measures had so recently used against him. "It certainly needs no argument," he wrote, "to prove that an act, compelling acceptance

---

[14] "How a Five-Twenty Bond Escaped a Rise," 1 August 1864, *Boston Daily Advertiser*, issue 26, col. C., available at 19th Century U.S. Newspapers, http://infotrac.gale-group.com.proxy.lib.duke.edu/itw/infomark/251/323/195719032w16/purl=rc1_NCNP_0_GT3006394100&dyn=9!xrn_3_0_GT3006394100&hst_1?sw_aep=duke_perkins.

[15] Legal Tender Act, 12 U.S. Statutes at Large 345 (1862).

in satisfaction of any other than stipulated payment, alters arbitrarily the terms of the contract and impairs its obligation.... Nor does it need argument to prove that the practical operation of such an act is contrary to justice and equity." Nothing could justify "the long train of evils which flow from the use of irredeemable paper money."[16]

In 1862, though, Chase followed the Legal Tender Act with a series of measures that solidified federal control of the currency. New legislation instituted a national banking system, creating incentives for state banks to join and taking away their power over the currency by taxing state bank notes out of existence. The centralization of financial policy proved complicated in practice and generated additional revisions over the course of the Civil War. Despite the problems, however, Chase's efforts legitimated the concept that federal involvement in the financial system constituted a necessary aspect of the nation's interests. Even his decision in 1870 in *Hepburn v. Griswold*, which was reversed the following year, could not dismantle what was put in place during the war years.[17]

Greenbacks and treasury notes brought the federal government into Americans' lives in immediate and intimate ways. They relieved a long-standing need for currency that reached back to the colonial period and that had made life extremely difficult for small producers and working people who had trouble obtaining notes of credit that wealthier people used as currency. Greenbacks quickly became a common – if not the most common – medium of exchange, because they were plentiful and dependable, despite their fluctuating value. Their practicality also imbued them with symbolic meaning. In fact, greenbacks and treasury notes literally brought the federal government directly into Americans' daily lives. When people pulled them out of their pocketbooks, they saw the United States – literally, engraved in large letters and personified in the solemn figures of federal officials. People, moreover, pulled them out

---

[16] *Hepburn v. Griswold*, 75 U.S. 603 (1870); quotes from 609 and 621. The opinion was overturned in the next term, *Legal Tender Cases*, 79 U.S. 457 (1871).

[17] National Currency Act (National Bank Act), 12 U.S. Statutes at Large 665 (1863).

often, with the faith that others would recognize and accept them. They were not disappointed, a marked contrast from the situation with other bank notes. With every transaction, every day, all across the country, Americans learned to associate the economy with the federal government.[18]

The federal government also raised revenue through new taxes. Congress laid direct taxes on a range of manufactured goods and passed an income tax in 1862. The income tax proved surprisingly popular, because it recognized sources of wealth that had become increasingly important as the economy developed in the nineteenth century. Until the income tax, taxes on land and goods provided the primary sources of revenue at the local, state, and national levels. It was a situation that placed the burden of taxation on farmers and small business owners, not those who were making fortunes in the form of salaries and other income in new segments of the economy. Those people also stood to gain from the war, given the demand for goods and services. So it only seemed fair that they, too, should contribute to the war effort. The income tax's graduated scale contributed to that sense of fairness, because only top earners ended up paying.[19]

The idea of the income tax also bolstered people's confidence in the nation. The American people could support the war effort without depending on foreign powers, self-interested banks, or other schemes that compromised their national independence. An article from the San Francisco *Daily Evening Bulletin* expresses the sentiment. Mixing an explanation of the practicalities of the tax with its ideals, and conveniently ignoring the fact that most of its readers would never pay the tax, the newspaper concluded that "every man may sit down at once and calculate to-night how much he must pay" for "the preservation of our liberties and our Union without which we can expect no permanent peace." "Let it be sacredly laid aside, as an offering on the altar of our country. It would be shameful to haggle about it, or to try to swear it down, or to postpone

---

[18] For the popularity of greenbacks, see Gretchen Ritter, *Goldbugs and Greenbacks: The Antimonopoly Tradition and the Politics of Finance in America* (New York, 1997).

[19] Revenue Act, 12 U.S. Statutes at Large, 432 (1862).

payment." In fact, the tax was so popular that there were protests when it was ended in 1873.[20]

Changes to the financial system unfolded at a certain remove from the American people, despite their popularity and the effect of tying them more closely to the federal government. Military mobilization, by contrast, required their physical participation. By the end of the Civil War, between two million and two and a half million men had served in the Union Army. The technology and tactics of the Civil War took all those who served to new places of horror. Military service also strengthened many soldiers' attachments to the nation. The men who made up the Union Army might disagree as to the substance of national values, but they all developed a common sense of themselves as American citizens through their experience as soldiers.[21]

The vast majority of the Union's troops were volunteers. Their numbers, however, ebbed and flowed. To keep recruits coming, the Union Army employed the carrot and the stick. The carrot took the form of bounties. By some estimates, bounties totaled $750 million – as much paid in regular salaries to the troops. The stick was conscription. The first effort came in 1862, when Congress authorized states to conscript troops to fill their militia quotas. This initial conscription effort ended in failure and had little impact on the lives of most Americans. It was not until 1863 that Congress created a national draft that applied to all men aged twenty-five to forty. Even then, the system had limited reach, particularly in comparison to Confederate policies. It conscripted only one soldier per family and offered a range of exemptions for health and family reasons. Some historians have described the system as a tax, because it exempted anyone who paid a $300 fee to the government (until the summer

---

[20] Quote from the San Francisco *Daily Evening Bulletin*, 12 January 1862, issue 88, col. B, available at 19th Century U.S. Newspapers, http://infotrac.galegroup.com. proxy.lib.duke.edu/itw/infomark/89/508/195722812w16/purl=rc1_NCNP_0_GT3000181676&dyn=4!xrn_1_0_GT3000181676&hst_1?sw_aep=duke_perkins. Richardson, *The Greatest Nation of the Earth*, pp. 115–38.

[21] Christian G. Samito, *Becoming American under Fire: Irish Americans, African Americans, and the Politics of Citizenship during the Civil War Era* (Ithaca, NY, 2009); Chandra Manning, *What This Cruel War Was Over: Soldiers, Slavery, and the Civil War* (New York, 2007).

of 1864) or who hired a substitute. Ultimately, African American volunteers, not draftees, met the demand for troops. Allowed into combat positions in 1863, black recruits from the United States and the Confederacy alleviated the need for more restrictive conscription policies. Only 2 percent of United States soldiers were draftees; 6 percent were paid substitutes.[22]

The draft, nonetheless, drew fire, because its exemptions were perceived as laying the burdens of service unevenly, demanding more of some than it did of others. While those with means could avoid service, poor people could not. Opposition to the draft used the rhetoric of slavery, a particularly powerful metaphor given the issues at stake in the Civil War. How could the U.S. government turn its white citizens into slaves to wage a war to free African Americans from slavery? Resentment exploded in the 1863 New York City draft riot, in which angry white mobs vented their ire on the city's African Americans: unable to punish the federal government, they destroyed the lives and property of those whom they identified as the beneficiaries of the war effort.[23]

ECONOMIC INDEPENDENCE AND THE LEGAL ORDER

All these wartime measures fit well within the Republican Party's larger political agenda, which emphasized labor as the source of all value and advocated policies that made labor more productive and more profitable. Republicans did not envision a change in the existing economic and legal order so much as an extension of it to the general population. Lincoln described it as "the right to rise": "When one starts poor, as most do in the race of life, free society is such that he knows he can better his condition; he knows that there is no fixed condition of labor, for his whole life." That goal was also evident in the Republican Party's slogan, "free soil, free labor, free men," which evoked a polity based on independent producers along the lines of the Jeffersonian ideal, although updated

---

[22] Conscription Act, 12 U.S. Statutes at Large 731 (1863). The figure on bounties is from Bensel, *Yankee Leviathan*, p. 138n82.

[23] Iver Bernstein, *The New York City Draft Riots: Their Significance for American Society and Politics in the Age of the Civil War* (New York, 1990).

to embrace the commercial expansion of the first half of the nineteenth century. In the Republican ideal, independent producers supplied their needs by selling goods to the market, instead of producing what they needed, as Jefferson envisioned. Yet Republicans still cleaved to the notion that free men owned the means of production (land, the tools of their trade, or – increasingly – their manufacturing enterprises), which allowed them to direct their own labor and to maintain their households. The economic independence of male producers grounded the legal order, because it entitled men to rights: access to the legal system through full civil rights as well as the ability to alter and create law through political rights. Economic independence thus secured the entire nation's future by ensuring a responsible, engaged citizenry, whose members were equal before the law.[24]

Republicans believed that government acted in the best interests of everyone by keeping economic opportunities open. As long as the system remained open, everyone's interests were of a piece: the interests of capital and labor aligned; so did the interests of business and government. Young men might labor for someone else for a time, but that would be a temporary stop on the way up the economic ladder. Some men might end up better off than others, but that was a result of their hard work. Their good fortune, moreover, redounded to the benefit of everyone else, by creating more opportunities for others to apply their labor. By promoting economic opportunities of all kinds, government encouraged the extension of this system, one that fostered a rough economic equality and a harmony of interests, rather than vast inequalities and endemic conflict.

Despite the rhetorical emphasis on equality, inequality was integral to the Republican Party's political vision. By the 1850s, most adult white men could vote and claim the full array of civil rights on the basis of their age, race, and sex. But for others, age, race, and sex resulted in inequalities. The legal status of male, independent producers, for instance, assumed the subordination of all domestic dependents – wives, children, and slaves – to a

---

[24] Quote from John G. Nicolay and John Hay eds., *Abraham Lincoln: Complete Works, Comprising His Speeches, State Papers, and Miscellaneous Writings* (New York, 1920), vol. 1, p. 625. Eric Foner, *Free Soil, Free Labor, Free Men: The Ideology of the Republican Party before the Civil War* (New York, 1970).

male head of household and the denial of rights to them.[25] Free African Americans were included in theory but not in practice. The free black population had increased in the decades following the Revolution, with abolition in northern states, the prohibition of slavery in many western territories, and individual emancipations in the South. Yet state and local governments had responded by replacing the disabilities of slavery with restrictions framed in terms of race.[26]

Even for free white men, the ideal of economic independence and legal equality never fully described reality. For those without access to capital, economic independence was difficult to achieve. Capitalist economic change in the antebellum period only accentuated that situation. At the same time, state legislatures uncoupled free white men's claims to rights from their ownership of productive property, eroding the long-standing association between economic and legal independence. While such changes protected the legal status of free white men who did not own productive property, they also affirmed permanent structural inequalities that made it impossible for all free white men to achieve the kind of independence promoted by the Republican Party. The rights enjoyed by free white men, moreover, did not always exempt them from various legal restrictions that applied to anyone without visible means of support and those who performed menial labor.[27]

The distance between the ideal and the reality troubled some in the Republican Party. That was particularly true when it came to the status of enslaved and free African Americans – which is the subject of Chapter 3. But the growing distance between those who benefited directly from commercial development and those who

---

[25] Stephanie McCurry, *Masters of Small Worlds: Yeoman Households, Gender Relations, and the Political Culture of the Antebellum South Carolina Low Country* (New York, 1995); Jeanne Boydston, *Home and Work: Housework, Wages, and the Ideology of Labor in the Early Republic* (New York, 1990).

[26] Leslie M. Harris, *In the Shadow of Slavery: African Americans in New York City, 1626–1863* (Chicago, 2003); Joanne Pope Melish, *Disowning Slavery: Gradual Emancipation and "Race" in New England, 1780–1860* (Ithaca, NY, 1998). Also see Barbara J. Fields, "Slavery, Race and Ideology in the United States of America," *New Left Review* no. 181 (1990): 95–118.

[27] Christopher L. Tomlins, *Law, Labor, and Ideology in the Early American Republic* (New York, 1993).

did not disturbed some Republicans as well.[28] In economic matters, however, the party focused on using federal power to create conditions favorable to independent producers during the Civil War. The goal was to open opportunities so that anyone with ambition could take advantage of them – anyone, that is, who could make contracts and own property in their own names. More to the point, Republican policies assumed a polity made up of individuals who fit the liberal ideal – self-interested and profit maximizing, with universal traits that made them essentially interchangeable.

Wartime policies magnified those tendencies, as the federal government embraced a more individualized vision of private property. Those conceptions are exemplified in the Confiscation Acts, best known for establishing the freedom of escaped slaves. When it came to other forms of property, however, the Confiscation Acts strengthened individuals' property rights, limiting the federal government's ability to redistribute wealth or regulate economic activity in the name of the public good.[29] That kind of individualism was the party's greatest strength and its greatest weakness. It fueled the party's most idealistic policies, particularly its advocacy of African Americans' civil and political rights. But it also blinded many Republican leaders to structural inequalities that prevented some individuals from making use of the opportunities that were, in theory, open to all. That blind spot ultimately would transform the implications of the Republican economic agenda: instead of creating a republic of independent producers, Republicans lay the foundation for an industrial order. Indeed, the Civil War and Republican policies accentuated the economic problems of working people.[30]

Secession gave Republicans a decisive majority in Congress and the opportunity to act on their ideals, which they did, even as the war raged around them. They turned first to agriculture, which

---

[28] For one such Republican, see Michael A. Ross, *Justice of Shattered Dreams: Samuel Miller Freeman and the Supreme Court during the Civil War Era* (Baton Rouge, LA, 2003a).

[29] Daniel W. Hamilton, *The Limits of Sovereignty: Property Confiscation in the Union and the Confederacy during the Civil War* (Chicago, 2007), particularly pp. 20–81; David Syrett, *The Civil War Confiscation Acts: Failing to Reconstruct the South* (New York, 2005).

[30] Philip Shaw Paludan, *A People's Contest: The Union and the Civil War, 1861–1865* (Lawrence, KS, 1996).

they identified as the anchor of the economy. More than any other occupation, farmers personified the ideal of the independent producer because they could produce what they needed, rather than purchasing it from others. Contemporary economic theory also characterized agriculture as foundational to the economy in ways that manufacturing was not, because agriculture created value from the application of labor to the land, instead of just refashioning existing resources into different forms. These assumptions found expression in the "free soil" component of the Republican Party's famous campaign slogan. Free soil referred to agricultural lands worked by free labor, not enslaved labor. It also referred to western lands that would be made available at little or no cost to those willing to work them.

Before the Civil War, Democrats from slave states had led the opposition to measures that made western lands available to settlement on favorable terms because they feared an increase in the number of free states. After secession, Democrats and eastern Republicans still had difficulty with the idea of giving land away instead of selling it, particularly given the desperate need for funds to pay for the war effort. But supporters carried the day by arguing that the nation's future lay in its ability to encourage its people's labor. The current system, they argued, stimulated speculation, which produced "land monopoly," kept land out of the hands of hardworking people, and undercut the economic growth of the nation as a whole. Land monopoly, railed a senator from Kansas, "entered like an iron into the soul of the laborer" and "deadened his hopes and extinguished his aspirations to rise in the scale of society."[31] Opening up lands for settlement at no cost would actually add to the federal government's coffers in the long run by increasing the nation's wealth. The result was the Homestead Act of 1862, which opened up new areas in the West for settlement and made land available to individuals who homesteaded for five years. The act also prohibited slavery in the new territories. Applicants had only to be a head of household or twenty-one years old, meaning that lands also were open to immigrants, African Americans, or unmarried women. To secure farmers' success, Congressional

---

[31] Quote from Richardson, *The Greatest Nation of the Earth*, p. 142.

Republicans provided for the development and dissemination of new agricultural methods through the Land-Grant College Act and a new federal agency, the Department of Agriculture.[32]

Republicans then sought to tie all these individual farms together into a national network with the transcontinental railroad. This vision – a truly national market created through transportation – reached back to the early nineteenth century. It had been central to the Whig Party's platform, and members of that party had worked to build the necessary infrastructure at the local, state, and national levels. The centerpiece was a railroad that would enable the economic development of the nation's midsection and tie the coasts together into one vast market. Detractors had argued that state governments and, particularly, the national government should not be involved in the economy to such a degree. The escalating politics of sectional difference quashed the idea completely, particularly at the national level. Among other things, sectionalism made it impossible to settle on a route. But even if that problem could have been resolved, supporters of slavery increasingly saw any assertion of federal authority as a threat to the institution.

With southern states out of the picture, Congress acted quickly, passing the 1862 Pacific Railroad Act, which supported construction of a transcontinental railroad by giving away millions of acres of land and millions of dollars in subsidies. Construction moved from two directions. The Pacific Railroad began at Council Bluffs, Iowa, at the southwestern corner of the state. From there, it traveled west across the northern part of Nebraska through Omaha, Colorado Territory, and Wyoming Territory, ending at Promontory Point, Utah, where it joined the Central Pacific Railroad. Starting in Sacramento California, the Central Pacific went east over the Sierra Nevada Mountains through Nevada and into Utah. Completed in 1869, it was a stunning technological accomplishment.[33]

The railroad also signaled the Republican Party's territorial vision of the nation. Like the tracks of the railroad, the jurisdictional boundaries of the United States would extend, unimpeded,

---

[32] Homestead Act, 12 U.S. Statues at Large 392 (1862). Coy F. Cox, *Justin Smith Morrill: Father of the Land-Grant Colleges* (East Lansing, MI, 1999).

[33] Richard White, *Railroaded: The Transcontinentals and the Making of Modern America* (New York, 2011).

east to west, across the continent. The new territories acquired in the Southwest and Pacific Northwest as well as areas in the continent's interior would become states, full members of the nation, with governing structures that mirrored those of existing states. The party's territorial ambitions ignored the presence of Indians, who claimed lands on the continent as their own. The conflict between Native people and the United States reached back to the Treaty of Paris, which had settled territorial claims following the Revolutionary War and in which Indians were not included. The transcontinental railroad only heightened existing tensions. Its tracks traversed territories occupied by various Indian tribes, who did not think the land was the federal government's to use or give away. More ominous to western Indian tribes was the implication that the federal government intended to bring all territory on the continent under its control. The result was violence. On the Civil War's far western front, the U.S. military engaged in a series of bloody efforts to subdue Indians and remove them from their lands. That part of the war, which was as much about the Republican Party's vision of national unity as the conflict to bring Confederate states back in the United States, stretched across the remaining decades of the nineteenth century.[34]

Although focused on agriculture, Republicans did not ignore manufacturing. Congressional Republicans passed protective tariffs intended to support the growth of industry. The war's insatiable appetite for materiel fueled manufacturing. Small firms expanded into large enterprises as they rushed to provide guns, ammunition, and other supplies. Wartime demand for goods also encouraged innovation that resulted in new products in related fields, such as agricultural implements, steel, textiles, and food processing.[35]

Republican economic policies were of piece, facilitating exchanges across the nation's vast expanses. At their most idealistic, Republicans hoped that their programs would enhance individual

[34] Alvin M. Josephy, *The Civil War in the American West* (New York, 1991); Heather Cox Richardson, *West from Appomattox: The Reconstruction of America after the Civil War* (New Haven, CT, 2007); Elliott West, *The Last Indian War: The Nez Perce Story* (New York, 2009).

[35] Alfred D. Chandler, *The Visible Hand: The Managerial Revolution in American Business* (Cambridge, MA, 1977); Harold C. Livesay, *Andrew Carnegie and the Rise of Big Business* (Boston, 1975).

rights, particularly those of free white male household heads. Yet, with the exception of western settlers, few ordinary farmers, artisans, and laborers benefited directly. Republican initiatives instead fueled a competitive, national economy that swallowed up small, independent producers. Railroad corporations gained most directly, absorbing millions of acres of public land and other federal incentives. The businesses that supplied the U.S. military or took advantage of wartime economic opportunities could not be the kind of small, independent producers posited in the Republican Party's ideal. The Civil War even transformed farmers, the most successful of whom presided over large, mechanized enterprises, sold most of what they produced, and bought most of what they consumed.[36]

The Republican Party's ideology made it difficult to acknowledge the increasing distance between the interests of industrialists and the rest of the population. Republicans assumed not only a rough equality among individuals, but also a harmony of interests among them and between their interests and those of the government. In the spring of 1861, when the banks refused to back government debt, Treasury Secretary Salmon P. Chase was genuinely dumbfounded, so certain was he that the bankers' interests aligned with those of the government and the people. That same sensibility marked the federal government's handling of various economic ventures, from the transcontinental railroad to military contracts. Even when facts on the ground suggested caution, officials did not anticipate the need for oversight, because they were confident that contractors and the government shared the same priorities. The businessmen working with the government, however, saw new opportunities to make a profit. Chase's disillusionment with the banks, for instance, opened up an opportunity for Jay Cooke, who made a fortune selling government bonds for commission. Many of the industrialists identified as robber barons in the late nineteenth century got their start in wartime government contracts, including Cornelius Vanderbilt, Andrew Carnegie, Leland Stanford, and Collis Huntington.

---

[36] Paludan, *A People's Contest*, emphasizes the connection between the wartime policies and capitalist transformation, arguing that the two are difficult to disentangle.

For most Americans, the economic future was one of wage labor, not independent production, despite wartime measures that opened up vast new areas of farmland. That created unforeseen contradictions, because the Republican legal order still envisioned a nation of independent producers, not of wage laborers. Wage laborers were included among the "free men" of Republican rhetoric, in the sense that they owned their own labor, could sell it at will, and could enjoy whatever they earned in doing so. If they were adult, white, and male, they also could claim full civil and political rights, at least in theory. But in practice, they were legally subordinate to their employers, who enjoyed rights as independent producers that wage workers did not. Property rights gave employers extensive authority over their factories. Those rights extended over laborers while they were on the job, where they could do little to alter working conditions on property that was not their own. In this context, the legal equality that wage workers theoretically enjoyed as citizens could actually compound their subordination. In law, Vanderbilt and his employees were contractual equals, even though they were clearly unequal in practice. As a property owner, moreover, Vanderbilt could do whatever he wished with his property, dictating the terms of labor to his employees, who had no recourse because of Vanderbilt's property rights.

The reluctance of many Republicans to expand federal authority further beyond its traditional bounds accentuated these problems. They were comfortable using federal power to promote economic growth, the principle of equality before the law, and the Union. But they were unwilling to use it to address the inequalities that resulted in practice, whether economic or legal. Doing so, they argued, pushed centralization too far, and threatened individual liberty.

That stance shaped popular perceptions of the federal government during the Civil War. Wartime rhetoric promised much more than the Republican Party actually delivered. During the war, the party encouraged the American people to see themselves as the center of the nation, and many started to think this way. Americans gave freely and generously during the Civil War, eagerly supporting the nation and proud to be a part of it. Yet encounters with the federal government were not always positive, even for those who supported the war effort. Despite Republican intentions to distribute existing economic opportunities and legal rights more broadly, most ordinary Americans actually experienced federal authority in terms of what the government asked of them: financial support and military service. The federal government did not give – it took. Many Americans, moreover, found it difficult to ignore growing inequalities that they saw all around them every day. To make their national vision work, Republican officials needed to close that gap between rhetoric and reality, to make the government reach the people. It was a tall order.

2

The Confederacy and Its Legal Contradictions

On March 18, 1863, a large group of very determined women marched through the streets of Salisbury, North Carolina. Between fifty and seventy in number, they were the widows and wives of Confederate soldiers who could no longer feed their families. So off they went to the railroad station where they heard that a merchant – a speculator, as they termed him – had stored some flour. The agent at the station tried to keep them out, insisting that there was nothing there. But he was no match for a passel of angry women, who came armed with hatchets and knew how to use them. As an eyewitness described it, they stormed past him and into the station. "The last I saw of the agent, he was sitting on a log blowing like a March wind." (Presumably, that meant he had been rendered as pointless as a winter wind come spring, howling loudly, but to no real effect.) The women "took ten barrels, and rolled them out and were setting on them, when I left, waiting for a wagon to haul them away."[1]

Such actions, often led by women, took place all over the Confederacy in 1863. The most notorious unfolded in Richmond, where a mass meeting devolved into a riot that cleaned out the city's business district. Observers then and historians now have explained

---

[1] *Salisbury Daily Carolina Watchman*, 23 March 1863. For similar actions on the part of white women, see Victoria E. Bynum, *Unruly Women: The Politics of Social and Sexual Control in the Old South* (Chapel Hill, NC, 1992), pp. 111–50; Jacqueline Glass Campbell, *When Sherman Marched North from the Sea: Resistance on the Confederate Home Front* (Chapel Hill, NC, 2003); Stephanie McCurry, *Confederate Reckonings: Power and Politics in the Civil War South* (Cambridge, MA, 2010).

women's actions primarily in terms of desperation. To be sure, there was more than enough desperation to go around at this point in the war, when the Confederacy was short of pretty much everything. The spring of 1863 proved particularly difficult because produce from the previous growing season had run out and that from the new season had yet to mature. As prices skyrocketed, patience wore thin and tempers flared, ending in actions like the ones in Salisbury and Richmond.

Bread riots, however, were as much about the precarious state of the Confederacy's legal order as they were about the scarcity of goods. In 1860, secession and states' rights were synonymous: secessionists expressed their opposition to the federal government's policies on slavery, the tariff, and internal improvements as a critique of centralized authority. That connection – between the content of policies and the structure of government – fell apart once southern states seceded. Instead of pursuing the kind of radical decentralization promised in the rhetoric of fire-eaters, Confederate leaders modeled their federal government after that of the United States. Neither did they institute change at the state or local level. In fact, as the war dragged on, Confederate leaders kept extending government authority, reaching deep into the daily lives of everyone within its jurisdiction, appropriating their labor, property, and lives for the nation, and leaving little for anything else. And so it was that a political movement based in a fundamental disdain for centralized government ended up producing a government far more centralized, at least in theory, than the one it left. To complicate matters, Confederate leaders maintained a rhetorical commitment to decentralization wholly at odds with their increasingly centralized governing structures.

Not everyone accepted – or even acknowledged – that outcome, particularly because centralization seemed to create more problems than it resolved. What riled the Salisbury women was the disparity between the authority that government claimed and what it actually delivered. As they explained, they could afford government prices for flour, referring either to the set price that the Confederate government paid for goods or its policies that made surplus provisions (a largely theoretical concept in 1863) available to the families of soldiers at prices below market value. These women felt entitled to government prices, as citizens of the Confederacy who had given so much to their nation's war effort. Yet government – be it local, state, or federal – could not deliver. So the women took matters into their own hands. More to the point, they took the law into their own hands, certain of the legitimacy of their actions and with the expectation of community support. It was an accurate assessment of the situation. No one – not even the feckless railroad agent – stopped them as they raided the station in broad daylight, rolled their flour barrels out to the street, and waited patiently for transportation.[2]

The centralization of government authority in the Confederacy created the conditions for its own demise. By 1863, it was no longer clear who held legal authority in the Confederacy, how it was defined, or what it should accomplish. The Salisbury women were not so much opposing their government as they were enforcing policies that they either attributed to it or thought it should be supporting. Following the example of their leaders, they applied the principles of decentralization, assumed the mantle of legal authority, and acted on their own conceptions of what the law prescribed. So did many others in the Confederacy. The resulting conflicts further eroded the Confederate government's legal legitimacy – and ultimately undermined governmental authority at all levels. It was not where secessionists imagined the rhetoric of states' rights would lead, but that was where it took them.

THE CENTRALIZED CONFEDERACY

Delegates met at the Montgomery Convention in February 1861 to create a provisional government and to frame a new constitution in accord with the political principles of the Confederacy. No one there suggested the adoption of the Articles of Confederation, with its radical affirmation of states' rights, as a model for the Confederate government. In fact, no one suggested radical change of any kind at all. "It is by abuse of language," President Jefferson Davis insisted in his inaugural address, that secession and the formation of a new nation "has been denominated a revolution." Confederates may have seceded from the United States, but not from its institutions

---

[2] *Salisbury Daily Carolina Watchman*, 23 March 1863.

or its ideals. "The Constitution framed by our fathers," Davis declared, "is that of these Confederate States." The Confederacy would reclaim and purify those structures, by separating from the corrupting influences that had taken over the United States.[3]

So it was. The basic institutional structure of the Confederate government – and its relationship to the states – duplicated that of the U.S. government. The delegates to the Montgomery Convention did make a few changes. Most notably, they added provisions to the Confederate Constitution that forbid Congress from "denying or impairing the right of property in negro slaves," establishing protective tariffs, or launching internal improvements – all key issues in the conflict that led to secession. In the Constitution's preamble, delegates also gestured grandly to states' rights, substituting the U.S Constitution's "we the people" with "we, the people of the Confederate States, each State acting in its sovereign and independent character." Those concessions to radical secessionists, however, sat uneasily in a document otherwise identical to the U.S. Constitution. Delegates retained a version of the supremacy clause, which subordinated state law to the Confederate Constitution, "the supreme law of the land." They also kept a "necessary and proper" clause, which allowed Congress wide legislative latitude in pursuing its delegated powers. Following through with that construction of federal power, delegates flatly rejected measures to allow secession and nullification. They further undercut states' rights in the controversial area of slavery, by continuing the federal prohibition on the international slave trade and the practice of counting slaves as three-fifths of the population for the purposes of representation in the federal government. Even the preamble muted its own states' rights rhetoric by affirming the establishment of a "permanent federal government."[4]

After the framing of the constitution, Confederate leaders proceeded to assimilate the laws, institutions, and installations of the

[3] Confederate States of America, Inaugural Address of the President of the Provisional Government, 18 February 1861, available at The Avalon Project, http://avalon. law.yale.edu/19th_century/csa_csainau.asp.
[4] Constitution of the Confederate States, 11 March 1861, available at The Avalon Project, http://avalon.law.yale.edu/19th_century/csa_csa.asp.

U.S. government. The delegates to the Montgomery Convention adopted all existing U.S. laws, until altered or appealed. After the Montgomery Convention, the new government took over existing federal institutions already in place in the region, including the postal system, federal courts, customs houses, lighthouses, arsenals, and – to the consternation of Union officials – the mint and all its gold and silver in New Orleans. In all these instances, the transition to the Confederacy was about as involved as taking down one sign and putting up another: the operations, even the personnel, remained the same. What the Confederacy could not absorb, it duplicated. The Confederate Quartermaster Bureau, according to historian Robert Black, "was a photographic reproduction of the United States organization." So were other bureaucracies in the Confederacy. Even the Confederate Congress adopted the same rules as those that governed the U.S. Congress.[5]

The ease with which the Confederacy adopted the institutions of the United States pointed to similarities between the two sections that remained, undisturbed, by secession. In fact, the rhetoric of states' rights can obscure the fact that the structure of the Confederate government owed more to the political legacy of the United States than it did to a uniquely southern governing tradition.[6] To be sure, slave states elaborated laws that sanctioned and regulated slavery. But that situation was the result of a constitutionally sanctioned legal order that gave states extensive authority over the legal status of state residents as well as all matters regarding the public health and welfare. The content of law varied from state to state, but the dynamic that produced those differences was common to all states. In that sense, secessionists purposefully overstated the differences between the two sections by equating policy differences with differences in governance that carried broader moral resonance: free states in the centralized (corrupt) North loomed as the ominous opposite of decentralized (virtuous) slaveholding states in the South.

[5] Quoted in Robert C. Black, *Railroads of the Confederacy* (Chapel Hill, NC, 1952), p. 50. Wilfred Buck Yearns, *The Confederate Congress* (Athens, GA, 1960), 32–5; Paul P. Van Riper and Harry N. Scheiber, "The Confederate Civil Service," *Journal of Southern History* 25 (1959): 448–70.

[6] Bensel, *Yankee Leviathan*.

By the 1850s, the institutions of governance in southern states looked a great deal like those elsewhere in the nation, with established institutional structures that exercised authority over a wide range of matters, both public and private. Since the end of the Revolution, political leaders across the region had worked to regularize the operations of law and government. Those efforts involved the centralization of legal authority at the state level, the subordination of local jurisdictions to state government, and the creation of rationalized bodies of law that applied uniformly, regardless of local conditions. To these ends, state leaders collected and organized existing statutes, created appellate courts with the power to set precedent, and clearly identified the state as the place where law was created and interpreted. If anything, the secession movement accelerated state centralization, by vesting states with even more power – both symbolic and actual – over individual rights and the public welfare. In theory, secessionists elevated state government over local jurisdictions as well as the federal government.[7]

Despite the rhetoric of states' rights, secession did not initially involve substantive changes in the structure or even the duties of state government. At their secession conventions, Deep South states passed new constitutions and a series of ordinances to set themselves up as independent governments. These new constitutions made only minor changes to the operation of state government and the rights of the people, because their focus was fixed firmly on the implications of separation from the United States. They affirmed that split, while the various ordinances buttressed state sovereignty by claiming all the powers formerly exercised by the U.S. federal government, including foreign relations and citizenship. But states never followed through in setting up these new departments, because of the adoption of the Confederate Constitution. Not only did that constitution give the Confederate federal government authority over most of the functions states had just claimed, but it also subordinated states within the new federal structure. That left states much as they had been before, although with a federal government located first in Montgomery and then in Richmond, rather

[7] Laura F. Edwards, *The People and Their Peace: Legal Culture and the Transformation of Inequality in the Post-Revolutionary South* (Chapel Hill, NC, 2009).

than in Washington, D.C. Upper South states, which seceded after the framing of the Confederate Constitution, did not even bother to frame new constitutions.[8]

In practice, moreover, governance in the region remained highly localized in southern states, despite the expansion of state government and the rhetoric of states' rights. The situation was actually similar in the North and West, where local areas also exercised considerable authority over a wide range of public issues that later migrated to state and, ultimately, federal jurisdictions. The most visible of these venues were circuit courts, which met on a regular schedule in county seats or court towns, held jury trials, and dealt with a wide range of business, including public welfare, markets, and morals. But circuit courts were only the most conspicuous part of a system dominated by even more localized legal proceedings, including magistrates' hearings and trials, inquests, and other ad hoc legal forums that were intended to preserve the peace – the social order – as defined in local areas. Magistrates not only screened cases and tried minor offenses, but also kept tabs on potential sources of disorder in their neighborhoods. In most legal matters, the interested parties collected evidence, gathered witnesses, and represented themselves. Cases were decided by common law in its traditional sense as a flexible collection of principles rooted in local custom, but that also included an array of texts and principles as potential sources for authoritative legal principles. Each jurisdiction produced inconsistent rulings, aimed at resolving particular matters, rather than producing a uniform, comprehensive body of law. Many saw that situation as natural and just: to them, it made no sense to impose arbitrary rules developed elsewhere without

---

[8] The Constitution of the State of Texas, available at Documenting the American South, http://docsouth.unc.edu/imls/texconst/menu.html; Journal of the Public and Secret Proceedings of the Convention of the People of Georgia, at http://docsouth.unc.edu/imls/georgia/georgia.html; Journal of the State Convention, and Ordinances and Resolutions Adopted in March 1861 (Mississippi), at http://docsouth.unc.edu/imls/msconven/msconven.html; Ordinances and Constitution of the State of Alabama, at http://docsouth.unc.edu/imls/alabama/menu.html; Ordinances and Constitution of the State of South Carolina, at http://docsouth.unc.edu/imls/southcar/menu.html. Compare to Ordinances and Resolutions Passed by the State Convention of North Carolina, 1861–2, at http://docsouth.unc.edu/imls/ncconven/ncconven.html.

paying attention to the particular attributes of local communities. Even as many white southerners found the rhetoric of states' rights attractive, they remained deeply enmeshed within the practice of local rule.[9]

The importance of local government did not distinguish southern states from states in the North or West. But localism had particular consequences in the context of the Confederacy, where the rhetoric of secession and its affirmation of decentralized authority in law and government gave new meaning to existing expectations of local control. Secessionists emphasized states as the primary units of law and government. But the rhetoric of secession encouraged expansive notions of decentralization, which went well beyond what Confederate leaders envisioned, let alone sanctioned. Proponents of localism went further, rooting legal authority in particular communities and rejecting centralizing tendencies at *both* the state and federal level. Circumstances in the Confederacy then allowed those notions of localism to flourish. Such notions, for instance, encouraged the actions of people whom Confederate leaders considered politically marginal – such as the women in Salisbury – but who saw themselves as fully authorized to act in their own communities' interests.

The demands of war foiled Confederate leaders' plans to move forward with a more purified version of the United States. The Confederacy lagged behind the United States in its ability to wage war by almost every measure – population, transportation, agricultural acreage, and manufacturing capacity. The figures are staggering. In 1861, the Confederate states had a population of nine million, 3.5 million of whom were enslaved. The population of the states that remained in the Union was twenty-two million. Confederate states had less than half the railroad mileage of the United States. Much of it was difficult to navigate, because the various railroad lines used different gauges, which meant unloading and reloading onto different cars at transfer points. Existing lines, moreover, did not connect areas of military and industrial significance. In 1860, manufacturers in states that would make up the Confederacy were valued at $69 million, in comparison to $388.2 million for the Middle states, $223.1 million for New England, and $201.7 million

---

[9] Edwards, *The People and Their Peace*, particularly pp. 26–99.

for the states in the West. In 1860, the states that would become the Confederacy produced only seventy-six thousand tons of iron ore, compared to 2.5 million tons in the rest of the United States, and less than one-sixteenth of the four hundred thousand tons of iron rolled in the Union. While on the eve of the Civil War, Confederate states produced four-fifths of the world's cotton, but they lagged far behind in textile production. In 1860, cotton mills in the states that became the Confederacy were valued at about one-tenth of the valuation of cotton mills in the United States.[10]

To marshal limited resources, the Confederate federal government extended its authority in unprecedented directions, going well beyond what the Union ever did. That happened almost immediately, early in 1862, when it became clear that the war would be neither short nor easy, and the first Confederate Congress passed a series of acts that charted their federal government's new course. Perhaps the most important was the Conscription Act of 1862, which made all able-bodied white men between the ages of eighteen and thirty-five eligible for service in the Confederate Army and extended the terms of those already enrolled for three years. In September of that year, Congress raised the age of eligibility from thirty-five to forty-five. The service requirements, alone, constituted an unprecedented exercise of federal authority. It was the first military draft ever instituted in North America, and it was rigorously enforced. The U.S. government did not follow suit until more than a year later. Even then, the U.S. draft appeared mild and ineffectual by comparison to its Confederate counterpart.[11]

Confederate conscription, however, did much more than scoop up men for military service. The draft nationalized the military, replacing state militias with a centralized command structure that assumed control over the supply as well the enlistment of troops – something that the United States never did. It also provided mechanisms for the exercise of broad authority over the economy through a schedule of occupations that qualified for exemptions, determined at the discretion of Confederate officials. The occupational

---

[10] Figures from Emory M. Thomas, *The Confederacy as a Revolutionary Experience* (Englewood Cliffs, NJ, 1970), pp. 79–80.

[11] Bensel, *Yankee Leviathan*, particularly pp. 135–9.

schedule not only enabled federal officials to exempt individual white men from service, but also allowed the federal government to provide select manufacturers in select industries with a labor force, be it free or enslaved, male or female. While the terms of the draft expanded and the occupations eligible for exemptions decreased over time, the federal government retained its power to allocate labor – but only to businesses that agreed to the terms of government contracts.[12]

The 1862 Conscription Act was the first of many policies that ultimately allowed the federal government to capture the region's productive capacity. Congress extended its control over labor in the same session, with an act that gave Confederate officials and military commanders the power to impress enslaved men at will. They did so with increasing frequency during the war, often over masters' protests. The government exercised its authority over labor early and often with the railroads, essentially nationalizing railway operations. Manufacturers soon felt the influence of federal authority as well. Existing manufacturers that produced war-related goods – particularly textiles, shoes, and leather – found that they lost access to labor, raw materials, and markets unless they supplied the government on its terms. The federal government also provided start-up loans to encourage the development of industries necessary for the war, but in which the region was weak, including iron, shipbuilding, weapons, and other war materiel. While all these businesses were privately held, none could operate without government contracts, which came with strict oversight, including ceilings on prices and profits as well as access to labor. As a result, the Confederate government ended up exercising extensive control over private industry, forcing it to work for the government, and then dictating the terms of production. Manufacturers who did not cooperate or who did not produce goods crucial to the war effort found it impossible to do business at all.[13]

---

[12] Charles W. Ramsdell, "The Control of Manufacturing by the Confederate Government," *Mississippi Valley Historical Review* 8 (1921): 231–49; Thomas, *The Confederacy as a Revolutionary Experience*, particularly pp. 61–2, 67–8.

[13] Ramsdell, "The Control of Manufacturing by the Confederate Government," 231–49; Thomas, *The Confederacy as a Revolutionary Experience*, particularly pp. 61–2, 67–8.

Other measures solidified federal control over the economy. As early as the fall of 1861, President Jefferson Davis was advocating federal support for railroad construction, despite the constitutional prohibition against it. Congress agreed and voted overwhelmingly to fund construction of a road between Danville, Virginia, and Greensboro, North Carolina, at its first session in February 1862. More funding followed for other railroads, the construction of which suffered more from a shortage of iron than a commitment to states' rights. Congress not only allocated funds to private firms in war-related production, but also allowed the military to set up works of its own. The results, as many historians have noted, transformed the region's economy. By the end of the Civil War, the Confederacy had significantly expanded its iron industry, increasing production in existing enterprises and building new ones from the ground up; it built a navy, along with all the materiel necessary to raise and outfit a fleet of ships; and it kept its military in arms and powder, which required the creation of whole new industries as well.[14]

Federal policies also harnessed agricultural production to the war effort. Early in the Civil War, before the U.S. Navy's blockade could lock down Confederate ports, the Davis administration organized an embargo on cotton, hoping to use Europeans' need for the staple to support the Confederacy. That never happened. Even if it had, the U.S. Navy's blockade ultimately destroyed the cotton trade. In an attempt to salvage something from the wreckage, the Davis administration engineered a federal takeover, in the form of the Cotton Bureau. With the approval of Congress, the bureau appropriated cotton for a uniform price and traded as best it could, with the proceeds going to the Confederacy's war coffers. With markets for cotton as well as the region's other key staples gone, farmers switched to food crops. But the federal government did for food crops what they did for cotton, allowing government agents to impress food and livestock at set prices, below market value. When that failed to bring in sufficient supplies for the military, Congress passed a 10 percent tax-in-kind on agricultural produce. Collection

[14] Black, *Railroads of the Confederacy*; Charles W. Ramsdell, "The Confederate Government and the Railroads," *American Historical Review* 22 (1917): 794–810

practices tended to blur the line between what the government took and what it paid for, with government agents showing up to carry away its 10 percent while also forcing the purchase of the rest for prices well below what farmers would have needed to replace what they had just lost. Increasingly, Confederate bureaus – particularly the Quartermaster's Department, which supplied the military – dominated the region's economy. One historian has described their dealings in pestilential terms, as "country and city teemed with officious agents of the new bureaucracy, who sometimes impressed into service what they could not buy."[15]

More than that, federal policies favored large units over small ones. A few months after the passage of the 1862 Conscription Act, Congress added exemptions for overseers – either hired or a family member – on farms with twenty or more slaves. Wildly unpopular, the "twenty nigger rule," as it was called, was phased out by 1864. While in place, however, the rule allotted additional labor to large plantations, while draining small farms of their key labor force, namely adult white men. Labor was already at a premium on small farms. Remaining family members – women, children, and the elderly – were all accustomed to the heavy labor required to keep a farm going, but they could not replace the lost labor of their menfolk. Procurement policies further eroded the viability of small farms, by slowly cannibalizing them. Planters on larger farms with more resources could survive longer, supplying the government and still setting aside – or hiding – enough to sell for higher prices on the civilian market. Those on small farms lost their means of production and their ability to support themselves. The result was a decaying agricultural economy in which farms lay idle and farm families could not feed themselves.

The Confederate government then reached even further into the daily life of the region. At its first session in 1862, the Confederate Congress suspended *habeas corpus* and sanctioned the imposition of martial law. Confederate officials made liberal use of both to silence dissent and to impose order on the civilian population. The crackdown was particularly brutal in East Tennessee, western Virginia, and western North Carolina, where Unionism remained

---

[15] Quoted in Bensel, *Yankee Leviathan*, pp. 146–7.

strong. Thousands of dissidents there were locked up and held without trial.[16]

Anyone who tried to move around in the Confederacy felt the effects of martial law. The military controlled the railroads, prioritizing its needs over those of civilians, who never knew how long they would wait for transport. Passengers also were subject to a pass system that required them to obtain permission to travel. Senator John W. Lewis found it incredible that he could not leave Richmond for his home in Georgia without obtaining a pass, as he put it, "like a negro." As Lewis well knew, armed military guards would check his pass repeatedly on his journey home. In 1863, a frustrated man from Dalton, Georgia asked if "it is in accordance with the Spirit of the Constitution of the Confederate Government" that martial law be "so rigidly executed" as to require people to produce passes every five or ten miles at each small town along the rail line. It was clearly a rhetorical question.[17]

Martial law also locked down many cities with tight curfews that kept residents off the streets and strict pass systems that limited access to outsiders. Those measures magnified food shortages. Produce headed for the civilian markets moldered in railway stations awaiting transport, and farmers quit carting their goods to urban markets because it took so long to get through checkpoints into town.

THE COLLAPSE OF LEGAL AUTHORITY

The rhetoric of states' rights nonetheless dominated political discourse, even as the Confederate government continued to centralize its authority. Debates over the extent of federal authority, reminiscent of those within the United States before secession, emerged almost immediately – although evidence of those debates comes from the press and other sources, not from the proceedings of the Confederate Congress, which conducted its business in secret

---

[16] Mark E. Neely Jr., *Southern Rights: Political Prisoners and the Myth of Confederate Constitutionalism* (Charlottesville, VA, 1999), pp. 99–150; Paul D. Escott, *Military Necessity: Civil-Military Relations in the Confederacy* (Westport, CT, 2006).

[17] Quotes from Neely, *Southern Rights*, pp. 3 and 4.

sessions. Richmond, the Confederacy's capital, developed a political culture of gossip, backbiting, and intrigue, as members of Congress, military commanders, and appointed officials charged each other with either failing or abandoning the Confederacy's true principles. Jefferson Davis endured the harshest criticism. Representative Henry Foote, of Tennessee, for example, characterized the 1862 Conscription Act as a "rank centralizing measure" intended "to put down all opposition" to Davis's "scheme of despotic domination."[18]

Such charges, and the conspiratorial paranoia that fueled them, contrasted sharply with the Confederate Congress's overwhelming support for centralizing initiatives. Some historians point to Congress's refusal to establish a Supreme Court as evidence of that body's principled commitment to states' rights, distinguishing opposition to a centralized court from measures passed of necessity to fight the war. But that distinction understates the structural implications of many wartime measures, which gave unprecedented authority to the federal government. In practice, moreover, the absence of a Supreme Court made little difference. The Confederate Attorney General took on the duties that the Supreme Court would have performed, reviewing state laws to assess their compatibility with the Confederate Constitution. Challenges to the federal government's assumption of power came to the state courts, instead of the federal courts. But state courts did not provide a sympathetic forum for states' rights activists: they upheld the federal government's position in every single case.[19]

Governors proved to be more formidable adversaries, although their efforts tended to protect centralizing efforts within their own states. In fact, state governments underwent a centralizing process similar to that at the federal level. During the Civil War, Confederate states enacted a slate of policies that concentrated more authority

---

[18] Quoted in Richard Franklin Bensel, "Southern Leviathan: The Development of Central State Authority in the Confederate States of America," *Studies in American Political Development* 2 (1987): 81. For the divisive aspect of the Confederacy's political culture, see George C. Rable, *The Confederate Republic: A Revolution against Politics* (Chapel Hill, NC, 1994).

[19] For the Confederate Congress, see Yearns, *The Confederate Congress*. For the absence of a Supreme Court, see Bensel, "Southern Leviathan," pp. 124–5.

at that level of government, which included raising troops; limiting the production of inedible staple crops; subsidizing the production of supplies and materiel for the military; and policing the civilian population. Governors Joseph Brown of Georgia and Zebulon Vance of North Carolina, in particular, openly obstructed federal policies that infringed on their own states' authority – and, thus, their authority. Among other things, Vance refused to comply with the Confederate Quartermaster's efforts to rationalize the army's purchase of textiles and to centralize the distribution of uniforms and other supplies. Instead, North Carolina developed its own policies for controlling textile production and outfitting its own troops. In a similar spirit of independence, Governor Joseph Brown of Georgia ignored the state's conscription quota on the grounds that the state needed troops at home.[20]

Both of these examples, however, reveal the centralizing tendencies inherent within the principle of states' rights. Faced with the question of whether authority would lie with the states or the federal government, state leaders chose – not surprisingly – their states. They pursued their own centralizing policies at the state level, similar to those at the federal level, during the Civil War. North Carolina's leaders fought a successful rearguard action to control its own textile industry, while Georgia's leaders did the same to retain control over the state's militia.

State leaders' efforts to derail unpopular federal policies met with support. But the centralization of state authority was as unpopular as the centralization of federal authority. What people in the Confederacy knew was that government officials kept asking more and more of them, without doing much to justify the sacrifices they were demanding. Public frustration over that disparity, while frequently noted, has not figured prominently in the scholarship on the Confederate government. Focusing on Confederate leaders' commitment to states' rights and the effectiveness of their policies, scholars tend to abstract government from the people it served and measure its effectiveness through the decisions of its officials, the

---

[20] Thomas, *The Confederacy as a Revolutionary Experience*, pp. 71–3. He is building on Ramsdell, "The Control of Manufacturing"; May Spencer Ringold, *The Role of State Legislatures in the Confederacy* (Athens, GA, 1966).

content of its policies, and the effects of both in waging war against the U.S. Army. The situation on the Confederate home front tells a different story. While increasingly centralized in its structure and policies, the Confederate state could never muster enough legitimacy to sustain its legal authority on the ground – not even in Richmond, the Confederate capital. In 1863, when rioters were looting the business district, President Jefferson Davis appeared personally to calm the crowd, to no effect. Rioters dispersed only when he ordered troops to fire on them. It was hardly a ringing endorsement of his leadership.[21]

The fact that counties and municipalities shouldered the burden of social welfare only magnified the gap between service and sacrifice. At the point when people needed services the most, local governments literally crumbled. Federal and state policies left local governments with too many needy people and too few resources. Not only were there no resources to distribute, there were not even enough men to fill the necessary positions, keep local courts running, and maintain a semblance of order. The bread riots of 1863 expressed the failure of local government as clearly as they did that of either the state or federal government. In Richmond, Jefferson Davis was called in to pacify the rioters because the efforts of the city's mayor and the state's governor had already failed.[22]

As conditions deteriorated, the Confederacy descended into a chaos of competing governing bodies, in which everyone claimed to be in charge and no one could actually do much to resolve the problems that people faced in their daily lives. Disgruntled officials – at the local, state, and federal levels – turned the rhetoric of decentralization against their own, using it to cut down any expression of

---

[21] For the Richmond Riot, see Emory M. Thomas, *The Confederate State of Richmond: A Biography of the Capital* (Austin, TX, 1971), pp. 111–19. For recent literature that raises question about the legitimacy of government, see Gregory P. Downs, *Declarations of Dependence: The Long Reconstruction of Popular Politics in the South, 1861–1908* (Chapel Hill, NC, 2011), particularly pp. 15–41; McCurry, *Confederate Reckonings*.

[22] One of the classic statements about the inadequacy of relief measures is Paul D. Escott, "Poverty and Governmental Aid for the Poor in Confederate North Carolina," *North Carolina Historical Review* 61 (1984): 462–80. By contrast, see William Alan Blair, *Virginia's Private War: Feeding Body and Soul in the Confederacy, 1861–1865* (New York, 1998).

legal authority with which they disagreed. Local officials ignored state officials, who disregarded federal officials, who plotted against each other, making coordinated efforts to address serious public issues – such as the shortage of food – even more difficult than they already were.

The collapse of slavery contributed to the crisis in legal authority. Many enslaved African Americans saw the war as an opportunity to undermine the institution, and they did everything in their power to do so. Emphasizing those efforts, recent scholarship has characterized slavery's collapse as resulting from the interplay between enslaved African Americans and U.S. officials and their policies. The next chapter focuses specifically on that dynamic. But African Americans' rejection of slavery also had profound implications for the Confederacy's legal order. White southerners depended on the institution of slavery in an immediate, material sense. They assumed a right not only to enslaved African Americans' labor, but also to a social order that subordinated all African Americans within a coercive system that reduced them to the position of property. Even free blacks did not escape slavery's grasp. In law, they had been classified as freed slaves, not to be confused with free people. The Confederacy embarked on its fight for national independence with more than a third of its population opposed to it. What is surprising is that Confederate leaders gave so little thought to that situation.[23]

In law, slavery fit within a system of governance that linked individuals to the state and defined their legal rights through their positions within households. Heads of household assumed moral, economic, and legal responsibility for all their domestic dependents, including African American slaves, white wives, and children. They also represented their dependents' interests in the public arena of politics. The position of household heads thus translated directly into civil and political rights. The exemplary household head was an adult, white, propertied male. As the logic went, these were the only people capable of the responsibilities of governance, whether

---

[23] Recent literature has emphasized the importance of enslaved people in destabilizing conditions on the Confederate home front. For further discussion, see Chapter 3.

in private households or public arenas. By contrast, white women and children and all African Americans were thought to require the protection and guidance of white men, because they lacked self-control and the capacity for reason. When African Americans ran to Union lines or otherwise challenged slavery, they threatened the structure of this entire legal order. If masters could not control their dependents and dependents could leave at will to direct their own lives, the basis of all white men's rights and the legitimacy of the entire system was called into question.[24]

The logic of the legal order led white southerners to equate social order with the physical presence of white men. As slavery began collapsing, many blamed the situation on the absence of white men, not a war that, by its nature, gave African Americans the opportunity to pry themselves loose from the institution. White southerners also linked slavery's end to the specter of bloody slave revolts, so certain were they that the institution, complete with its necessary masters, was what kept African Americans in line. Those concerns spurred the addition of exemptions for overseers on plantations with twenty or more slaves in 1862. As the war dragged on, some Confederate leaders demanded that troops be pulled from the front and stationed in local areas. Barring that, they asked that more white men be left on the home front to maintain slavery and, with it, the social order that they identified as the Confederacy's founding mission. The Confederate government, however, privileged battles with the Union army over the legal crisis unfolding on the home front, creating tension between its policies and its professed principles. At the end of the war, the Confederate Congress even approved a measure that would have enlisted and armed slaves in exchange for their freedom.[25]

---

[24] Peter Winthrop Bardaglio, *Reconstructing the Household: Families, Sex, and the Law in the Nineteenth-Century South* (Chapel Hill, NC, 1995), particularly 3–26. Also see Chapter 1, note 21.

[25] Robert Franklin Durden, *The Gray and the Black: The Confederate Debate on Emancipation* (Baton Rouge, LA, 1972); Bruce C. Levine, *Confederate Emancipation: Southern Plans to Free and Arm Slaves during the Civil War* (New York, 2006). As Crystal Feimster has argued, the notion that white men failed to protect their women and children fueled the political mobilization of white women after the Civil War; see *Southern Horrors: Women and the Politics of Rape and Lynching in the American South* (Cambridge, MA, 2009).

White southerners expected more of their government. Quick to express their dissatisfaction, they did so with candor and assertiveness. They also cast a wide net, venting their ire about whatever policy they opposed to whatever official happened to be handy, regardless of jurisdiction. That was because white southerners identified the location of legal authority differently than did their political leaders, whose concerns centered on the theoretical balance of power between the federal government and the states. White Confederates thought that legal authority rested – at least in part – with them. That presumption was derived from a tradition of local governance, which accommodated the customs of particular communities. The rhetoric that led them into war, with its emphasis on decentralized government and the importance of individual white men's interests, only raised expectations that government – at all levels – would respond directly to their needs.

The early offers to raise militia companies suggest the presence of localism and the potential of states' rights rhetoric to legitimize that particular vision of governance. Those who initially agreed to support the war had their own terms. In 1861, before passage of the Conscription Act, the Confederate War Department received hundreds of letters from men who were willing to raise volunteer companies, but only if they could serve less than the standard service requirement – the standard varied, given that states controlled the mustering of troops initially, but the Confederate federal government had indicated a preference for three years. As one man explained, "many of us here is anxious to serve our country if needed." But "we are mostly men of famileys and cannot leave our families for so long a term as three years." "If a company ... will be received for twelve months," he continued, "we will ... be ready to report for service in five days." A company in Georgia had conditions about the place as well as the amount of time served. As they explained to the governor, they wanted to remain "in our State & feel that twelve months will be best for us & our families." "Please let me know," their representative concluded, "if you will receive as above." It made sense that the war should be conducted on their terms, because they saw both the conflict and the government that managed that conflict as an extension of their interests.[26]

The terms of conscription clashed with those expectations. When white southerners had had enough, they simply withdrew their support through evasion or desertion. Efforts to force them into service failed miserably. Confederate military officials who rode through the countryside hunting down the country's own citizens and pressuring women and children to reveal the whereabouts of neighbors and kin accomplished little other than the further erosion of faith in government. By 1864, the head of the Confederacy's Bureau of Conscription reported that desertion had become so common "that it has, in popular estimation, lost the stigma that justly pertains to it, and therefore the criminals are everywhere shielded by their families and by the sympathies of many communities."[27]

That situation reflected a general sense that government was not doing right by its people. In the oft-quoted phrase, it was a rich man's war and a poor man's fight. For many, the best example was the exemption for overseers on plantations with twenty or more slaves. Although added to address concerns about the collapse of slavery, it smacked of arrogance and class privilege to other whites. The wealthy, complained a group of white women in Georgia, "dont care what becomes of the poor class of people" as long as "they can save there niggroes."[28] They were not the only ones who spoke out. The exemption came under such vocal attack that it was soon modified and slowly fazed out. Eventually, so was

---

[26] A. G. Hammock, 1 June 1861, Letters Received, Confederate Secretary of War, RG 109, reel 3, M1106, National Archives. John R. Allen, 7 Sept. 1861, box 22, Gov. Joseph Emerson Brown Papers, Incoming Correspondence (IC), Georgia Department of Archives and History (GDAH). These tensions were evident from the beginning of the Confederacy: Daniel W. Crofts, *Reluctant Confederates: Upper South Unionists in the Secession Crisis* (Chapel Hill, NC, 1989); William W. Freehling, *The South vs. the South: How Anti-Confederate Southerners Shaped the Course of the Civil War* (New York, 2001).

[27] Quote from Bruce Catton, *Never Call Retreat* (New York, 1965), 436. Albert Burton Moore, *Conscription and Conflict in the Confederacy* (New York, 1924); Ella Lonn, *Desertion during the Civil War* (New York, 1928); Mark A. Weitz, *More Damning than Slaughter: Desertion in the Confederate Army* (Lincoln, NE, 2005).

[28] The Ladies of Spaulding County, 25 June 1864, box 22, Gov. Joseph Emerson Brown Papers, IC, GDAH.

the hiring of substitutes, another way the wealthy slipped out of military service.

The sense of injustice, however, persisted and escalated. It was painfully obvious to many whites on the Confederate home front that the wealthy still had food, labor, and family, while they did not. Letters flooded the offices of government officials complaining about high prices, scarce goods, the lack of labor, and the deterioration of social order more generally. An anonymous Georgian summed up these frustrations: "old Mr. Stuard had 5 sons in the army ... Stuard is a poor man. Lee is rich and his sons are all at home, and it is so with other familys. They want other people do all the fighting and let them ly at home. Such people ought to be drafted and made go." She put the blame squarely on the government: "Do for Gods sake put an end to this unrighteous war!" Otherwise "we shall be eaten up by Confederate office holders and speculators."[29] By Confederate officials, letter writers did not necessarily mean federal officials; they meant all those connected with government at any level.

When their entreaties met with silence, white southerners took the law into their own hands. The result was not always lawlessness. Instead, people acted on their own notions of justice, grounded in local values and suited to the situation at hand. Those who sheltered deserters and who participated in food riots are examples of a wider effort to reclaim the social order. People not only appropriated needed goods, but also redistributed them to those who did not have enough. They set up an underground economy invisible to outsiders, particularly those who wanted to collect taxes. African Americans took over plantations, with the expectation of running them on their own. But so did dispossessed whites, who moved onto lands abandoned by slaveholders fleeing at the approach of Union troops.[30]

But with no identifiable center of authority, conditions did degenerate into lawlessness. Guerrilla war broke out in many areas

---

[29] Anonymous, Tunnell Hill, Catoosa County, no date; Anonymous, no place, no date; both in box 22, Gov. Joseph Emerson Brown Papers, IC, GDAH.

[30] In addition to note 1, see Wayne K. Durrill, *War of Another Kind: A Southern Community in the Great Rebellion* (New York, 1990).

of the Confederate home front, as ordinary people battled for the authority that the government could no longer command. In some places, the lines of demarcation were between Unionists and Confederates. In Jones County, Mississippi, for instance, Unionists seized control and seceded from the Confederacy to form the Free State of Jones, which became a haven for Unionists in surrounding counties as well. In other places, though, opportunistic mobs ransacked the countryside, taking what they could and doing as they wished, regardless of political affiliation.[31]

The rhetoric of states' rights was never realized in the governing structures of the Confederacy because such a system was so unworkable. Its contradictions, nonetheless, folded in on each other, bringing the Confederacy down with them. States' rights justified the centralization of legal authority at the state and federal level to preserve the nation it created, while also resulting in a collapse of authority so profound that anarchy ensued in some areas. By the end of the war, it was no longer clear who was in charge in many parts of the region. The Confederacy not only lost the war, it also lost its own home front. More accurately, the Confederacy's government lost legitimacy with its own citizens. Many die-hard Confederates had difficulty accepting General Robert E. Lee's surrender to General Ulysses S. Grant. But at least that side of the war did have an identifiable end. The other side of the war – the one that tore through the Confederate home front and destroyed its legal order – did not. Unresolved and largely relegated to a secondary position during the military conflict, those issues and their legal implications became the central focus of Reconstruction.

---

[31] Victoria E. Bynum, *The Free State of Jones: Mississippi's Longest Civil War* (Chapel Hill, NC, 2001); Michael Fellman, *Inside War: The Guerilla Conflict in Missouri during the American Civil War* (New York, 1989); Thomas Goodrich, *Black Flag: Guerilla Warfare on the Western Border, 1861–1865* (Bloomington, IN, 1995); Daniel Sutherland, *A Savage Conflict: The Decisive Role of Guerrillas in the American Civil War* (Chapel Hill, NC, 2009).

3

Enslaved Americans, Emancipation, and the Future Legal Order

Although slavery figured prominently in the rhetoric of political leaders on the eve of the Civil War, enslaved African Americans did not. When Abraham Lincoln was elected in 1860, he promised not to touch slavery in those states where it already existed. He did oppose the extension of slavery into western territories, in keeping with the Republican Party platform. But, otherwise, he vowed to keep the federal government out of the institution, leaving its regulation and the status of enslaved African Americans to the states. "I have no purpose, directly or indirectly, to interfere with the institution of slavery in the States where it exists," promised Lincoln in his inaugural address. "I believe I have no lawful right to do so, and I have no inclination to do so." Those words provided no consolation to Confederate leaders, who thought Lincoln's election would lead inevitably to slavery's demise. Even so, they gave surprisingly little consideration to the implications of war for those they held in bondage.[1]

Enslaved African Americans felt differently. They began leaving slavery in the summer of 1861, even before secession devolved into

---

[1] First Inaugural Address of Abraham Lincoln, 4 March 1861, available at The Avalon Project, http://avalon.law.yale.edu/19th_century/lincoln1.asp. Recently, James Oakes, *Freedom National: The Destruction of Slavery in the United States* (New York, 2013), has argued that the meaning of Lincoln's rhetoric has been interpreted too narrowly. In fact, he saw slavery as a perversion of federal law and never intended to keep the federal government out of the institution. But, whatever Lincoln intended, his early speeches signaled limited interference – which proponents of slavery did not believe. Policy, moreover, developed over time from limited to active interference.

war. More accurately, they left slavery for freedom, which moved geographically closer in 1861 than it had ever been before, particularly for those along the coast of the eastern seaboard. Where they once had to travel hundreds of miles to free states in the North, they were now within hailing distance of those states' representatives: the U.S. Navy, which patrolled the Confederate coast in its blockade, and the U.S. Army, which occupied federal forts offshore in Virginia, Georgia, North Carolina, and South Carolina. Enslaved African Americans along the South Carolina coast began fleeing to U.S. naval vessels as soon as the state seceded. By July 1861, about nine hundred of slavery's refugees had sought asylum with General Benjamin Butler's army at Fortress Monroe, Virginia.

It was not just the physical presence of the U.S. military that encouraged enslaved African Americans. Like everyone else in the country, they had been following news of the brewing sectional conflict. Unlike white Americans, however, enslaved African Americans saw the outbreak of war as an opportunity to reshape the terms of their own lives. Armed conflict – even the threat of armed conflict – exposed the fragility of the power structure on which slavery rested, rendering individual masters and the entire system vulnerable. So it was that enslaved African Americans, who lived along the Mississippi River near Vicksburg, also began leaving their plantations in the summer of 1861, even though the U.S. military was nowhere near. "The runaways," wrote Kate Stone, the daughter of one planter, "are numerous and bold."[2] Stone continued to describe slavery's collapse in clear and vivid detail in her diary over the next months. But she never acknowledged the actions of enslaved people for what they were: political opposition to the Confederacy and support for the United States. And it certainly never occurred to her that the people she spoke of in such patronizing tones fundamentally changed the terms of the war, turning it into something much more than an effort to keep Confederate states in the Union.

Recent scholarship acknowledges what Kate Stone and even later historians could not: that enslaved African Americans helped make emancipation a reality in the United States. Slaves were not

---

[2] Quoted in Sarah Katherine Stone (Holmes), *Brokenburn: The Journal of Kate Stone, 1861–1868*, edited by John Q. Anderson (Baton Rouge, LA, 1955), p. 27.

freed; they freed themselves.[3] Yet, in its focus on the social dynamics of emancipation, this scholarship has not fully explored the relationship between the actions of enslaved African Americans and the legal changes that abolished slavery. Running through much of the literature is the assumption that *individual* efforts to obtain freedom would inevitably result in the *legal* abolition of slavery throughout the entire United States. The leap from individual claims to a fundamental change in the nation's legal order, however, was much less certain than the historiography suggests. Individuals could be free without changing a legal order that sanctioned slavery. Nor was emancipation solely a matter of political will. To be sure, the politics of emancipation were formidable, involving a delicate balance among seemingly irreconcilable concerns: the differing views on slavery, federal power, and the nation's war goals as well as the immediate needs of military commanders in the field. But the nation's political leaders could do nothing until they confronted a legal structure that gave the federal government very little power over the legal status of individuals. In fact, the only way *federal* lawmakers could end slavery was to change the U.S. Constitution. That it was amended underscores the importance of enslaved African Americans, whose refusal to act as slaves not only made it impossible for federal officials to ignore slavery, but also forced them to confront the place of slavery within the nation's legal order.

What began with enslaved African Americans reaching for new lives ended in structural changes to the nation's legal order. Federal

---

[3] This point is most closely associated with the work of the Freedmen and Southern Society Project, which has done so much to make the wartime records relating to slavery and African Americans available. See Berlin et al., *Freedom: A Documentary History of Emancipation, 1861–1867*, Series 2: *The Black Military Experience* (New York, 1982); Series 1, Vol. 1: *The Destruction of Slavery* (New York, 1985); Series 1, Vol. 3: *The Wartime Genesis of Free Labor: The Lower South* (New York, 1990); Series 1, Vol. 2: *The Wartime Genesis of Free Labor: The Upper South* (New York, 1993); Steven Hahn et al., *Freedom: A Documentary History of Emancipation, 1861–1867*, Series 3, Vol. 1: *Land and Labor, 1865* (Chapel Hill, NC, 2008). But the larger point – that African Americans played a central role in destroying slavery – was first made by African American historians in the early twentieth century: W. E. B. DuBois, *Black Reconstruction: An Essay toward a History of the Part Which Black Folk Played in the Attempt to Reconstruct Democracy in America, 1860–1880* (New York, 1935); Benjamin Quarles, *The Negro in the Civil War* (Boston, 1953).

policy responded to the actions of individuals. But ultimately the implications extended well beyond those who sought freedom from slavery. The Thirteenth Amendment solidified an expansion of federal authority present in other wartime measures, but that might otherwise have contracted once the military crisis passed. More than that, it wrote the Republican Party's rhetorical promises into law, connecting the federal government to the people in unprecedented ways.

THE LEGAL PROBLEM OF EMANCIPATION

The nation's legal order joined slavery to constitutional questions about the balance of power between the states and federal government. The U.S. Constitution gave states broad authority over the people and their welfare, making it difficult for the federal government to legislate or, ultimately, mediate on the issue of slavery. Even those in relative agreement on slavery stumbled over the balance between state and federal authority, as the Republican Party's 1860 platform suggests. The second plank made a politically idealistic connection between the Declaration of Independence and the Constitution, asserting the party's support for "principles promulgated in the Declaration of Independence and embodied in the Federal Constitution": "'That all men are created equal; that they are endowed by their Creator with certain inalienable rights; that among these are life, liberty and the pursuit of happiness; that to secure these rights, governments are instituted among men, deriving their just powers from the consent of the governed." The plank reflected the recent rhetoric of party leaders, notably Lincoln, who had framed their position on slavery in terms of Revolutionary principles. In his widely republished speech at the Cooper Institute, Lincoln had argued that freedom was the national default. Slavery did not accord with the nation's founding principles, he argued, and the Founding Fathers never had intended its spread outside the states where it already existed. Yet, in connecting the Declaration of Independence to the U.S. Constitution, this plank conflated politics and law: it turned political ideology that animated the nation's founding into legal principles over which the federal government had unquestioned jurisdiction. That was not the case. As Lincoln and his peers well knew, the Declaration of Independence was not a charter for government; the U.S. Constitution was, and it positioned states, not the federal government, as the arbiters of individual rights. States determined who could vote, who could exercise civil rights, when the public interest took precedence over individual rights, and even whether human bondage would be permitted. Given the structure of the nation's legal institutions, which allowed for the evolution and interpretation of basic legal principles, the political ideals of the Declaration of Independence *could* make their way into law. In fact, a strong strand of antislavery constitutionalism did emerge in the decades between the Revolution and the Civil War that attempted to draw the kinds of connections between the Declaration and the Constitution that the Republican Party posited. But those connections were not clearly established in legal practice, because the U.S. Constitution proved maddeningly vague about the federal government's authority over most matters involving the legal status of individuals, including the status of slavery. By contrast, it was quite clear in giving the states broad authority in that area. Most Americans accepted and approved of this situation.[4]

The tension between the Republican Party's political ideals and the nation's legal structure proved impossible to ignore as the party's 1860 platform moved from the ideology of the Revolution to the very real issue of slavery. Rather than argue for expansive federal authority to weaken or abolish slavery, the Republicans used states' rights to condemn the U.S. Supreme Court's 1857 decision in *Dred Scott* and the Buchanan administration's subsequent backing of the proslavery LeCompton Constitution in Kansas in 1858. *Dred Scott*, which nationalized the recognition of slave property by allowing individuals to take slaves into free states as well as the territories, provided the rationale for President James Buchanan to

---

[4] "TRE Platform," 18 May 1860, *New York Times*, p. 1, available at Proquest Historical Newspapers, http://search.proquest.com.proxy.lib.duke.edu/hnpnewyorktimes/docview/91552854/13BB3E042AB6FF2A762/6?accountid=10598. William M. Wiecek, *The Sources of Anti-Slavery Constitutionalism in America, 1760–1848* (Ithaca, NY, 1977). Federal courts became more involved in individual rights over the course of the nineteenth century, particularly in personal liberty cases, which dealt with cases, such as that involving Dred Scott, of African Americans challenging enslavement. The federal government's jurisdiction, however, applied only in specific instances.

admit Kansas as a slave state. Such actions, the Republican platform claimed, constituted a perversion of federal power, because the U.S. Constitution gave states the right to "order and control [their] own domestic institutions."[5]

The federal territories, however, presented an altogether different situation, because the federal government had jurisdiction there. Federal policy, according to the Republican Party, should contain slavery to the states where it already existed. The *Dred Scott* decision challenged that position, with its implication that residents of the territories were not permitted to outlaw slavery, even if a majority wished to do so. In their platform, Republicans answered by summoning the nation's legal past. That past, according to the platform, proved that "the normal condition of all the territory of the United States is that of freedom." The evidence lay in the relationship between the Declaration of Independence, the U.S. Constitution, and the Northwest Territorial Ordinance: "That, as our Republican fathers, when they had abolished slavery in all our national territory, ordained that 'no persons should be deprived of life, liberty or property without due process of law,' it becomes our duty, by legislation, whenever such legislation is necessary, to maintain this provision of the Constitution against all attempts to violate it; and we deny the authority of Congress, of a territorial legislature, or of any individuals, to give legal existence to slavery in any territory of the United States." Therefore, it would be unconstitutional for the federal government to follow the U.S. Supreme Court's decision in *Dred Scott* and allow slavery in the territories.[6]

The Republicans' struggle to square their political principles with the existing legal order spoke volumes about the national culture, characterized by a combination of pride and insecurity in the accomplishment of founding a new republic. The country's leaders were committed to making their political experiment work, not challenging or changing it. Amending the Constitution did not figure as a solution to governing problems in the early nineteenth century, even when questions of constitutional interpretation suggested the need for greater clarity. That was particularly true on the issue of

---

[5] "TRE Platform," 18 May 1860, *New York Times.*
[6] Ibid.

slavery. No one in either party, for example, proposed constitutional amendments as a means of addressing the fallout from *Dred Scott*, which included opposition to the federal government in northern states nearly as heated as that in southern states after the election of Lincoln. *Dred Scott* heightened long-standing opposition to the Fugitive Slave Act (1850). In the decision's wake, many northerners believed the U.S. Supreme Court would soon extend its ruling from federal territories to the states and insist, contrary to decades of actual practice, that states could not outlaw slavery. In response, several state legislatures passed personal liberty laws, which effectively nullified both the Fugitive Slave Act and *Dred Scott*. In Wisconsin, the State Supreme Court went so far to declare the Fugitive Slave Act unconstitutional. When the U.S. Supreme Court reversed that decision in *Ableman v. Booth* (1859), the state legislature passed a resolution affirming the state's sovereignty.[7] Yet the conflict, while clearly focused on constitutional issues, never generated demands for a constitutional amendment. In fact, before the Civil War, even abolitionists did not advocate a constitutional amendment as a means of ending slavery. Congress entertained only a handful of amendments relating to slavery in the decades following the ratification of the Constitution and the first twelve amendments (all of which were added in the eighteenth century).[8]

When Americans did finally reach for amendments to resolve the crisis over slavery, they did so in a way that suggested their hesitance to change the existing legal structure. After Lincoln's election in 1860, Congress received about 150 amendments, offered by a wide range of Americans desperate to save the nation. Almost all of them recommended restricting the federal government's power in order to protect slavery and to leave authority over it to the states. Americans found it difficult to think outside the existing constitutional box – to imagine an active role for the federal government,

[7] Fugitive Slave Act. *Dred Scott v. Sandford. Ableman v. Booth* 62 U.S. 506 (1859). Don E. Fehrenbacher, *The Dred Scott Case: Its Significance in American Law and Politics* (New York, 1978); Mark Graber, *Dred Scott and the Problem of Constitutional Evil* (New York, 2006).

[8] Michael Kammen, *A Machine That Would Go of Itself: The Constitution in American Culture* (New York, 1986); David E. Kyvig, *Explicit and Authentic Acts: Amending the U.S. Constitution, 1776–1995* (Lawrence, KS, 1996).

particularly in determining the legal status of individuals. Even when faced with the dissolution of the nation, they left those issues where they had been since the Revolution, with the states.[9]

Americans might not be able to imagine a federal government that could end slavery, but many of them still thought the war would result in abolition, the Republican Party's assurances to the contrary notwithstanding. From the outset of the Civil War, free blacks in the North tried to turn the conflict into one for the abolition of slavery and the legal equality of all free people, regardless of race. Not all white abolitionists supported racial equality, but they still saw the war as an opportunity to end slavery. Americans less committed to the political cause of abolition also assumed that the conflict would end in abolition. But these conversations were all largely theoretical: at the beginning of the Civil War, there was very little that anyone could do to alter the legal status of slavery, short of upending the existing constitutional order. As Frederick Douglass wrote, the challenge was finding a way of "translating antislavery sentiment into antislavery action," given the limits of the existing legal system.[10]

The actions of enslaved African Americans in the Confederacy forced practical solutions to these theoretical conundrums. In May, 1861, three enslaved men "delivered themselves up" to General Benjamin F. Butler's picket guards at Fortress Monroe, located off the southern tip of the Virginia peninsula. What to do? The Fugitive Slave Act mandated that all runaways be returned, and Abraham Lincoln still insisted that nothing would be done to interfere with slavery in the states where it already existed, despite the outbreak of war. Current law and Republican policy statements, however, did not anticipate the situation that Butler faced: three African American men who sought shelter with U.S. troops because they

---

[9] For the slavery amendments in 1860, see Michael Vorenberg, *Final Freedom: The Civil War, the Abolition of Slavery, and the Thirteenth Amendment* (New York, 2001), pp. 18–22. The most influential were the Crittenden Amendments; see Amendments Proposed in Congress by Senator John J. Crittenden: 18 December 1860, available at The Avalon Project, http://avalon.law.yale.edu/19th_century/critten.asp.

[10] Quoted in Eric Foner, *The Fiery Trial: Abraham Lincoln and American Slavery* (New York, 2010), pp. 72–3.

did not want to work for the Confederate commander to whom they were enslaved. Butler saw an opportunity. "I had great need of labor in my quartermaster's department," he explained to General-in-Chief Winfield Scott. So he put the men to work. Shall the Confederates, Butler asked rhetorically, "be allowed the use of this property against the United States, and we not be allowed its use in aid of the United States?" Then he put the issue in legal terms, defining the African Americans as "contraband," property seized as a consequence of war. Suspecting that these three men constituted the beginning of what could be a mass exodus, Butler was informing this commander of the situation, asking for clarification as to the military's policy, and trying to frame the issue in his own terms. Scott responded that he found "much to praise ... and nothing to condemn" in Butler's handling of the matter, and Secretary of War Simon Cameron concurred. But neither Scott nor Cameron offered any specific statement about what, exactly, Butler's creative solution meant for either the status of the enslaved men now in his command or, by extension, federal policy on slavery.[11]

It was federal policy that had Butler – and every other military commander – boxed in when it came to the handling of escaped slaves. Butler found a way out of the conundrum by invoking international law, which allowed for the seizure and use of enemy property and therefore – theoretically – slaves. If slaves were appropriated as contraband, then Butler and other military commanders could act without contradicting federal policy that prohibited interference in slavery. Yet the principle of "contraband of war" was meant to apply only to property seized from neutral parties who were shipping war materiel to the enemy. There were no neutral parties at Fortress Monroe, unless African Africans were defined as both the neutral parties and the war materiel. Butler knew he was applying the concept of "contraband" loosely, but he believed it was the only way to resolve the dilemma posed by enslaved people who were seeking refuge at Fortress Monroe. "The truth is," Butler wrote of the contraband argument in his 1892 memoir, "as a lawyer

[11] Commander of the Department of Virginia to the General-in-Chief of the Army, 27 May 1861, available at the Freedmen and Southern Society Project, http://www.history.umd.edu/Freedmen/Butler.html.

I was never very proud of it, but as an executive officer I was very much comforted with it as a means of doing my duty."[12]

It did not take long for the actions of enslaved African Americans to upset the legal fiction of contraband. "Since I wrote my last dispatch," Butler informed Scott three days after the initial letter about the first refugees, "the question in regard to slave property is becoming one of very serious magnitude." Enslaved men were being forced to work on Confederate fortifications, and there were rumors that enslaved women and children would be shipped out of the area. Families with children were now asking for shelter at Fortress Monroe, which made it impossible for Butler to continue to maintain that he was holding the slaves as contraband of war, claiming their labor as property confiscated from the enemy. So Butler recognized the refugees for what they were: families, not property. As he explained, "I have therefore determined to employ, as I can do very profitably, the able-bodied persons in the party, issuing proper food for the support of all, and charging against their services the expense of care and sustenance of the non-laborers, keeping a strict and accurate account as well of the services as of the expenditure having the worth of the services and the cost of the expenditure determined by a board of Survey hereafter to be detailed."[13]

Butler knew that he was on increasingly shaky legal ground. So he justified his actions in strategic terms. If the African Americans in his charge were still enslaved, he informed General-in-Chief Scott, they would be worth somewhere in the neighborhood of sixty thousand dollars, which represented a significant loss for the Confederacy. Without their labor, moreover, Confederate forces could not have constructed fortifications as quickly as they had. But Butler could not hide the fact that his handling of the situation involved more than considerations about the strategic value of slavery in the war effort. That was clear in the questions that he posed to General-in-Chief Scott: "As a political question and a question of humanity can I receive the services of a Father and a Mother

---

[12] Quoted in Kate Masur, "'A Rare Phenomenon of Philological Vegetation': The Word 'Contraband' and the Meanings of Emancipation in the United States," *Journal of American History* 93 (2007): 1054.

[13] Commander of the Department of Virginia to the General-in-Chief of the Army.

and not take the children? Of the humanitarian aspect I have no doubt. Of the political one I have no right to judge." As Butler saw it, mothers, fathers, and children could not actually be dealt with as either slaves or contraband, despite what the law said.[14]

The African Americans who sought shelter at Fortress Monroe were shaping Butler's decisions. Butler did not support slavery. But neither was he an abolitionist – at least, not at the outset of the Civil War. In 1860, he was a Democrat, sympathetic to states' rights, who had voted for Stephen A. Douglas, not Abraham Lincoln. Previously, when in command in Maryland, he assured that state's governor that he would not interfere in slavery and even offered to put down any "servile insurrections" there. The Civil War gave African Americans the opportunity to change Butler's mind, by exploiting the fundamental legal contradiction of slavery: people were not the same as other forms of inanimate property, which made it extremely difficult to apply property law to them. It was because African Americans were human beings with feelings, desires, and the capacity for rational decision making that they kept coming to Union lines. Butler and other military commanders found it impossible to ignore their actions, if only because laws premised on the assumption that people could be governed in the same way as inanimate property tended to fall apart in practice.[15]

Butler's position, however, remained controversial in 1861, despite the tacit support of both the general-in-chief and the secretary of war. Drawn into questions about slavery unwittingly and unwillingly, the War Department responded in an ad hoc fashion, leaving decisions on the matter with commanders on the ground. The result was a patchwork of policies, dependent largely on the inclinations of the particular commanders. At the same time that Butler was struggling with the situation at Fortress Monroe, Brigadier General William S. Harney assured a Missouri Unionist that the U.S. military had no intention of interfering with slavery in that state or any other slave state, even those in the Confederacy.

---

[14] Ibid.

[15] Manning, *What This Cruel War Was About*, has argued that many white soldiers in the U.S. Army ended up opposing slavery, because of their experiences in the war.

Butler would have been surprised to hear Harney's take on military policy: "Already since the commencement of these unhappy disturbances, slaves have escaped from their owners, and have sought refuge in the camps of United States troops," but they were "carefully sent back to their owners."[16] Later, in November 1861, when a Union commander in Kentucky proposed to do what Butler had done, General William T. Sherman forbid it. "I have no instructions from Government on the subject of Negroes," wrote Sherman, and it is "my opinion ... that the laws of the state of Kentucky are in full force and that negroes must be surrendered on application of their masters or agents or delivered over to the sheriff of the County." In 1861, commanders in Maryland and Missouri also refused to shelter African Americans fleeing from slavery. To be sure, the situation in these states was different because they remained in the United States and it was easier to argue that existing laws supporting slavery were still in effect. Still, the differing responses suggest the ad hoc nature of the policy.[17]

The rapid adoption of the term "contraband" in popular culture highlights the uphill battle that enslaved African Americans faced. Military commanders in the field were the first to confront the fact that war made it impossible to leave slavery intact in the states where it already existed. That realization, however, did not lead them to abandon their convictions about slavery and race. The term "contraband" retained cultural currency long after the legal argument was abandoned, precisely because it captured both the ambiguities of African Americans' legal position and the reservations of many Americans about abolition. Those reservations were especially clear in one letter from General T. S. Sherman, from South Carolina. The "contraband" in question had been left behind

---

[16] Missouri Unionist to the Commander of the Department of the West, and the Commander's Reply, 14 May 1861, available at the Freedmen and Southern Society Project, http://www.history.umd.edu/Freedmen/Gantt-Harney.html.

[17] Commander at Camp Nevin, Kentucky, to the Commander of the Department of the Cumberland; and the Latter's Reply, 5 November 1861, available at the Freedmen and Southern Society Project, http://www.history.umd.edu/Freedmen/McCook-Sherman.html. For the unevenness of federal policy, see Louis Gerteis, *From Contraband to Freedman: Federal Policy toward Southern Blacks, 1861–1865* (Westport, CT, 1973).

by slaveholders fleeing the U.S. military and had set about working the lands abandoned by their former masters. Unimpressed, the general described them as "naturally slothful and indolent" and doubted that they would work without the threat of the lash or starvation. Sherman, like so many white Americans, evidently considered enslaved African Americans either too stunted by the institution of slavery or too inferior racially to act as free people. The term "contraband" expressed the general's discomfort, distancing him from slavery while still condemning those who had been slaves by rhetorically pushing them closer to the status of property, not free people.[18]

"It is really a question for the Government," T. S. Sherman concluded, "to decide what is to be done with the Contrabands." So it was. But when the nation's lawmakers took up the issue, late in 1861, they ran into the same problem that military commanders had: it was difficult to deal with the situation of escaped slaves without altering federal policy on slavery and, ultimately, confronting the constitutional issues involved in doing so. To say that federal policy inched toward emancipation one small step at a time, as so much of the literature in social and political history does, is to misconstrue the profound difficulties in accomplishing abolition in law. That scholarship focuses on the moral and ethical dimensions of the problem, charting lawmakers' course in grappling with their own feelings about slavery and their efforts to persuade others to act, assuming that abolition could be accomplished once the tide of opinion turned. But the law made it difficult for even the most principled official to use federal power to end slavery. Government policy during the war years reflected those legal constraints as clearly as it did federal officials' convictions about abolition.

With the First Confiscation Act, passed in August 1861, Congress allowed for the seizure of all property used in support of the rebellion, including enslaved African Americans. The

---

[18] Commander of the South Carolina Expeditionary Corps to the Adjutant General of the Army, 15 December 1861, available at the Freedmen and Southern Society Project, http://www.history.umd.edu/Freedmen/T%20W%20Sherman.html. Masur, "A Rare Phenomenon of Philological Vegetation."

act resolved questions about whether the military could shelter refugees. But it also reflected deep differences among lawmakers about federal control over private property. While distinguishing enslaved property from other forms of property, it left slavery in place, and even extended it behind Union lines, putting the federal government in the awkward position of sanctioning slavery and, perhaps, possessing slaves.[19]

A few months later, in December 1861, Secretary of War Simon Cameron addressed that dilemma in an impassioned annual report that advocated both the aggressive seizure of slave property, emancipation for all enslaved people who came within the jurisdiction of the U.S. military, and military service for African Americans. "It would be national suicide," wrote Cameron, to leave the Confederacy in "peaceful and secure possession of slave property, more valuable and efficient to them for war than forage, cotton, and military stores." But once slaves moved into the jurisdiction of the U.S. military, they could no longer be slaves, because the federal government did not have the legal power to keep them in bondage. Cameron maintained that the U.S. military should employ former slaves in active duty or some other capacity. "But in whatever manner they may be used by the Government," Cameron argued, "it is plain that, once liberated by the rebellious act of their masters, they should never again be restored to bondage. By the master's treason and rebellion he forfeits all right to the labor and service of his slave; and the slave of the rebellious master, by his service to the Government, becomes justly entitled to freedom and protection." In a dramatic rebuke, Lincoln forced Cameron to remove the references to the employment of slaves and emancipation. The final report, which cut the original twelve paragraphs down to a mere two, also watered down Cameron's position on the strategic necessity of seizing slave property. Soon after, Lincoln replaced Cameron with Edward Stanton – although

---

[19] First Confiscation Act, 12 U.S. Statutes at Large 319 (1861). James Oakes, in *Freedom National*, argues that the First Confiscation Act was not as ambiguous and largely resolved the status of enslaved people who made it to Union lines. In a larger context, however, the act and its application reflected the difficulty of legislating in the area of property rights, an issue that also framed questions regarding Indians' land claims.

the replacement had as much to do with Cameron's inventive use of patronage in allotting military contracts as it did with his position on slavery. The issues Cameron raised, however, were not so easily dismissed.[20]

Lawmakers felt more comfortable legislating against slavery in areas where the federal government had always exercised clear authority. In April 1862, Congress abolished slavery in the District of Columbia, over which the federal government had jurisdiction. But it did so by compensating loyal slaveholders and promoting the colonization of former slaves outside the United States. In previous congressional debates, compensation had come under fire precisely because it implied national recognition of slavery: if the federal government paid slaveholders for their slaves, it implicitly recognized the legitimacy of property in people. In June, Congress abolished slavery in all federal territories, without compensation – after all, many Republicans thought slavery never should have existed there in the first place.[21]

The question of slavery's status in states where it already existed in law, however, remained vexed. In March 1862, Congress buttressed the position of enslaved African Americans who sought refuge with the U.S. military with an article of war that forbid commanders from returning them to their owners. But it remained silent as to the legal status of those people. Two months later, in May 1862, General David Hunter created an uproar when he unilaterally abolished slavery in South Carolina, Georgia, and Florida, the states in his department of command and in which the U.S. military had a significant presence. Faced with the task of governing occupied areas, Hunter declared martial law and leaped from there to emancipation. "Slavery and martial law in a free country," as he put it, being "altogether incompatible," therefore, "the persons in these

---

[20] Draft and Final Versions of a Passage in the Secretary of War's Annual Report, available at the Freedmen and Southern Society Project, http://www.history.umd.edu/Freedmen/cameron.htm. Silvana Sidali, *From Property to Person: Slavery and the Confiscation Acts, 1861–1862* (Baton Rouge, LA, 2005), pp. 95–119.

[21] An Act for the Release of Certain Persons Held to Service of Labor in the District of Columbia, 12 U.S. Statutes at Large, 376 (1862); Law Enacting Emancipation in the Federal Territories, 12 U.S. Statutes at Large 432 (1862).

three States – Georgia, Florida and South Carolina – heretofore held as slaves, are therefore declared forever free."[22]

Hunter's order echoed that of General John C. Fremont, who used martial law to abolish slavery in Missouri in September 1861 and whom Lincoln promptly had removed from command. Hunter, however, was operating within Confederate territory, while Fremont had emancipated slaves in a border state that remained within the United States. Moreover, by the spring of 1862, U.S. military commanders faced a growing influx of African American refugees. Hunter now raised the same question as Secretary of War Simon Cameron: How could the military, an extension of the federal government, sanction slavery or, even more problematically, possess slaves? Lincoln immediately nullified Hunter's order, maintaining that the legal status of slavery involved "totally different questions from those of police regulations in armies and camps." He did admit that it might be necessary for the federal government to exercise authority over slavery at some point, as "a necessity indispensable to the maintenance of the government." But he reserved that power to himself, as commander-in-chief of the U.S. military.[23]

War powers provided a constitutional means to end slavery without upsetting the balance of powers between states and the federal government. Since the beginning of the war, abolitionists had been urging Lincoln to use the war powers of the president to end slavery in the Confederacy. During the secession crisis, Congressman John A. Bingham read excerpts of a speech by John Quincy Adams, who in 1842 identified the "war power" as the means to take down all the other constitutional barriers that protected slavery. As historian Eric Foner tells the story, "Charles Sumner rushed to the White House" after the attack on Fort Sumter "and told the president 'that under the war power the right had come to him to emancipate the slaves.'" The logic was that war gave the president broad powers to do what was necessary to deal with the crisis, thus giving the

---

[22] Proclamation by the President, 19 May 1862, available at the Freedmen and Southern Society Project, http://www.history.umd.edu/Freedmen/hunter.htm#HUNTER.

[23] Proclamation by the President, 19 May 1862.

federal government jurisdiction over issues that it would not have had otherwise.[24]

Lincoln's response to Hunter's order did cast emancipation as something that could be accomplished through war powers, although only under certain circumstances. But Lincoln did not accept the abolitionists' broad interpretation, which used war powers as simply a convenient means to bypass other elements of the Constitution and achieve emancipation. He believed that the federal government had the power to attack slavery in the states only if it was required by military necessity. Otherwise abolition did not fall within federal purview. Until the military crisis demanded intervention, Lincoln maintained the legal status quo, which left control over slavery to the states.

The use of war powers to end slavery in states that remained in the Union, however, was neither politically feasible nor legally tenable. Debates over the Confiscation Acts made that abundantly clear. The discussion, which extended beyond the halls of Congress, linked the seizure of rebel property to larger constitutional questions, with opponents calling the fate of the Union into question if the U.S. Constitution was interpreted in such a way as to violate the sanctity of private property. Faced with this conundrum, Lincoln hoped to bypass state authority by enticing individual slaveholders to let go of their slaves. In 1862, at Lincoln's request, Congress pledged compensation to slaveholders who had remained loyal to the United States, if they voluntarily freed their slaves. He made the same overture when he overrode Hunter's order, urging slaveholders in border states to consider compensated emancipation.[25]

The Second Confiscation Act, passed in July 1862, continued to cast the federal government's authority over slavery as a product of the war. It dealt with the status of escaped slaves, not the status of slavery, specifying the circumstances under which certain individuals would be freed, rather than issuing blanket statements that dealt with the status of slavery in the nation as a whole. The

---

[24] Quotes from Foner, *The Fiery Trial*, p. 164.
[25] Congressional Joint Resolution on Compensated Emancipation, 12 U.S. Statutes at Large 617 (1862).

first part of the act went into great detail in justifying the military's seizure of slave property as an aspect of war. Only toward the end of the document did enslaved African Americans emerge as something other than property. Those owned by masters defined as rebels within the terms of the act and who lived within the jurisdiction of the U.S. military would be "forever free of their servitude, and not again held as slaves." But the act freed only specific individuals as an accommodation to the military crisis. It did so through the legal route of confiscation, which required the recognition of slaves as property. Like the First Confiscation Act, moreover, the second one reflected deep divisions over the federal government's authority over private property, even as it moved away from the concept that property in people was legally legitimate.[26]

By the summer of 1862, however, Lincoln was convinced that the military conflict had reached a point that justified his use of war powers to abolish slavery. Yet, so concerned was he about the implications of reversing his previous position that he issued a preliminary proclamation one hundred days before the official Emancipation Proclamation to give fair warning of his intentions. The Proclamation followed on the logic of the Second Confiscation Act, linking emancipation to slaveholders' status as rebels who were at war against the United States. It also drew on the evolving conceptions of property, particularly the separation of slavery from other forms of property, in its policy of uncompensated emancipation. The Proclamation allowed slaveholders in the Confederacy to keep their slaves if their states returned to the United States within one hundred days. Otherwise all slaves within Confederate states would be declared free. But the Emancipation Proclamation defined abolition as a result of war. It did not signal a change in the constitutional order or imply an interpretation of federal authority that would allow for a greater role in determining the rights of individuals. In practice, moreover, the Emancipation Proclamation did not make a universal offer of freedom, even within the Confederate States. Enslaved people had to leave for areas occupied by federal forces to take advantage of their promised freedom, because the Confederacy did not recognize U.S. authority. Even then, huge

---

[26] Second Confiscation Act, 12 U.S. Statutes at Large 589 (1863).

swaths of occupied territory, including the entire state of Tennessee, were excluded.

In some ways, the Emancipation Proclamation did nothing more than legitimize what enslaved African Americans had been doing since 1861. But, in so doing, it escalated the terms of the conflict, moving beyond the battlefield to make war on the Confederacy's basic social structures. It also solidified the legal status of those who escaped to Union lines. But the Emancipation Proclamation did not legally abolish slavery. It did what the Second Confiscation Act and other federal legislation did, acknowledging the freedom of certain individuals, while leaving the institution of slavery in place. The limitations of the Emancipation Proclamation and of federal policy reflect divisions among lawmakers and white Americans: there was as yet no consensus on the future of slavery in the United States. But those same limitations also underscore the power of escaped slaves' actions, which forced both lawmakers and white Americans to confront an issue many wished to avoid.[27]

THE LEGAL LIMITS OF EMANCIPATION

If anything, federal policy only complicated the legal status of individual African Americans who came within the federal government's jurisdiction. Wartime enactments established the freedom of African Americans who found their way to Union lines, but not the meaning of freedom. Questions relating to the legal status and rights of individuals lay with states and localities, which meant that those who escaped slavery found themselves in a legal netherworld. Occupied areas were controlled by the federal government and governed by martial law, which held out the promise of more equitable treatment than state or local courts that had kept African Americans enslaved. But these venues were ill equipped to handle the legal problems of formerly enslaved

---

[27] The Emancipation Proclamation, 1 January 1863, available at The Avalon Project, http://avalon.law.yale.edu/19th_century/emancipa.asp. Also see The Preliminary Emancipation Proclamation, available at the Freedmen and Southern Society Project, http://www.history.umd.edu/Freedmen/prelep.htm. Hamilton, *The Limits of Sovereignty*.

people, because such matters previously had been handled within the jurisdiction of states and localities, not the federal government or the military.

All states placed definite legal limits on the rights of all free African Americans to varying degrees. The enactment of racially restrictive legislation followed hard on the heels of abolition in northern states, reflecting an enduring connection between racism and abolition. Many white Americans who opposed slavery still believed that African Americans were inferior to whites and incapable of exercising civil or political rights responsibly. Given those racist presumptions, it followed that legal restrictions were necessary to police free blacks and to protect the larger public. By 1860, free blacks could vote in only six states: Maine, Massachusetts, New Hampshire, Rhode Island, Vermont, and New York, which had substantial property requirements for free blacks that did not apply to whites. Legal limits extended to free blacks' civil rights and included restrictions on their ability to testify in court, enter contracts, hold property, and congregate. States in the Old Northwest – Illinois, Indiana, Iowa, Ohio, Michigan, and Wisconsin – enacted particularly draconian measures. Some denied free blacks entry altogether. Local ordinances and custom further limited free blacks, segregating them in the least desirable locations, forcing them into the most menial jobs, and policing their behavior in host of other ways.

States' traditional authority over the rights of all individuals – including the rights accorded to all U.S. citizens – complicated the federal government's jurisdiction over free blacks. On the eve of the Civil War, it was not entirely clear whether free blacks were citizens of the United States and, if so, what that meant. The 1790 Naturalization Act limited citizenship to those who were free and white. But that act and subsequent legislation addressed the situation of new immigrants who sought application for naturalization. What of those who resided in the United States at its inception and never applied for citizenship because they already considered themselves citizens? States did not usually question the citizenship status of such people. That position extended even to free blacks, although there was considerable discussion about the rights and citizenship status of free blacks, particularly in slaveholding states in the decades immediately preceding the Civil War.[28] Those debates culminated in the U.S. Supreme Court's decision in *Dred Scott*, which stated that people of African descent were not citizens of the United States. But the *Dred Scott* decision's statement of black citizenship was controversial precisely because it upset the status quo and stepped on the traditional prerogatives of states. In the context of growing sectional tensions, the implications of *Dred Scott* were unclear and authority over the rights of free blacks remained with localities and states, which maintained their rigid racial restrictions.[29]

Free blacks in the states that remained in the United States hoped to use the war effort to achieve racial equality as well as abolition. Initially, they focused on military service, not changes in federal law. Through military service, African American men could prove their loyalty to the nation, making it impossible – or, at least, more difficult – to deny them rights. "Why does the Government reject the Negro? Is he not a man? Can he not wield a sword, fire a gun, march and countermarch, and obey orders like any other?" asked Frederick Douglass. His answers to those questions were clear. But more than that, "We do believe that such soldiers, if allowed to take up arms in defence [*sic*] of the Government, and made to feel that they are hereafter to be recognized as persons having rights, would

---

[28] Naturalization Act, 1 U.S. Statutes at Large 103 (1790). James H. Kettner, *The Development of American Citizenship, 1608–1870* (Chapel Hill, NC, 1978). As Martha S. Jones shows in "*Hughes v. Jackson*: Race and Rights beyond Dred Scott," *North Carolina Law Review* 91 (2013): 1757–83, free blacks claimed rights and also the connection between rights and citizenship, claims that were recognized at the state level.

[29] *Dred Scott v. Sandford*. In the 1830s and 1840s, northern courts adopted the position that slave law could not reach into their states; see Leonard W. Levy, *The Law of the Commonwealth and Chief Justice Shaw* (Cambridge, MA, 1957); Paul Finkelman, *An Imperfect Union: Slavery, Federalism, and Comity* (Chapel Hill, NC, 1981). Literature on African Americans' attempts to sue for freedom suggests how legally ambiguous the distinction between slavery and freedom was for African Americans in the decades between the Revolution and the Civil War: Martha S. Jones, "Time, Space, and Jurisdiction in Atlantic World Slavery: The Volunbrun Household in Gradual Emancipation New York," *Law and History Review* 29 (2011): 1031–60; Eldie L. Wong, *Neither Fugitive nor Free: Atlantic Slavery, Freedom Suits, and the Legal Culture of Travel* (New York, 2009). Questions about freedom were tied to questions about racial identity, which were not easy to resolve either; see Ariela J. Gross, *What Blood Won't Tell: A History of Race on Trial in America* (Cambridge, MA, 2008).

set the highest example of order and general good behavior to their fellow soldiers, and in every way add to the national power." In 1862, Congress passed a new Militia Act that allowed African Americans to serve in the military.[30]

Military service, however, did not immediately alter the legal restrictions that proliferated at the state and local level. African Americans took advantage of their proximity to federal lawmakers in Washington, D.C. to push for great civil and political equality there during the war. But they faced an uphill battle. It was even more difficult for African Americans in places without such a high concentration of progressive policy makers who advocated abolition and full civil and political rights for African Americans.[31]

Racial inequality also followed black troops into the military. It was not until June 1864 that Congress passed legislation equalizing pay for black soldiers. The racism that fueled reduced pay also resulted in deplorable conditions in the field. The commander of a North Carolina regiment was outraged to find that his troops had been ordered to prepare camp for white regiments. He put the issue bluntly: "It IS a draw-back that they are regarded as, and called 'd – d Niggers' by so-called 'gentleman' in uniform of U.S. Officers, but when they are set to menial work doing for white regiments what those Regiments are entitled to do for themselves, it simply throws them back where they were before and reduces them to the position of slaves again."[32]

The rights of refugees also varied widely, depending on the military commander. In December of 1862, a committee of "chaplains and surgeons" from Helena, Arkansas, complained of conditions all too common throughout occupied areas of the Confederacy. "The

---

[30] The quote is from "Fighting the Rebels with One Hand," September 1861, in Frederick Douglass, *The Life and Writings of Frederick Douglass*, Philip Foner, ed. (New York, 1950–75) 3:151–4. For the importance of military service as a means for African Americans to demonstrate fitness for full civil and political rights: Berlin et al., *The Black Military Experience*; Samito, *Becoming American under Fire*.

[31] Kate Masur, *An Example for All the Land: Emancipation and the Struggle over Equality in Washington, D.C.* (Chapel Hill, NC, 2010).

[32] Commander of a North Carolina Regiment to Commander of a Black Brigade, 13 September 1863, available at the Freedmen and Southern Society Project, http://www.history.umd.edu/Freedmen/Beecher.html.

Contrabands within our lines," they wrote to the commander of the Department of Missouri, "are experiencing hardships oppression & neglect the removal of which calls loudly for the intervention of authority." That situation had allowed soldiers in the U.S. military to rob refugees, rape the women and attack the men who tried to intervene, and refuse to pay them for their work. "For the sake of humanity, for the sake of christianity, for the good name of our army, for the honor of our country," they begged, "cannot something be done to prevent this oppression & to stop its demoralizing influences upon the Soldiers themselves?"[33]

Those military policies that did exist, moreover, significantly circumscribed the range of possibilities for refugees. The system of compulsory labor was particularly important. Military officials considered such a coercive system consistent with free labor in the sense that former slaves entered into contractual agreements and were compensated for their labor. The logic reflected fundamental assumptions about the individual rights of wage workers within a free labor system more generally: freedom was not measured in terms of either the circumstances that brought a person into a labor contract or the terms of that contract, but in the ability to contract. Advocates of free labor, moreover, expected force in establishing such a system: people unused to it would have to be coerced into labor contracts and subjected to harsh contractual terms, until they understood its dynamics and accepted its benefits. Racism tended to narrow this vision still further. Many free labor proponents in the Union believed that former slaves might eventually internalize the values that made reliable, manual workers, if instructed properly and carefully. But until then, they needed to be kept in line – by whatever means necessary. In fact, some doubted that former slaves would ever learn and saw legal coercion as an essential, permanent component of freedom. Such policies blurred the line between wage labor and slavery, particularly when commanders held workers' wages until the end of the contract or applied them to payment for supplies instead of paying them directly. Complaints

---

[33] Committee of Chaplains and Surgeons to the Commander of the Department of Missouri, 29 December 1862, Freedmen and Southern Society Project, http://www.history.umd.edu/Freedmen/Sawyer.html.

about compulsory service, with little or no pay, streamed into the War Department from sympathetic white observers as well as the African Americans forced to labor.[34]

Slavery would remain legal in the United States until the ratification of the Thirteenth Amendment, after the end of the war. Despite all the legal efforts to dismantle slavery during the war, it was impossible to eliminate it without a constitutional amendment. Even so, the dynamics culminating in passage of the Thirteenth Amendment were, simultaneously, definitive and ambiguous. They were definitive in the sense that the growing popular consensus for an amendment underscored how much had changed as a result of the Civil War. Historian Michael Vorenberg describes the scene in Congress, when the House of Representatives voted for the amendment, in particularly vivid detail: "For a moment there was only a disbelieving, hollow silence. Then the House exploded in cheers.... The normally staid Victorian audience lost its emotional bearings. Witnesses to the great event roared their approval, wept, embraced."[35]

The unity of that moment passed, leaving uncertainty in its wake. When the amendment moved from Congress to the states, it was subjected to considerable debate, particularly in the states of the Old Northwest, which had the most racially restrictive laws. Iowa, for instance, did not approve the amendment until 1866, after it had been ratified by two-thirds of the states. The approval process ran into difficulties in other states with a significant Democratic presence as well, including New York and New Jersey. The states of the former Confederacy were all but required to pass it as part of President Andrew Johnson's Reconstruction plan. Even then, state representatives debated the amendment as if they still had choice in the matter.

The difficulties of ratification reflected larger divisions over the Thirteenth Amendment's legal meaning. Republican leaders who supported abolition and racial equality saw it as a means to both

---

[34] Gerteis, *From Contraband to Freedman*; Thomas C. Holt, "'An Empire over the Mind': Emancipation, Race, and Ideology in the British West Indies and the American South," in *Region, Race, and Reconstruction: Essays in Honor of C. Vann Woodward*, edited by J. Morgan Kousser and James McPherson (New York, 1982), pp. 283–331.

[35] Vorenberg, *Final Freedom*, p. 207.

ends. For them, the abolition of slavery would also mean full civil and political equality for African Americans. That interpretation did not sit well with Democrats and moderate Republicans, who supported abolition, but not equality for African Americans. The politics of ratifying the amendment further muddied the legal waters. Given the opposition at the state level, the amendment's supporters downplayed its implications, emphasizing abolition but not racial equality in order to secure its passage. President Johnson made explicit assurances to the representatives of former Confederate states to obtain the required votes. The amendment was ratified on December 6, 1865, when Georgia approved it. Nine of the thirty-six states then in the Union did not pass it until after ratification. Of those, Delaware waited until 1901; Kentucky until 1976; and Mississippi until 1995.[36]

The Thirteenth Amendment wrote the rhetoric of the Republican Party into the Constitution: it reached into the states to establish direct legal ties between the federal government and the people by announcing one key area in which states could no longer determine the people's rights. In mandating the end of slavery, the Thirteenth Amendment extended the federal government's authority in unprecedented ways and encompassed all states in the Union, not just those in the former Confederacy. It did so not as a necessity of war, but as an element of the nation's legal order. As such, the Thirteenth Amendment brought more substantive and permanent changes than other wartime policies, at least in theory. Now, for the first time, the Constitution gave the federal government the power to trump the authority of the states in matters of individual rights.

Yet abolition opened up more questions than it resolved, because it was unclear what it really meant for the federal government to abolish slavery. Even if most Americans – even white Americans – expected the Civil War's outcome to be abolition, they did not necessarily anticipate the implications of the resulting constitutional changes. What would those changes mean for governance? What would they mean for the legal status of African Americans? Or all Americans, for that matter? African Americans, in particular, had forged a direct relationship to the federal government during the

---

[36] Ibid., particularly pp. 221–50.

Civil War. Even though that relationship was often fraught, federal officials were more reliable allies than local, state, or Confederate officials. A return to the terms that existed before the war would give Confederate states the ability to define and direct their post-war social order, something that white Americans who remained loyal to the United States did not want either. Even so, many white Americans were reluctant to extend the scope of federal authority, particularly into the area of individual rights. They had gone through the war to preserve, not to change the polity they had known, even if it made for a federal government that promised to do more for its people.

4

The Federal Government and the Reconstruction of the Legal Order

Tennessee had been exempted from the Emancipation Proclamation, as had parts of the Confederacy occupied by U.S. troops in 1863. Slavery did not end in those states or in slave states that had remained in the Union until they adopted new constitutions that prohibited slavery or the Thirteenth Amendment's ratification resolved the issue for them. Tennessee approved a new constitution with provisions to end slavery in February 1865, before the Confederacy surrendered. But the end of slavery did not end the problems faced by those who had once been enslaved. With Tennessee's new constitution, wrote a group of African Americans from the state, we "became formally and legally free, our prayers were answered, and the secret hopes of our hearts were realized." The problem was that the legislature "failed, as we think, to pass the necessary laws, to recognize our standing, and secure to us by law, our rights as freemen." They continued, "As we are now the old slave laws of the State remaining unrepealed, and the oath of the colored man not being received by our Courts, as against the whites, we have no where to look for protection, save to the United States Authority." "In those authorities," they wrote, "we have the fullest confidence: but we want some way of easily bringing our cases before them."[1]

Therein lay the problem. The federal government's jurisdiction did not extend to matters of the kind that plagued this group of

[1] Tennessee Freedmen to the Freedmen's Bureau Assistant Commissioner for Kentucky, Tennessee, and Northern Alabama, 27 July 1865, available at the Freedmen and Southern Society Project, http://www.history.umd.edu/Freedmen/Bright.htm.

African Americans. In fact, the states' broad authority over the legal status of the American people – the issue that brought the nation to war – remained unchanged, despite everything that had happened between 1860 and 1865. It was not just an issue for African Americans who lived in the former Confederacy. It was an issue all over the United States, where states and localities routinely restricted the rights of African Americans, all women, and a range of other racial, ethnic, and religious minorities as well. That situation, once accepted without comment, appeared increasingly problematic because of the national vision pursued by Republican Party leaders during the Civil War. Theirs was the nation depicted by Lincoln in the Gettysburg Address, the one "our fathers brought forth on this continent ... conceived in liberty and dedicated to the proposition that all men are created equal." But this portrayal fell apart if states could interpret national ideals on their own and produce multiple, even conflicting outcomes. Reconstruction-era policies addressed that situation by taking the nationalizing political rhetoric of the war years and writing it into the legal order of the nation. The results ultimately extended the federal government's jurisdiction, although not so far that it subsumed the legal authority traditionally exercised by states. Those institutional changes were accompanied by an even more profound change in the nation's legal culture: the federal government, not the states, came to be seen as the guarantor of liberty and equality.[2]

The Republican Party's national vision, however, contained another important element that complicates easy assumptions about the positive potential of enhanced federal authority. The nation Lincoln invoked in the Gettysburg Address was continental in reach, stretching from the Atlantic to the Pacific and incorporating that vast space into a single, unified jurisdictional entity. That United States bore little resemblance to the one established by the Founding Fathers. It emerged during the war years, as federal policy lured settlers west and cleared the way for their arrival by subduing Native populations. Traditionally, historians have treated the imposition of federal authority in the West separately from the policy

---

[2] Gettysburg Address.

changes of Reconstruction, the historiography of which is arrayed along a north-south axis, focused on the eastern part of the country and dealing with policies relating to the former Confederacy and the status of African Americans. Recent scholarship, however, has challenged that separation, arguing that federal policy in the West should be seen as an extension of the Republican Party's vision of national unity. A continental view of the nation, one that includes areas where people did not wish to be a part of the national project, also changes the terms of the analysis, making it impossible to mask the coercive dimensions of the national vision that fueled the extension of federal power. The African Americans of Lincoln County, Tennessee, looked to the federal government to help them. Indians might have advised caution in placing such faith in federal authority, despite its lofty promises.

FEDERAL OVERSIGHT OF RIGHTS

Lincoln did not wish to alter the fundamental legal order of the nation, particularly the balance of power between the federal government and the states. For that reason, he was not a fan of the Thirteenth Amendment when it was first proposed in 1864. As he saw it, secession was legally impossible and therefore states that claimed to have joined the Confederacy were, in reality, still in the United States. Lincoln believed the relationship between those states and the Union remained the same as it always had been, and Confederate states would retain authority over the status of all those living within their borders, including former slaves.

That logic shaped Lincoln's proposal, dubbed the Ten Percent Plan, for establishing pro-Union governments in the states of the Confederacy. Announced in December 1863, the Ten Percent Plan neither extended the federal government's jurisdiction over the states that claimed to be in rebellion against it nor diminished the authority of those states. That was because Lincoln identified the disloyalty of individuals, not the structure of government, as the problem. The Ten Percent Plan aimed to reconnect those individuals to the Union. It offered a full pardon to all adult white men living in the Confederacy who took an oath of loyalty to the United States, which included a pledge to accept the abolition of slavery.

With the oath came the restoration of all rights, except property rights in slaves. Only high-ranking Confederate officials and those who had abused Union soldiers were ineligible. When the number of men who took the loyalty oath equaled 10 percent of the votes cast in that state in the 1860 elections, that minority could form a new state government and frame a new constitution. Those state constitutions had to abolish slavery and provide for the education of former slaves. Once those conditions were met, the states returned to the status quo antebellum. The imposition of federal power never negated states' traditional powers in the Ten Percent Plan, even when it came to abolition. The plan directed states to abolish slavery, but ultimately it would be the elected delegates to state constitutional conventions who performed the legal work necessary to accomplish abolition, not the president, the U.S. Congress, or any other part of the federal government.

Lincoln's Ten Percent Plan has not fared well in the scholarship since World War II. Many historians have seen it as a telling example of the failures that would ultimately derail Reconstruction: failure in apprehending the destructive rage of former Confederates; failure in supporting full civil and political equality for African Americans; failure in grasping the magnitude of the political problems attendant in reconstructing the Union; and, most damning of all, Republicans' failure in pursuing the political principles they purported to value. But the Ten Percent Plan is revealing for what it says about Lincoln's – and many other Americans' – remarkable faith in the existing structure of government, particularly the authority given to states, a faith so strong that it ultimately survived the acrimony and violence of the war.[3] The principles of the Ten Percent Plan would later generate opposition that led to a different Reconstruction plan, in which the federal government took a much more active role. But Lincoln's plan met with widespread approval when it was first announced in 1863, even among those who ultimately opposed it. At that time, the Ten Percent Plan represented a significant and, as many saw it, positive departure from the administration's previous positions. In particular, it affirmed a national

[3] William C. Harris, *With Charity for All: Lincoln and the Restoration of the Union* (Lexington, KY, 1997).

commitment to abolition, even if abolition would be accomplished through the states, not the federal government.

Lincoln followed through, using the Ten Percent Plan to push border states to write new constitutions that abolished slavery. Maryland, Missouri, and West Virginia all did so by the end of the Civil War. It was also hoped that the plan would help end the war by bringing occupied Confederate states back into the Union and then encouraging others to come along. Arkansas, Louisiana, and Tennessee all organized new governments under the plan, abolished slavery, and returned to the United States before the surrender of the Confederacy.

Those outcomes suggested that Lincoln's faith in the existing structures of government was not misplaced. But there were warning signs as well. The pressure brought to bear on political leaders in the slave states of Kentucky and Delaware went nowhere, and their intransigence presented a serious challenge to Lincoln's strategy. If states that had stayed in the United States refused to let go of slavery, then how could leaders of Confederate states be persuaded to do so? The notion that Unionists in the Confederacy would leap at the opportunity to reorganize their states also proved illusory, dashing hopes that Confederate states could be easily reabsorbed by the United States. Then, in 1864, Republicans faced a significant challenge from the Democratic Party, which opposed a national commitment to abolition. Republican leaders, including Lincoln, feared that the nation might well return to its situation before the war, divided into free and slave states, if Democrats won the presidency and decisions about slavery remained with the states.

As the political winds shifted, moderates in the Republican Party began to embrace the idea that the federal government would have to assume more power over states of the former Confederacy if they hoped to maintain control over a reunited nation after the war. The more radical wing of the Republican Party had advocated such a position from the beginning of the Civil War. Moderates, including Lincoln, required persuasion. The trajectory of support for the Thirteenth Amendment is indicative of their transformation. When the amendment was first proposed in February 1864, Lincoln opposed it, as did other moderates. While the Senate approved it in April 1864, the House of Representatives turned it down. The greater presence of the Democratic Party in the House guided the outcome, but so did the ambivalence of many Republicans who, like Lincoln, still hoped that abolition could be accomplished through the states. Then, in June 1864, Congress signaled a shift in course with its repeal of the Fugitive Slave Act. Although the act was no longer enforced, its repeal symbolized a significant change in prevailing notions about the appropriate balance of power between the federal government and states on the issue of slavery: no longer would the federal government protect states' authority in this area. By the fall of 1864, Lincoln threw his support behind the Thirteenth Amendment and made sure it was added to the party's platform. In January 1865, after Lincoln's reelection and Republican victories in congressional elections, the House of Representatives passed the Thirteenth Amendment in a decisive vote of 119 to 56. Then the Republican Party went one step further, establishing federal supervision over the transition from slavery to freedom. In March 1865, at Lincoln's request, Congress created the Bureau of Freedmen and Abandoned Lands, a temporary federal agency, operated through the military and charged with handling conflicts that resulted from the end of slavery.[4]

The wartime connections forged between the American people and their nation placed pressure on Republican leaders. African Americans, like so many other Americans, took the Republican Party at its word: they saw the federal government as the representative of a nation that supported liberty and equality and they assumed they could call on federal officials for assistance in such matters. In fact, African Americans, particularly those from the South, had tried to use federal authority to protect their interests since the war's outset. State and local laws negated the rights of the enslaved and limited the rights of free blacks, so African Americans went instead to military authorities and other federal officials, turning the federal government into a legal intermediary and anticipating the legal changes that would come with the Reconstruction Amendments.[5]

---

[4] First Freedmen's Bureau Act, 13 U.S. Statutes at Large 507 (1865).

[5] The volumes of the Freedmen and Southern Society Project provide the most compelling picture of African Americans' efforts to use federal authority, although examples also run through much of the literature. See Chapter 3, note 3.

The petition of the African Americans from Tennessee is representative. They had little patience with the authority granted to their state by the U.S. Constitution, given the way their state's new constitution kept them in legal subordination. Instead, they cast state authority – and the inequalities it generated – as a problem to be overcome, not an indisputable truth to be revered and accepted. And they had a solution: they could bring their issues to legal officials who represented their nation, not their state. It is hard to resist the irony of this request, coming as it did from people who lived in Lincoln County, Tennessee. The county, of course, was not named for the president; its namesake was Major General Benjamin Lincoln, an officer in the American Revolution. Nor did any of President Lincoln's plans for reconstructing the nation provide the inspiration for the petitioners' request, in which the federal government would take over the traditional legal authority of states. Nonetheless, it was Lincoln's wartime policies that made it possible for Americans, including this group of African Americans, to imagine the federal government as a legal ally – as a place they could go to uphold their rights, as they defined them, when other legal venues had failed them.[6]

Political events, combined with the actions of African Americans, worked to create a climate favorable to the extension of federal power into areas once governed solely by states. General Robert E. Lee surrendered to Ulysses S. Grant on April 9, 1865, marking the official end of the Civil War. Five days later, President Abraham Lincoln was shot by an assassin's bullet. He died early the next morning, leaving Vice President Andrew Johnson – the only U.S. senator from a Confederate state to remain loyal to the Union and keep his seat during the Civil War – as president.

With the nation in turmoil and Congress in recess, Johnson moved unilaterally to reconstruct the country. Acting on the basics of Lincoln's Ten Percent Plan, although going far beyond it, he tried to return the Union to what it had been before the war, only without slavery. Specifically, he indicated that the states of the former Confederacy would resume their standing in the United States after

---

[6] Tennessee Freedmen to the Freedmen's Bureau Assistant Commissioner for Kentucky, Tennessee, and Northern Alabama.

they repudiated the Confederate debt and created new state constitutions that negated the ordinances of secession and abolished slavery. Johnson feared that states might not take steps to abolish slavery, so he directly lobbied political leaders in states of the former Confederacy to adopt the Thirteenth Amendment, promising them that it did not imply civil and political equality for African Americans and would not be used that way. He did disfranchise high-ranking Confederate officials, but he allowed for amnesty if they applied for it personally.

In the summer of 1865, while Congress was still in recess, the states of the former Confederacy began reorganizing under Johnson's plan. The resulting constitutions did withdraw the secession ordinances and abolish slavery, but they otherwise left their states' basic structures of governance in place. State legislatures then passed a series of laws, derived from antebellum measures that had restricted free blacks, which denied African Americans civil and political rights. The Black Codes, as they were called, were the kind of laws that African Americans in Lincoln County, Tennessee, found so problematic. Although the specific restrictions varied, states of the former Confederacy allowed African Americans few rights beyond the ability to contract and to access criminal and civil courts. Most states excluded them from juries, limited their testimony against whites, and required them to work, carry passes from their employers when they traveled, and obtain permission when buying and selling property. The terms used to refer to African Americans are also suggestive. They were "negroes," "persons of color," men and women who were "lately slaves," and "inhabitants of this state." Although free, African Americans were not to be confused with citizens.[7]

That fall, the Confederate states' new representatives arrived to take their seats in the U.S. Congress. In many instances, they were the same men who had headed the Confederacy just a few months before. By Johnson's standards, the results were a success. National reunion had been accomplished quickly and without radical change. He congratulated himself on a job well done and called it a day – or, at least, he tried to do so.

---

[7] The Black Codes are reprinted in Laws in Relation to Freedmen, 39th Cong., Senate Executive Doc. No. 6.

Congressional Republicans felt differently. They also had the backing of the American people – at least those who had sided with the Union. Even those who had been sympathetic to Lincoln's Ten Percent Plan found Johnson's application of that plan's principles to be utterly unacceptable. The results seemed like a blatant attempt to deny the war's outcome. The same political leaders, who had led their states out of the Union and plunged the nation into a conflict unparalleled in its destruction, now led those states back into the Union along paths largely of their own choosing.

Congressional Republicans' objections to Johnson's Reconstruction plan were as much legal as they were political. Johnson, like Lincoln, maintained that secession was a constitutional impossibility. Confederate states, therefore, remained in the Union and decision-making power over them lay with the president, in his capacity as commander-in-chief of a nation in the midst of war. But leaders of the radical wing of the Republican Party never accepted that view. As they had argued since the beginning of the Civil War, Confederate leaders negated their states' relationship to the Union when they seceded and declared war. According to this logic, when the Confederacy surrendered, the federal government had great authority to shape how and under what terms the regions that had seceded came back into the United States. At times, Congressional Republicans characterized federal authority in terms of war powers, which they extended to Congress as well as the president. Some also justified such power as similar to the federal government's control over territories. Either way, though, Congressional Republicans claimed the legal authority to legislate for these areas. This position, once the exclusive domain of radicals, acquired the support of moderates, as opposition to the results of Johnson's Reconstruction plan mounted.[8]

Congressional Republicans were not always consistent in their legal logic, and individual Republicans strategically picked up and put down legal points as needed. Nonetheless, they took care to explain their policies in constitutional terms. To buttress their proposed extension of federal authority, they pointed to the Thirteenth

---

[8] Herman Belz, *Reconstructing the Union: Theory and Policy during the Civil War* (Ithaca, NY, 1969).

Amendment and the "guarantee clause," the clause in Article 4 of the U.S. Constitution that directs the federal government to "guarantee to every State in this Union a Republican Form of Government."[9] The guarantee clause had not attracted much attention since the Constitution's framing because it spoke directly to concerns of that moment: the presence of violent post-Revolutionary conflicts, such as Shays's Rebellion, that had threatened the new republic's stability and raised the possibility that states might veer toward authoritarian forms of governance. The clause was also an unreliable legal ally because it did not specify what, exactly, constituted a republican form of government. But some Congressional Republicans saw possibility where others had seen ambiguity, perhaps because they had such a clear vision of the national legal order to guide them. Breathing new life into the guarantee clause, they argued that the federal government could intervene in states that failed to meet the standards – that is, the Republican Party's standards – of republican government. As these Republicans saw it, the Thirteenth Amendment gave constitutional substance to the guarantee clause. In fact, a core group of Republicans had always seen the Thirteenth Amendment as a means of establishing civil and political equality for African Americans as well as abolishing slavery. The logic was straightforward: the legal disabilities of slavery prevented a person from exercising civil and political rights, so once those restrictions were removed, full civil and political rights were obtained. Moderates used that interpretation as a way to justify the use of federal power to intervene in states of the former Confederacy. The Thirteenth Amendment, argued Senator Lyman Trumbull, empowered Congress to eliminate all vestiges of "the badge of servitude," including the discriminatory Black Codes passed under Johnson's Reconstruction plan.[10]

Congressional Republicans' constitutional invocations flowed from the nationalizing political rhetoric that had served the party so well during the Civil War. During the war, only the radical wing

---

[9] U.S. Const., amend. XIII. U.S. Const., art. 4, sec. 4.

[10] Quote from Eric Foner, *Reconstruction: America's Unfinished Revolution* (New York, 1988), pp. 232–3. William M. Wiecek, *The Guarantee Clause of the U.S. Constitution* (Ithaca, NY, 1972).

of the party had interpreted such rhetoric to mean a permanent, expanded federal presence in the lives of the American people. When Congress reconvened in 1866, however, even moderates incorporated elements of that vision into their understanding of the nation's legal order. At that point, the party coalesced around a new consensus, which called not just for national reunion, but also for fundamental changes within the former Confederacy. The first thing Congressional Republicans did when Congress reconvened was to refuse recognition to delegations from the states of the former Confederacy that had been reconstructed under Johnson's plan. To underscore the point, the Republican leadership also withheld funds to cover their living expenses in Washington. As one excluded southern representative quipped, the options were "to go home or starve." Congressional Republicans also appointed a Joint Committee on Reconstruction to investigate conditions in the states of the former Confederacy, an act that signaled their intent to revise Johnson's Reconstruction Plan.[11]

Early in 1866, Congressional Republicans recommended two bills, the Civil Rights Act and the Second Freedmen's Bureau Act, to rectify what they identified as the problems with Johnson's Reconstruction Plan. The formal title of the Civil Rights Act, "An Act to protect all Persons in the United States in their Civil Rights, and furnish the Means of their Vindication" expressed its intent. The act clarified the vexing question of African Americans' citizenship and negated *Dred Scott* by declaring "all persons born in the United States and not subject to any foreign power, excluding Indians not taxed" to be citizens. All those citizens, "of every race and color, without regard to any previous condition of slavery or involuntary servitude shall have":

the same right, in every State and Territory in the United States, to make and enforce contracts, to sue, be parties, and give evidence, to inherit, purchase, lease, sell, hold, and convey real and personal property, and to full and equal benefit of all laws and proceedings for the security of person and property, as is enjoyed by white citizens, and shall be subject to like punishment, pains, and penalties, and to none other, any law, statute, ordinance, regulation, or custom, to the contrary notwithstanding.

[11]   Quote from Foner, *Reconstruction*, p. 239.

The act made the denial of rights a crime and prescribed penalties for convicted offenders. It also provided for the removal of such cases to federal courts, allowing defendants to bypass hostile state and local jurisdictions.[12]

The Civil Rights Act's provision for the removal of cases to federal courts responded to the problem identified by the African American petitioners of Lincoln County, Tennessee – one pointed out repeatedly by African Americans in states of the former Confederacy as well as sympathetic military commanders and federal officials. African Americans could now, at least in theory, challenge discriminatory state and local laws. But the right to remove their cases to federal courts, as provided for in the Civil Rights Act, was not exactly what the African Americans of Lincoln County had in mind. Like other African Americans who suffered under state-mandated legal restrictions, they wanted to bypass the state court system altogether. The Civil Rights Act, however, affirmed that state jurisdiction took priority: an aggrieved party would have to go to courts in the state's jurisdiction first and then prove discriminatory treatment to remove the matter to the federal level. Federal courts, moreover, had neither the presence nor the personnel to handle the resulting cases. Congressional Republicans acknowledged these problems in the Second Freedmen's Bureau Act, which gave agents the authority to adjudicate a range of legal matters, particularly economic disputes between freedpeople and their employers. The Second Freedmen's Bureau Act also made it possible for agents to fulfill their new obligations by regularizing the bureau's funding and extending its life. But it was still just a drop in the bucket. Bureau agents, many of whom had no legal training, could not manage the caseload. The legislation also made it clear that the bureau would be a temporary salve for an acute crisis, not a permanent remedy to a chronic condition.

President Johnson promptly vetoed both the Second Freedmen's Bureau Act and the Civil Rights Act. Those vetoes felt like a sharp slap in the face to moderate Republicans, who still hoped to work with Johnson to revise the terms of his Reconstruction plan and

[12] Civil Rights Act, 14 U.S. Statutes at Large 27 (1866). Second Freedmen's Bureau Act, 14 U.S. Statutes at Large 173 (1866).

who had been confident of his support on these two measures. Johnson's vetoes also drew a legal line in the sand. He cast the Second Freedmen's Bureau Act as an unconstitutional expansion of federal authority that undermined the traditional purview of states, subverted established legal processes, and thereby threatened the rights of all American citizens. "The exercise of power over which there is no legal supervision, by so vast a number of agents as is contemplated by the bill," he wrote, "must, by the very nature of man, be attended by acts of caprice, injustice, and passion." The constitutional cost, Johnson maintained, was unwarranted, because the assistance offered to former slaves was entirely misguided anyway. Furthermore, federal intervention, of the kind established by the Second Freedmen's Bureau Act, would consign freedpeople to a permanent state of poverty and distress, keeping them dependent and incapable of taking care of themselves.[13]

Johnson's veto of the Civil Rights Act was, if anything, even more caustic. In a racist screed, he rejected every aspect of the bill, not just the federal government's authority to assure civil equality among its citizens, but also the very principle of civil equality. He scoffed at the idea of making "our entire colored population ... citizens of the United States." "Four millions of them have just emerged from slavery into freedom," he wrote. "Can it be reasonably supposed that they possess the requisite qualifications to entitle them to all the privileges and immunities of citizenship of the United States?" Obviously not. As Johnson saw it, states needed discriminatory laws, given the challenges of governing such a difficult population.[14]

Congressional Republicans mustered the votes necessary to override Johnson's veto of the Civil Rights Act – the first time Congress ever enacted such a consequential piece of legislation over a president's objections. Unable to override his veto of the Freedmen's Bureau Act on the first try, they passed a new bill, nearly identical to the first. Johnson rejected it again, but this time Congressional

[13] Andrew Johnson, Veto of the Freedmen's Bureau Bill, 19 February 1866, available at TeachingAmericanHistory.org, http://teachingamericanhistory.org/library/index.asp?document=1940.

[14] Andrew Johnson, Veto of the Civil Rights Bill, 27 March 1866, available at TeachingAmericanHistory.org, http://teachingamericanhistory.org/library/index.asp?document=1944.

Republicans overrode his veto. Johnson, still certain that he held the winning hand, took his case directly to the American people in a speaking tour during the summer of 1866. It was ill-advised. He rambled and ranted, looking anything but presidential and setting the stage for a Republican landslide in the fall of 1866.

Although politically inept, Johnson did raise a good legal question: What made Congressional Republicans think that they could exercise legal authority over civil rights, an area over which states had long exercised exclusive power? Many Congressional Republicans did not consider states of the former Confederacy to be within the United States, despite what Johnson said or did. Johnson's Reconstruction plan nonetheless created facts on the ground by readmitting Confederate states over the objections of Congress. It forced Congressional Republicans onto rocky constitutional terrain, making it difficult to assert that the federal government could exercise direct control over the states of the former Confederacy – as Congress could over territories and as many Congressional Republicans wished to do – without setting a precedent that might be used against other states in the future.

Debates over the Thirteenth Amendment's passage underscored the precarious constitutional foundation of the Civil Rights Act, the Second Freedmen's Bureau Act, and Congressional Republicans' approach to Reconstruction more generally. Republicans now commanded solid popular support. But their constitutional arguments exposed deep divisions among the American people over the goals of federal policy. A broad reading of the Thirteenth Amendment – as a means of establishing African Americans' civil and even political rights as well as abolishing slavery – was not widely shared, even at the amendment's most popular point, when Congress approved it in January 1865. For many white Americans, the elimination of slavery meant only that and no more. In their minds, the Thirteenth Amendment gave the federal government jurisdiction over that *one* aspect of individuals' legal status. The arm-twisting and horse-trading necessary to secure the amendment's ratification at the state level validated that narrow reading, burying what was left of its idealism in practical assurances that it would never be used to secure civil and political rights to African Americans or to extend federal jurisdiction over these issues. By the time Congress passed the Civil

Rights Act, it was clear that the Thirteenth Amendment would not be a reliable constitutional ally in Congressional Republicans' Reconstruction plans. The guarantee clause, given its ambiguity and the lack of precedent, was equally problematic.[15]

Such constitutional concerns led the Joint Committee on Reconstruction to recommend that the Civil Rights Act's provisions be written into the U.S. Constitution in the form of a new amendment – what would become the Fourteenth Amendment. The committee made that recommendation before Johnson's vetoes, highlighting the legal dimension of what is often cast, primarily, as a political battle between Congressional Republicans and an increasingly recalcitrant president. Proponents of the Civil Rights Act feared that it would always be vulnerable without a secure constitutional footing. Initially, they were less concerned about Johnson than they were about the inherently ephemeral nature of all legislation. The U.S. Supreme Court could declare the Civil Rights Act unconstitutional at any time, either then or at some point in the future. If it escaped that fate, a future Congress might gut it or repeal it altogether, a possibility that seemed all too real, particularly because emancipation would boost the relative power in Congress of many southern states. When congressional seats were reapportioned with the 1870 census, politicians realized, states in the former Confederacy would likely gain representatives, because African Americans would no longer be counted as only three-fifths of a white person for purposes of federal representation. That advantage struck Congressional Republicans as problematic in the extreme. Why should former Confederates be rewarded after seceding, forcing the nation into war, opposing abolition, and then denying civil and political rights to the African Americans whose presence now enhanced their own political power? But Congressional Republicans also had their sights set on the nation's future. What if states of the former Confederacy combined with northern Democrats to overturn everything that Congressional Republicans had worked to accomplish? The shifting sands of politics led Congressional Republicans to the firmer ground of constitutional change. That Congressional Republicans – both moderates and radicals – felt the need to turn the Civil Rights

[15] Vorenberg, *Final Freedom*, particularly pp. 211–50.

Act into a constitutional amendment, so soon after ratification of the Thirteenth Amendment, also says a great deal about their sense of historical mission at that particular moment. They were so certain of their political principles that they felt justified in making them a permanent part of the nation's legal order.

The Fourteenth Amendment's first and most famous provision restated the Civil Rights Act's basic principles. The opening sentence clarified the definition of U.S. citizenship: "All persons born or naturalized in the United States, and subject to the jurisdiction thereof, are citizens of the United States and of the State wherein they reside." In so doing, the amendment went beyond the Civil Rights Act, which affirmed the citizenship of African Americans and, thus, referred only to those born in the United States. The Fourteenth Amendment included naturalized citizens because it was intended to offer a general definition of citizenship. That definition echoed existing understandings of citizenship, current in both law and popular culture, as a status that could be assumed through a voluntary affirmation of political allegiance as well as birth. Nonetheless, it is difficult to overstate the legal significance of the amendment's first sentence. Until the Fourteenth Amendment, the United States had no definitive statement about who could claim citizenship and by what means. Like so many legal issues, questions about citizenship had resisted a uniform, national definition because they resided in both federal and state jurisdictions, which produced their own renderings of who was a citizen and what that meant. The new amendment asserted federal authority, applying a uniform definition that applied in all the states throughout the nation.[16]

The remaining sentences of the first provision connected citizenship to civil rights, turning the Civil Rights Act's lengthy list of guaranteed rights into more general promises of equity. "No State," the amendment promised, "shall make or enforce any law which shall abridge the privileges or immunities of citizens of the United States; nor shall any State deprive any person of life, liberty, or property, without due process of law; nor deny to any person within its jurisdiction the equal protection of the laws."[17] Those general statements

---

[16] U.S. Const., amend. XIV, sec. 1.
[17] Ibid.

captured the political conflicts of the moment and preserved them in legal amber: What were the privileges and immunities of citizens? While the deprivation of life seemed clear, what counted as the deprivation of liberty and property? What constituted due process of law and equal protection? In fact, there were no clear answers to those questions at the time. Although Congressional Republicans and their constituents could agree that all citizens should be able to claim rights, consensus broke down on the particulars.[18]

In the legal culture of the time, rights fell out on a continuum. There were natural rights (fundamentals such as life, liberty, and the ever-illusive happiness that all people claimed as part of the human condition and that could not be abridged); civil rights (that involved equal protection in the courts in civil and criminal cases and were conferred by government); political rights (privileges granted to those qualified to make decisions in the interest of the larger public); and social rights (matters of personal affiliation in which it was thought the government had no interest). The Fourteenth Amendment's language invoked both natural rights and civil rights. But what, exactly, those categories included remained open at the time, with some people advocating much more expansive views of rights than others – the subject of Chapter 5. Yet, while vague, even purposefully so, the Fourteenth Amendment's connection between citizenship and rights took the nation in an utterly

[18] There is considerable debate among legal scholars about the original intent of the Fourteenth Amendment, with a particular focus on the meaning of "privileges and immunities" clause and whether the framers intended it to incorporate the Bill of Rights (i.e., to extend those constitutional rights to all American citizens, regardless of state laws in those areas). For an example of the proincorporationist argument, see Richard L. Aynes, "On Misreading John Bingham and the Fourteenth Amendment," *Yale Law Journal* 107 (1993): 57–104; Kurt T. Lash, "The Origins of the Privileges and Immunities Clause, Part 1: 'Privileges and Immunities' as an Antebellum Term of Art," *Georgetown Law Journal* 98 (2010): 1241–1302; Kurt T. Lash, "The Origins of the Privileges and Immunities Clause, Part II: John Bingham and the Second Draft of the Fourteenth Amendment," *Georgetown Law Journal* 99 (2011): 329–433. For the antiincorporationist argument, see Phillip Hamburger, "Privileges or Immunities," *Northwestern University Law Review* 105 (2011): 61–148. Placing the Fourteenth Amendment in a broader political context, however, recasts questions of original intent, by highlighting the irreconcilable political conflicts that the amendment embodied. Robert J. Kaczorowski, "Searching for the Intent of the Framers of the Fourteenth Amendment," *Connecticut Law Review* 5 (1972–3): 368–98.

new legal direction. Citizenship, granted by the federal government, had never before implied such broad claims to rights.

The Fourteenth Amendment charged the federal government with the protection of those rights, but framed its power in the passive voice. It promised that "No state ... shall abridge" citizens' rights.[19] But to whom would citizens appeal, should states abridge their rights? Who would determine which rights were included in those that could not be abridged? The amendment's passive construction spoke volumes about contemporary political currents, particularly widespread, deep-seated doubts about the wisdom of extending federal authority into areas once exclusively controlled by the states. "No political idea," Frederick Douglass remarked around the time the Civil Rights Act was being debated, was "more deeply rooted in the minds of men of all sections of the country [than] the right of each State to control its own affairs."[20] It was not until the final clause that the rhetorical curtain was lifted to reveal the enhanced authority of the federal government: "The Congress shall have power to enforce, by appropriate legislation, the provisions of this article." That statement, remarkable in its brevity, nonetheless turned what might have been mere political aspirations into tangible goals by giving Congress the power of enforcement.[21]

The passive voice, however, was not just rhetorical. It applied to the actual construction of federal authority as well. The Fourteenth Amendment did not give the federal government *direct* authority over individuals' civil rights, even though many Congressional Republicans had argued for that. In fact, the amendment did not grant rights to anyone at all, not even African Americans. The Fourteenth Amendment, like the Civil Rights Act, gave the federal government a negative power: to *prohibit* states from *discriminating* on the basis of race or previous servitude. That situation left states with great authority to determine the rights of all American citizens. African Americans could only claim the same rights that their states gave – or not – to others. It also made the link between American citizenship and rights all the more maddeningly vague,

[19] U.S. Const., amend. XIV, sec. 1.
[20] Frederick Douglass quoted in Foner, *Reconstruction*, p. 251.
[21] U.S. Const., amend. XIV, sec. 5.

because substantive authority over the distribution and meaning of rights lay with the states, not the federal government. In that sense, the Fourteenth Amendment was something of an empty vessel: it delegated the federal government to protect rights that it had no power to grant or define.

The Fourteenth Amendment also made clear that political rights were not fundamental rights of citizenship. Articles 2 and 3 penalized states that enacted suffrage restrictions on adult males and denied high-ranking Confederate officials the right to hold federal office. Section 4 eliminated the federal government's liability for Confederates' losses as a result of the Civil War, including the loss of property in slaves. While the provisions encouraged the enfranchisement of African American men, the Fourteenth Amendment did not link political rights to citizenship in the same way that it did civil rights.[22] That separation accorded with contemporary legal thought, which held that political rights were of a different, higher order than civil rights. The civil rights granted to all citizens were the ones that allowed them to handle the business, primarily the economic business, of their own lives. Political rights, by contrast, involved a much larger responsibility – to the future of the polity and all its people, not just to one's own, individual interests. The distinction was clear in the Civil Rights Act, which did provide a list of protected rights and defined them largely in terms of the procedures necessary to own and convey property: "to make and enforce contracts, to sue, be parties, and give evidence, to inherit, purchase, lease, sell, hold, and convey real and personal property, and to full and equal benefit of all laws and proceedings for the security of person and property." Political rights were a privilege; not everyone was worthy of them. In 1866, when the Fourteenth Amendment was framed, Congressional Republicans and their white constituents did not believe African American men were worthy.[23]

That changed by the end of 1866, just a few months later. Republicans won a decisive victory in the elections that fall. Emboldened, they abandoned any pretense of working with Johnson,

[22] U.S. Const., amend. XIV, sec. 2.
[23] Civil Rights Act (1866).

and went their own way. In 1867, Congressional Republicans passed the Reconstruction Acts, which negated Johnson's Reconstruction plan, divided the former Confederacy into military districts, and placed them under federal authority. Johnson immediately vetoed the first act, in a determined, if meaningless gesture. His signature was hardly dry on the page before Congress overrode him and set about reconstructing the Confederacy without him. They ultimately instituted impeachment proceedings against him.[24]

Under the congressional plan, Confederate states would be reconstituted and readmitted to the Union only if they accepted major changes in their laws and government. Those terms included political as well as civil rights for African Americans, in addition to the abolition of slavery and the repeal of nullification ordinances. Specifically, the former Confederate states had to ratify the Fourteenth Amendment, which prohibited legal distinctions on the basis of race in state law. Then they had to square their constitutions and their laws with those principles. The delegates charged with making new state constitutions had to be selected by an electorate that included African American men and excluded all high-ranking Confederate officials. Suffrage would be extended to others involved in the Confederacy only after they had sworn loyalty oaths.

At the constitutional conventions mandated by Congressional Reconstruction, delegates created some of the most democratic state governments in the nation. In addition to extending full civil and political rights to African Americans, they opened the legal system and government at both the state and local levels to whites of poor and moderate means. African Americans and poor whites began to prosecute cases and sit on juries, participating directly in formal legal arenas. They elected local officials, such as sheriffs and magistrates, who played crucial roles in the administration of law. They also selected representatives to their legislatures, which solidified and built on the democratic changes in their states' constitutions, including public education. The extension of suffrage to African American men, in particular, turned former Confederate states

---

[24] Articles of Impeachment Against President Andrew Johnson, 4 March 1866, *Supplement to the Congressional Globe*, 40th Cong., 2nd Sess., 1868.

with large black populations into Republican strongholds, supporting further legal change at the state and federal levels in keeping
with the spirit of Congressional Reconstruction – sometimes more
strongly than in states that had remained in the Union.[25]

The Fifteenth Amendment, which protected political rights
more specifically, was ratified soon thereafter, in 1870, when the
newly reconstructed states were part of the Union. The Fifteenth
Amendment followed the logic of the Fourteenth Amendment
by giving the federal government a negative power: the power to
respond to the denial of suffrage, when done on the basis of "race,
color, or previous condition of servitude." But, just as the Fourteenth
Amendment left states authority over civil rights, the Fifteenth
Amendment left them authority over suffrage. States could – and
did – restrict the vote in various other ways and for various other
reasons.[26]

THE LEGAL ORDER AND THE INHERENT
LIMITS OF FEDERAL OVERSIGHT

The political transformation that resulted from Congressional
Reconstruction and the democratization of state governments in
the South was profound, but ephemeral, as Chapters 5 and 6
will show. Change was fragile, in part, because federal policy did
not establish a firm basis for legal equality among U.S. citizens.
While the Reconstruction Amendments affirmed the principle
of civil and political equality among men and promised federal
protection of those principles, they left basic authority over individuals' legal status to the states, where race and slavery had
never been the only reason for restricting rights or for defining
them in ways that clearly benefited one group of people over
another. Many of these legal inequalities disadvantaged African
Americans as much as restrictions that were framed explicitly in
terms of race.

---

[25] For the kinds of changes at the state level, see Paul D. Escott, *Many Excellent
People: Power and Privilege in North Carolina, 1850–1900* (Chapel Hill, NC,
1985), particularly pp. 85–170.

[26] U.S. Const., amend. XV, sec. 1.

The legal status of women provides the most obvious example. Not only were free white women denied the same civil and political rights as white men, but they were also subject to a host of disabilities that men were not. African American women acquired all those legal disabilities upon emancipation. The Fourteenth and Fifteenth Amendments did nothing to alter that situation, and even made it more difficult to address by affirming the states' denial of rights to women. The Fourteenth Amendment penalized states only for denying adult men the vote, a clause that implicitly sanctioned states' denial of political rights to women. It was the first gendered reference in the U.S. Constitution, one that infuriated women's rights activists, who had supported the extension of the vote to African American men and assumed that suffrage would be given to women as well. The Fifteenth Amendment finished what the Fourteenth Amendment started, by extending federal protection only when the vote was denied on the basis of "race, color, or previous condition of servitude" and leaving states free to disfranchise women.[27]

The legal status of ethnic minorities, particularly in the West, provides another striking example of legally sanctioned inequality. The admission of California to the Union as a free state in 1850, for instance, did not really end slavery there. Southern slaveholders brought slaves with them to work in the mines, while the booming economy encouraged forms of labor that closely resembled slavery. Although "free" in the sense that they were contractual, these labor arrangements locked workers into a lifetime of service, from which there was almost no hope of escape. Most California laborers in such contracts were immigrants from China, Mexico, and other parts of Latin America, who received wages in the form of transportation, food, and lodging, but who found themselves in an endless cycle of debt in which their earnings never exceeded their living expenses. Provisions in the Reconstruction Amendments, particularly the connection between citizenship and rights, limited their ability to protect immigrant laborers. In fact, California's political

---

[27] U.S. Const. amend. XIV, sec. 2. U.S. Const., amend. XV, sec. 1. Ellen Carol DuBois, *Feminism and Suffrage: The Emergence of an Independent Women's Movement in America, 1848–1869* (Ithaca, NY, 1978).

leaders used the Reconstruction Amendments to support a host of legal prohibitions against people from China, including immigration restrictions, arguing that Chinese immigrants worked in conditions akin to slavery and, therefore, represented a threat to freedom and liberty.[28]

All African Americans, moreover, found themselves subject to the legal inequalities that had always disadvantaged the poor. States handled the rights of white men in ways that reinforced existing economic inequalities. In law, individuals who were obviously unequal were treated as equal, obscuring structural inequalities that were often inseparable from the legal issues. A poor laborer had the right to enter contracts, as did his employer. Both could sue. Both were entitled to property rights. But those rights did not make them equal, not even in law, particularly if one party owned property and the other did not. If there was ever a conflict, a court would likely uphold the property rights of the employer over the claims of the employee, whose labor had become the employer's property through the labor contract. Those inequalities, which the Civil Rights Act and the Fourteenth Amendment did not touch, affected African Americans disproportionately because of their economic circumstances.

In fact, Congressional Republicans flatly refused to address the economic condition of former slaves, a situation attributable to conceptions of rights and property that, in turn, meshed with their views of Indians, western lands, and the nation's destiny. Some more radical members of the party did advocate measures to confiscate former slaveholders' land and distribute it to former slaves. Such efforts came from a basic sense of justice and a practical assessment of what freedpeople would need to succeed economically. Concerns about freedpeople also connected with general economic precepts held by many in the Republican Party, particularly the rejection of a permanent landholding class. Indeed, opposition to a landed monopoly fueled support for a range of popular wartime policies, particularly the Homestead Act and other measures designed to secure the interests of those who worked the land. Yet this economic

---

[28] Stacey Smith, *Freedom's Frontier: California and the Struggle over Unfree Labor, Emancipation, and Reconstruction* (Chapel Hill, NC, 2013).

vision depended on conceptions of private property that, ultimately, militated against economic policies that would have helped African Americans emerging from slavery and secured the future of working Americans more generally.[29]

The implications of those assumptions were most clear in the West. Many Republicans, like many white Americans, did not see western land in the same terms as land in the South or, for that matter, anywhere else in the United States. They considered western lands to be unoccupied, despite the obvious presence of Indians and numerous treaties that clearly established Indian land claims. More than that, the rules of property law, particularly the rules establishing ownership, did not apply to Indians, who were not part of the United States or its legal system. In a series of cases from the 1820s and 1830s, beginning with *Johnson v. McIntosh* (1823), the U.S. Supreme Court had defined Indian tribes as, essentially, sovereign nations without land of their own. It was a legal fiction that applied in no other context and allowed the federal government extensive authority over Indians, while denying them direct representation in the federal government. *Johnson v. McIntosh* arose from a common source of tension in areas where white settlers were encroaching on Indian lands: Was the sale of land by one Indian to a third party valid when it was done without consent of the tribe? In other contexts, property transactions among private parties would have been unremarkable. But when they involved Indians, they implicated federal authority because they involved treaties that promised federal recognition of Indian lands and, with that recognition, protection against the aggressive efforts of white settlers to appropriate it. At issue was also the federal government's authority at this early moment in its history, when it faced challenges from both within and outside its borders. If it hoped to survive, the federal government had to persuade its own people – at the very least – to

---

[29] The classic statement of the connection between Republicans' view of labor and property and their policies in regard to former slaves is David Montgomery, *Beyond Equality: Labor and the Radical Republicans, 1862–1872* (New York, 1967). For a compelling interpretation of private property and the U.S. Constitution, see Jennifer Nedelsky, *Private Property and the Limits of American Constitutionalism* (Chicago, 1990).

respect its authority, particularly over lands over which it claimed jurisdiction.[30]

Johnson v. McIntosh gave with one hand and took away with the other. John Marshall, writing for the majority, recognized Indian sovereignty, but hemmed it in with so many exclusions that it meant very little. While sovereign, Indians existed as conquered nations, whose land had been stripped away by European powers long before the founding of the United States. That situation, as Marshall argued, was an unavoidable tragedy: "The tribes of Indians inhabiting this country were fierce savages, whose occupation was war, and whose subsistence was drawn chiefly from the forest. To leave them in possession of their country, was to leave the country a wilderness; to govern them as a distinct people, was impossible, because they were as brave and as high spirited as they were fierce, and were ready to repel by arms every attempt on their independence." Europeans had no choice but to subdue the Indians or leave the country to them, which was unthinkable, because that deprived an entire continent of civilization. The whole unfortunate situation had been foisted on the United States, which was now forced to deal with its implications.[31]

Marshall's tone of helpless resignation would become common in federal discourse on Indian policy in the nineteenth century. Of course, Marshall was anything but helpless, because he was in complete control of the historical narrative he was writing and on which he based his legal conclusions. That history, according to Marshall, meant that Europeans' claims to the continent had transferred to the United States. Indians therefore occupied land at the discretion of the federal government; they did not own it or exercise any of the

---

[30] *Johnson v. McIntosh*, 21 U.S. (8 Wheat.) 543 (1823); *Cherokee Nation v. Georgia*, 30 U.S. (5 Pet.) 1 (1831); *Worcester v. Georgia*, 31 U.S. (6 Pet.) 515 (1832). For the importance of law regarding the seizure of Indian lands, see Stuart Banner, *How the Indians Lost Their Land: Law and Power on the Frontier* (Cambridge, MA, 2005).

[31] *Johnson v. McIntosh*. Tim Alan Garrison, *The Legal Ideology of Removal: The Southern Judiciary and the Sovereignty of Native American Nations* (Athens, GA, 2002) argues that state decisions in this period undermined Indian sovereignty. Property claims were actually much more complicated, see Maria Montoya, *Translating Property: The Maxwell Land Grant and the Conflict over Land in the American West, 1840–1900* (Berkeley, 2002).

powers that came with ownership. In negating Indian land claims, *Johnson v. McIntosh* hollowed out the core of Indian sovereignty to the point where it collapsed in on itself. Indians maintained the right to govern themselves, but only on matters internal to their own tribes. Otherwise they were subject to the authority of the United States. And they did not own the land on which they lived.[32]

Johnson v. McIntosh put a positive gloss on what was, in fact, a relationship of extreme subordination, describing it as a means for the federal government to protect a vulnerable, uncivilized people who were powerless to protect themselves against the encroachments of the modern world, particularly the settlers who pushed at their borders. The kind of sovereignty granted in *Johnson v. McIntosh*, however, also eliminated any leverage Indians could mobilize as individuals with rights within the federal government. As sovereign nations, Indians had no legal or political presence within the government that "protected" them. They could not even access its law or its legal system, as the U.S. Supreme Court affirmed in *Cherokee Nation v. Georgia* (1831). Writing for the court, John Marshall refused to hear the Cherokee's charges against the state of Georgia's aggressive seizure of their lands, arguing that doing so would undermine the principle of Indian sovereignty. Indian nations would not be sovereign if they were subject to the laws of the United States. But Marshall's respect for Indian sovereignty only went so far. He described them as "domestic dependent nations." "The relationship of the tribes to the United States," he wrote, "resembles that of a 'ward to its guardian.'"[33]

These U.S. Supreme Court cases laid the basic legal framework that governed Indian relations for much of the rest of the nineteenth century. The historical narrative they spun out, however, did not describe the situation on the ground. Marshall – and many white Americans – may have thought that the continent had been wrested from the Indians by Europeans, whose claims then accrued to the

---

[32] *Johnson v. McIntosh*. Also see *Worcester v. Georgia*. Lindsay G. Robertson, *Conquest by Law: How the Discovery of America Dispossessed Indigenous Peoples of Their Lands* (New York, 2005).

[33] *Cherokee Nation v. Georgia*. Marshall softened his language in *Worcester v. Georgia*; some say that was because he regretted the ways that previous decisions had been applied to justify Georgia's oppression of the Cherokee.

United States through treaty. But Indians had not participated in or consented to most of those agreements. Many still considered the land on which they lived to be their own, and conflicts continued into the Civil War and beyond.

The wartime policies of Congressional Republicans heightened existing tensions. During the Civil War, Congress had quickly organized the West into territories and enticed settlers with the Homestead Act and new transportation projects, including the transcontinental railroad. Colorado, Nevada, and Dakota were made territories in 1861; Idaho and Arizona in 1863; and Montana in 1864. The discovery of gold and silver in various western territories, including Colorado, Washington, Idaho, Montana, and Oregon, produced stampedes into those areas, with whole cities mushrooming out of nowhere overnight. As Indians laid claims to the land on which they lived, and which formed the material base of their economies and cultures, sporadic conflict devolved into full-scale war in many parts of the trans-Mississippi West. Military commanders were brutal in their response. They did not feel bound by the usual rules of engagement because they did not see the conflict as a war, in the formal sense of the term, but rather as operations designed to subdue an inconvenient population and clear the way for settlement as envisioned by the land's rightful claimants: the federal government and, through it, the American people. Even when federal policies were couched in the guise of protecting Indians, they involved force. Treaties shrunk Indian lands or moved Indians onto reservations in places that no one else wanted and that offered no means for economic subsistence, let alone cultural continuity. Federal assistance, although promised, failed to materialize, leaving Indians in truly desperate circumstances, with no legal recourse.

By the end of the Civil War, the situation had deteriorated to the point where it became the focus of intense public debate. While new settlers in the West encouraged even more aggressive action, many easterners were horrified by reports of the appalling conditions in which Indians were forced to live. In 1865, while in the midst of formulating its policies for Reconstruction, Congress created a special commission to look into Indians' problems. They recommended peace: "to conquer by kindness." That recommendation signaled a shift in policy aimed at turning Indians into U.S. citizens – which

Chapter 6 will discuss in more detail. The language of Congressional Reconstruction highlights the deep ambiguities that attended such policies. Both the Civil Rights Act and the Fourteenth Amendment followed federal judicial decisions of the early nineteenth century in excluding "Indians not taxed" from both citizenship and the rights attached to that status. Not that Indians wanted citizenship. But the line between civilized and savage, which was so deeply embedded within the nation's law and culture, made it difficult for most white Americans to imagine that Indians had any legal standing as individual citizens entitled to rights. To admit that would be to question the nation's territorial integrity – and its very existence.[34]

The Republican Party encouraged settlement of the continent as part of its national vision. White Americans would bring the nation's core values with them, plant them on western soil, and bring the wild parts of the continent into the national family. Nearly a half century later, Frederick Jackson Turner would turn the Republican Party's political aspirations into historical description with his frontier thesis, which explained the development of the nation's political culture in terms of waves of westward settlement. Each time they picked up and moved, American settlers constructed democratic institutions anew. Private property lay at the center of this process, which assumed that democratic institutions grew from ground carved up into individually owned plots and that their chief duty was to protect the owners' property rights. The centrality of private property to the nation's legal regime was why Marshall, Turner, and host of other officials and commentators took pains to differentiate Indian lands from other kinds of property, the ownership of which was protected by the legal system. For Marshall and Turner, civilization required the appropriation of Indian land. Congress agreed. From the Northwest Territorial Ordinance (1787) forward, the thrust of federal policy was taking Indian land and redistributing it to American citizens as private property. Yet the centrality of private property ownership also made the seizure of Indian land potentially problematic: if some private property could be appropriated without reason or due process, then all claims to private property might be endangered. That was why so much ink

---

[34] West, *The Last Indian War.*

was expended in explaining the legalities of what was, essentially, the uncompensated seizure of property without due process of law. Marshall put it off on European powers, whose actions had pre-dated the founding of the United States. Turner denied it altogether, erasing Indians from the land and rendering the West as empty ter-ritory, ripe for the taking. Either way, the story went, the federal government's claims to the land were legal and the Indians' claims were not.[35]

That same commitment to private property also described Reconstruction policy back East. Congressional Republicans refused to negate the property rights of white Confederates, apart from the abolition of slavery. Not secession, not Civil War, not the treason-ous acts of individual Confederates, not the political and practical arguments offered on behalf of former slaves, and not even the legal sanction offered in the Confiscation Acts changed the situation. The majority of Republicans stood by Confederates' property rights in their land, stock, and tools. That vision of rights – one centered on the importance of protecting individual property ownership – also grounded the Reconstruction Amendments.[36]

In the political rhetoric of the time, the rights protected in the Fourteenth and Fifteenth Amendments were soaring and expansive. At times they seemed to fulfill the promise of the Declaration of Independence, as in Lincoln's Gettysburg Address: a nation "con-ceived in liberty and dedicated to the proposition that all men are created equal." In the context of the legal system, however, those rights could take on very different forms. The idealism of the era's political rhetoric has often made Reconstruction's failures all the more glaring and disappointing. Historians in the early twentieth century, particularly those associated with the Dunning School, saw those ideals as the problem. As they maintained, Congressional Republicans improperly – and unjustly and unconstitutionally – imposed their political vision on the rest of the nation. The resulting expansion of federal power had toxic results: chaos in the South, a national government infested with corruption and cronyism,

---

[35] Frederick Jackson Turner, *The United States, 1830–1860: The Nation and Its Sections* (New York, 1935).

[36] Hamilton, *The Limits of Sovereignty.*

inappropriate intervention in issues best left to the states, and a general disregard for individual liberties. The pendulum swung the other direction after World War II. The problem, according to revisionist historians, was not the Republicans' ideals, but their unwillingness to follow through and use federal authority to its full effect. Yet both strands of the historiography tend to confuse politics and the law, conflating the expansion of the federal government's *legal* authority with *political* efforts to extend civil and political rights to African Americans – as if federal authority and the attendant legal changes of the Reconstruction era would always and only be used to realize the political principles with which historians associated them. The resulting studies suggested that the federal government's enhanced authority should have allowed it to achieve racial equality – which, after World War II, the historiography identified as a positive, unrealized goal. To be sure, enhanced federal authority did offer an important counterweight to efforts on the state and local levels to restrict the rights of African Americans, particularly in the former Confederacy. But accomplishing the kind of equality promised in political rhetoric would take far more than extending federal oversight over areas once controlled by the states. Federal oversight, moreover, never guaranteed egalitarian outcomes. The situation in the West – where federal authority resulted in the seizure of Indian land, the opening of that land to capitalist development, and the systematic annihilation of Indian culture – served as a cautionary tale. Indeed, Reconstruction in the West makes the federal government's subsequent abdication of authority in the South less anomalous. In the South, as in the West, the federal government followed a particular legal vision, one that upheld the rights of private property and generated inequality in the name of preserving formal legal equality.

5

The Possibilities of Rights

Bella Newton was one of many Americans who gave meaning to
the broad legal changes put in place by Congressional Republicans.
Newton, an African American woman in North Carolina, did not
set out to involve herself in the major constitutional questions
of the day. She wanted only to defend her children, William and
Susan, against the actions of an angry white neighbor, Alexander
Noblin. The incident began in the spring of 1869 when William and
Susan took a short cut across Noblin's land on the way home from
school. Noblin ordered the children off. From there, the situation
deteriorated rapidly. Noblin tried to assault Susan. William threw a
rock at Noblin's head, frustrating his attempt. Then, as the children
made their escape, Noblin tried to assert his authority one final
time. In William's words, he "shook his penis at us." After learning
of the incident, Bella Newton's first response was in keeping with
local customs. She publicized her complaint in the neighborhood
and then made an informal bargain with Noblin, agreeing to drop
the matter in exchange for one dollar and ten pounds of bacon.
Noblin delivered on his end of the deal, but Newton had a change
of heart and filed charges with the justice of the peace, turning the
incident into a legal matter involving her rights and those of her
children. Much to his chagrin, Noblin learned that his actions carried different consequences than they had before the enactment of
the Reconstruction Amendments: Noblin was indicted for assault
at the spring term of the Superior Court.[1]

[1] *State v. Alexander Noblin*, 1869, Granville County Criminal Action Papers, North
Carolina Department of Archives and History. Also see Laura F. Edwards, "Sexual

Congressional Republicans rallied in support of the extension of federal power to bring the states of the former Confederacy in line with what they saw as broad, national principles. But consensus fell apart after that: even within the Republican Party, there was no agreement as to what, exactly, the Reconstruction Amendments were meant to accomplish. Reliance on the compliance of state governments only muddied the waters, dispersing responsibility for enforcing the amendments and, in the process, diluting their meaning.

The commitment to civil and political equality at the state level was uneven, at best – and not just in the South. If anything, it was the states of the former Confederacy that embraced the Reconstruction Amendments the most enthusiastically. In the years immediately following their reorganization under Congressional Reconstruction, many of those states' leaders were fully committed to the realization of the new amendments' principles. But even state governments supportive of the Reconstruction Amendments were limited in what they could do because they did not have direct authority over most incidents involving breaches of civil and political rights. Those cases were tried by local courts, which operated at a remove from state government even though they followed state law. Cases reached state or federal jurisdictions on appeal: given the Reconstruction Amendments' provisions, the only way to challenge local or state rulings that failed to recognize an individual's rights was for aggrieved individuals to file suit themselves. That jurisdictional situation applied throughout the United States, making it difficult for anyone to make use of the rights guaranteed by state and federal law – even in the most ideal of circumstances.

It was left to people like Bella Newton to claim and define their rights. African Americans in the states of the former Confederacy did so in profoundly difficult circumstances, where even routine social interactions, such as William and Susan Newton's unfortunate shortcut home from school, erupted in violence. In the South, such confrontations were notable for their extremes: the extreme rage and extreme forms of violence that white southerners let

Violence, Gender, Reconstruction, and the Extension of Patriarchy in Granville County, North Carolina," *North Carolina Historical Review* 68 (1991): 237–60.

loose on African Americans over what would have been, in other contexts, the most minor of incidents. But if the conditions of African Americans' lives were unique, their legal claims and their uses of the law were not. In fact, their efforts echoed those of other Americans across the country, who identified with the principles that informed the Reconstruction Amendments, picked them up, and used them for their own purposes. The legal dimension of such efforts has not fully registered in the historiography. Legal historians rarely find their way to the venues where ordinary people made their claims, while scholars who study those people most engaged in the project of Reconstruction – namely African American men, laboring people, and all women – rarely find their way to legal history. Americans, however, had definite expectations of the law. They expected the legal system to serve as a venue of social change, not just a bastion of the status quo. They also expected the idiom of rights, once linked to individual interests, to produce social justice. Their efforts to write those expectations into the legal order ultimately produced a powerful backlash, not just in the South, but throughout the United States as well. But even as the forces of reaction crushed the hopes and dreams of many Americans, they also testified to the success of ordinary people, like Bella Newton, in reshaping the nation's legal culture.

THE INTRANSIGENCE OF INEQUALITY IN THE EXISTING LEGAL ORDER

Federal troops remained when former Confederate states reorganized under the terms of Congressional Reconstruction and rejoined the Union. But Congressional Republicans phased out the Freedmen's Bureau, which had been the most visible extension of federal legal authority in the South. In 1865, when the bureau was formed, its agents had fanned out across the region, working in local areas to explain the concept of wage labor, to supervise the signing of labor contracts, and to make sure the terms of those contracts were met. One year later, Congressional Republicans buttressed the bureau's authority in conjunction with the Civil Rights Act of 1866 and the Second Freedmen's Bureau Act, giving agents jurisdiction in a range of legal matters where state law did not recognize African

Americans' civil rights. Bureau agents dealt with a wide range of other issues as well, including the distribution of aid to indigent whites and blacks, the reunion of families that had been separated by slavery or the war, and the establishment of schools.[2]

The bureau's authority, moreover, was more limited than some radical Republicans and most freedpeople wanted. Instead of using their legal authority and developing their own court system, bureau agents placed their faith in the existing system, endeavoring to persuade states and localities to recognize the civil and political rights of African Americans. Congress never authorized the redistribution of land or property, which left bureau agents with the task of convincing – or forcing – African Americans to enter into labor contracts to work the lands of their former masters. Even then, the bureau's effectiveness varied widely, depending on the commitment of local agents. In some states, governors elected under Johnson's Reconstruction Plan appointed agents who were hostile to the Freedmen's Bureau's mission. In other states, however, the bureau provided a stabilizing presence at a moment of profound economic dislocation and wrenching social transformation. States' compliance with the terms of Congressional Reconstruction, however, did not entirely resolve African Americans' legal problems, which involved discrimination not just in the letter of the law, but also its administration and enforcement. To be effective, the bureau needed to remain in the South much longer. Yet many Republican leaders insisted that the bureau's presence was no longer necessary or justifiable once states had been reconstituted in a way that recognized all citizens' legal rights. Jurisdiction of those matters should revert to the states. "Now that the colored men have been endowed with the same civil and political rights as the whites," wrote a South Carolina Freedmen's Bureau agent who was fully committed to the principles of Congressional Reconstruction, "it is a question whether they ought longer to be subjects for special legislation."[3]

---

[2] First Freedmen's Bureau Act. Civil Rights Act (1866). Second Freedmen's Bureau Act.

[3] Quote from Suzanne Stone Johnson and Robert Allison Johnson, eds., *Bitter Freedom: William Stone's Record of Service in the Freedmen's Bureau* (Columbia, SC, 2008), p. xii. Paul A. Cimbala, *Under the Guardianship of the Nation: The*

Congressional Republicans placed their faith in the existing logic of the law as well as the existing legal system. Their policies, as expressed in the Thirteenth, Fourteenth, and Fifteenth Amendments, were structured around the presumption that slavery could be removed from the legal order without changing much of anything else. Once the Thirteenth Amendment eliminated slavery, the Fourteenth and Fifteenth Amendments denied its existence by making African Americans indistinguishable from other Americans in law: they became legal individuals with the same civil and political rights as all other legal individuals, as if they had never been anything else. That legal transformation, however, was not so easily accomplished. The Reconstruction Amendments, along with southern states' new constitutions, created legal equality by denying the past – a past in which legal jurisdictions, at all levels, had allowed for African Americans' systematic exploitation on the basis of race. But race had worked its way so thoroughly into the legal order, particularly in slave states, that it was impossible to remove simply by insisting that it no longer mattered.

Slavery was an extreme manifestation of a dynamic that characterized the nation's legal order more generally: the identification of adult white men as the paradigmatic legal individuals. That situation grew from conceptions of household governance with deep roots in Anglo-American law. In the logic of household governance, only adult white men had the capacity for independence necessary to head households, which entailed the assumption of economic and moral responsibility for their dependents in addition to the fulfillment of public duties as members of the polity. The legal regimes of slaveholding states took that logic to its extreme, stretching conceptions of domestic dependency to include enslaved African Americans. But the same assumptions also restricted the rights of women and racial minorities in free states. It was no accident that John Marshall reached for domestic dependency as an analogy to describe Indian nations' subordinate relationship to the United States in *Cherokee Nation v. Georgia* (1831). Indians were to the

Freedmen's Bureau and the Reconstruction of Georgia, 1865–1870 (Athens, GA, 1997); Donald G. Nieman, *To Set the Law in Motion: The Freedmen's Bureau and the Legal Rights of Blacks, 1865–1868* (Millwood, NY, 1980).

United States as wards were to guardians, with power firmly fixed on one side of the relationship. Indians and other people of color also suffered from the laws that sanctioned racial slavery. Indeed, the presence of slavery, an unrestricted legal form of human debasement, encouraged particularly twisted forms of racism throughout the country against all people of color.[4]

Race and gender acquired increasing significance in the legal framework of household governance in the decades between the American Revolution and the Civil War. Conceptions of independence and dependence, once attached to an individual's structural place within households, became linked to an individual's race and gender. African Americans were denied rights, not just because of their status as slaves, but because of their race, which made them innately dependent and incapable of exercising them. By the same token, all women were denied rights, not because of their status as wives, but because of their gender. All white men could exercise the full range of civil and political rights, not because they actually were household heads, but because of their race and gender, which made them innately independent. More to the point, white men were constituted as freemen through their rights *over* those without rights. Political rhetoric in the decades leading up to the Civil War construed those rights broadly, linking them to freedom, liberty, and even equality.[5]

The idiom of rights was commonplace in both parties in the mid-nineteenth century. Confederate leaders had been as invested in the defense of rights at the war's outset as radical Republicans were in their extension at its conclusion. After the Civil War, Democrats as well as Republicans drew heavily on the rhetoric and imagery of rights. All these political leaders, regardless of party affiliation, invoked rights in positive terms, often in connection to liberty and equality. But they rarely explained the connection. In fact, most

---

[4] *Johnson v. McIntosh.* Carole Pateman, *The Sexual Contract* (Stanford, CA, 1988); Catherine Hall, *White, Male, and Middle-Class: Explorations in Feminism and History* (New York, 1992); Cheryl I. Harris, "Whiteness as Property." *Harvard Law Review* 106 (1993): 1923–2015.

[5] Edwards, *The People and Their Peace*, particularly pp. 205–98; Barbara Young Welke, *Law and the Borders of Belonging in the Long Nineteenth Century United States* (New York, 2010).

political leaders attached specific, if unarticulated, meanings to their words: they were referring to the rights that provided access to the legal system and to mechanisms that allowed for the ownership and transfer of property, particularly the ability to enter into contracts. Political rights were an altogether different category of rights, a privilege accorded to those capable of putting their individual interests aside so as to make reasoned decisions about the public good. Political leaders differed over who could claim those rights, not what they were. That was true even for Republican leaders, who wished to extend political rights to African American men. As they saw it, equality was accomplished if everyone – or, at least, all men – had the same rights. There was no need to change anything else.[6]

That conception of rights narrowed further once it moved from the realm of political discourse to the legal system, where access was only the beginning. Rights, like other legal principles, did specific work within the legal process. Their practical task was the resolution of competing claims among individuals through the identification of winners and losers – a situation that undercut the link between rights and equality in the political rhetoric. Rights also held a privileged position, along with other legal principles, in the legal system. The courts' duty was to those legal principles and existing laws, not the rights-bearing individuals who brought their problems to court. While the legal process weighed individual claims, the point was to uphold existing laws and legal principles. As such, the application of rights could produce outcomes of questionable justice for the actual people involved: a conviction overturned because of an improperly framed indictment; the seizure of property because of a faulty bill of sale; or a worker denied six months of wages for a minor infraction because statutes specified strict adherence to labor contracts. Such outcomes did not necessarily conform to popular conceptions of liberty, freedom, and equality, let alone justice.

Even so, at the outset of the Civil War, white men could claim rights not just in their property and their own labor, but also in the labor and bodies of their dependents and, through the abstractions of gender and race, over the lives of other subordinate people as

---

[6] See Foner, *Reconstruction*, particularly pp. 124–75, 228–80; Richardson, *The Greatest Nation of the Earth*.

well. Their authority in this body of law extended over all black persons, slave or free, and no black person fully possessed his or her own body or the product of his or her labor, even in free states. The logic naturalized the inequalities of domestic dependency, including slavery, as expressions of immutable qualities of race and gender. It also turned their exercise into a zero sum game. Because the rights of white men included authority over women and racial minorities, then the extension of rights to those people represented a loss to white men. Alexander Noblin's parting gesture to William and Susan Newton spoke volumes about that situation: with it, Noblin sought to convey the authority he once claimed, by right, as a white man.

REMAKING RIGHTS AND RECLAIMING THE LEGAL ORDER

That construction of rights made it difficult to alter the legal status of African Americans in any way, particularly in the states of the former Confederacy where slavery had become so central to the legal order. The legal fallout from slavery's collapse began during the Civil War. As military commanders and federal officials struggled to define the formal legal status of slavery's refugees, those refugees tackled even more intransigent legal issues. They tried to establish their own lives within a legal order that denied that possibility to them: they left slavery; they brought their families with them; they lived in their own households; they moved around as they saw fit; they did work that they wanted to do and demanded pay for it; they learned to read and write; they worshipped as they pleased; they formed their own community organizations; and they insisted on respect from others. In all these ways African Americans rejected the legal order and their position as legal dependents within households headed by white men. More than that, African American men took the position of household head, a legal status previously reserved for white men. African American women located themselves within those households, where they assumed both the roles and legal privileges that had previously only applied to white women.[7]

---

[7] These efforts have been documented in the volumes of the Freedmen and Southern Society Project; see ch. 3, note 3. For the legal implications of African Americans

Both whites and African Americans understood such efforts for what they were: overt challenges to the existing legal order – now a crumbling legal order that had supported slavery and, in turn, had been constituted by it. That legal order locked enslaved people into positions of extreme subordination. The law did not recognize slaves' marriages, their claims to their own children, or their ownership of any property. The law mandated where slaves could go, requiring written permission for them to move beyond the bounds of their owners' land and prohibiting assembly not supervised by whites. It even regulated slaves' interaction with their masters and other whites, specifying that they show due deference, excusing violence against them if they did not, and barring the use of force to defend themselves, even when their lives were in danger.

The legal changes initiated during the Civil War and Reconstruction prohibited restrictions on the basis of race, opening up the possibility for change. But for those laws to have meaning, there had to be change in an entirely different arena, namely the social relations that structured people's daily lives. African Americans started that process long before Congressional Republicans seized control of the Reconstruction process. As recent scholarship has emphasized, African Americans actively seized rights; they were not passive recipients of them. Former slaves followed events closely, assessed their meanings carefully, and passed that information along quickly to others, creating a tightly woven, but wide-reaching network that stretched across the South. The hope and optimism of that moment is hard to miss. They were free. But what did freedom mean? Historians who study African Americans' efforts to establish independent lives of their own usually do so from a perspective that isolates the law from those struggles. The law figures in this scholarship as a tool, entering into the narrative only to the extent that it supported – or not – African Americans' claims. Such an approach, however, misses not only the profound legal implications of African

efforts to set up households of their own, see Nancy D. Bercaw, *Gendered Freedoms: Race, Rights, and the Politics of Household in the Delta, 1861–1875* (Gainesville, FL, 2003); Laura F. Edwards, *Gendered Strife and Confusion: The Political Culture of Reconstruction* (Urbana, IL, 1997).

Americans' actions, but also the importance of law in the lives of all Americans.[8]

African Americans understood the importance of law. In fact, they tried to mobilize the legal system from the outset of the Civil War, by framing their problems in legal terms, questioning existing law, and suggesting changes to it. They did so even before emancipation, with refugees and black soldiers firing off letters and complaints to military commanders, federal officials, and elected representatives. They continued after the Civil War, under Presidential Reconstruction and the notorious state Black Codes, which limited African Americans' individual rights and barred them from using local and state courts in most instances. African Americans nonetheless brought complaints to military commanders and Freedmen's Bureau officials, turning them into legal intermediaries even before passage of the Civil Rights Act and Freedmen's Bureau Act in 1866 gave the bureau jurisdiction over such matters. After the passage of the Fourteenth Amendment and the restructuring of southern state governments, African Americans made valiant efforts to use all the new legal arenas open to them, at the local, state, and federal levels.[9]

In their efforts, they pushed the legal process along, participating actively in the major policy debates of the era. The petition from the African Americans of Lincoln County, Tennessee, which began Chapter 4, was not unusual in this regard. Writing in the summer of 1865, while Johnson was implementing his Reconstruction plan, these petitioners anticipated many of the legal changes that

[8] Leon F. Litwack, *Been in the Storm So Long: The Aftermath of Slavery* (New York, 1979). In addition to the scholarship from the Freedmen and Southern Society Project, also see Barbara J. Fields, *Slavery and Freedom on the Middle Ground: Maryland during the Nineteenth Century* (New Haven, CT, 1985); Eric Foner, *Nothing But Freedom: Emancipation and Its Legacy* (Baton Rouge, LA, 1983).

[9] Recent work emphasizes enslaved African Americans' familiarity and involvement with the legal system in slavery: Edwards, *The People and Their Peace*; Ariela J. Gross, *Double Character: Slavery and Mastery in the Antebellum Southern Courtroom* (Princeton, NJ, 2000); Dylan C. Penningroth, *The Claims of Kinfolk: African American Property and Community in the Nineteenth-Century South* (Chapel Hill, NC, 2003).

would come later with Congressional Reconstruction. They asked
for rights that would give them access to the legal system and that
would secure their property, including property in their labor. "We
now, simply ask," they wrote, "that we may be secured as others,
in the just fruits of our toil: protected from unjust, and illegal pun-
ishments." They framed that request in terms of Republican political rhetoric that not only identified the American people as the
source of the nation's wealth, but also connected them closely to
the nation through their legal status as citizens: "We are sure we
will keep our families from want and do our part as good citizens
of the United States to add to the wealth and glory of the Country."
Lawmakers in the nation's capital had yet to confer citizenship on
African Americans; they approved the Civil Rights Act and the
Fourteenth Amendment later, in 1866. Yet these petitioners thought
that they, too, could claim a place among the nation's citizens and,
more than that, claim legal rights on the basis of citizenship: "We
are recognized as men by the Constitution of the land: we only ask
to be treated as such, and we will, in the future as in the past, be
law abiding men."[10] The petitioners in Lincoln County, Tennessee,
were not alone. In 1865 and 1866, African Americans across the
country formed Equal Rights Leagues and other similar organizations, met in conventions, and issued statements intended to sway
public opinion.

By 1866, and even before, African Americans in these organizations were advocating the extension of political as well as civil
rights to all black men, a position that put them way out in front of
the debate in Washington. To be sure, many African American leaders in the North had long supported full civil and political equality.
But they also accepted legal conventions of the time that characterized suffrage as a higher order of rights than mere civil rights. That
was one reason why African American leaders pushed so hard for
black military service during the Civil War: they hoped that military
service, the most extreme form that commitment to the polity could
take, would demonstrate fitness for the privilege of political rights.
The argument gained some traction by the end of the Civil War.

---

[10] Tennessee Freedmen to the Freedmen's Bureau Assistant Commissioner for
Kentucky, Tennessee, and Northern Alabama.

Even Lincoln, who was certainly not on the leading edge in the promotion of African Americans' rights, found it compelling enough to support the extension of political rights to black veterans when Louisiana was readmitted to the Union in 1865.

It was, nonetheless, an enormous step from the enfranchisement of a handful of black veterans in one state to the enfranchisement of all African American men throughout the entire nation. And that was what African Americans were advocating in 1866, even in southern states where the extension of political rights would entail a radical restructuring of the electorate and, by implication, the government. They did so at a particularly difficult moment, when the outcome of the conflict between Johnson and Congressional Republicans was unclear and a public stance on such a controversial issue might have ended badly for many African Americans, particularly in the South. Yet, as recent scholarship has shown, these meetings had a profound effect in convincing Republican leaders and their northern constituents that African Americans deserved political as well as civil rights. Their orderly demeanor, reasoned requests, and public spirit presented a convincing case – and a stark contrast with Johnson's politically tone-deaf policies and the reactionary actions of ex-Confederates who claimed power as a result.[11]

African Americans also stretched the framework of rights to cover a whole new range of issues. Specifically, they turned issues that had been considered social rights into civil rights. Civil rights implied universal standards that everyone could claim. Social rights, by contrast, included access to public services and space, privileges that were established in context and thus varied from one community to another.

One of the earliest, most common demands from African American organizations in both the North and South was equal access to education. In northern states, many of which had well-established public school systems, African Americans advocated

---

[11] Foner's *Reconstruction* and *Fiery Trial* capture the evolution in the historiography, with its increasing emphasis on African Americans' role in influencing policy. *Reconstruction*, pp. 228–345, focuses on Congressional Republicans in its discussion of Reconstruction policy and brings in African Americans once their civil and political rights were established; *The Fiery Trial*, by contrast, positions African Americans as central actors on those debates throughout the book.

desegregation as the best way to provide equal access. The problem of access took a different form in southern states, most of which did not have public schools at all. There, African Americans called for the creation of public education systems, funded through state government, which would serve all the states' residents, white and black. African Americans characterized education as a right: it was something to which everyone deserved equal access because it was such a fundamental component of American life. That characterization stuck, both in popular conceptions of education and the law. The Reconstruction-era constitutions of many southern states gave education all the trappings of a right: a universal claim that was available to everyone within the state and that the state was bound to protect. North Carolina's 1868 constitution even named education as a right. "The people," it declared, "have a right to the privilege of education, and it is the duty of the state to guard and maintain that right."[12]

African Americans also insisted on access to other public venues and services, including streetcars, railroads, restaurants, hotels, and even government jobs. Businesses providing transport and accommodation were not wholly private in law, even though they were privately owned: because they provided services that the public needed and could not do without, they always had been subject to more government regulation than other forms of private property. Such regulation, however, did not guarantee equal access. Even access to public property – sidewalks, streets, parks, and jobs – had never been unrestricted. Local ordinances and long-standing customary practices determined who could use public space and under what circumstances. All these measures coalesced into constraints

---

[12] North Carolina's constitution quoted in Emily Zackin, *Looking for Rights in all the Wrong Places: Why State Constitutions Contain America's Positive Rights* (Princeton, NJ, 2014), p. 68n4; see pp. 67–105 for a discussion of states' recognition of education as a right. Zackin argues that states recognized an array of positive rights in the late nineteenth century, often at the behest of citizens who actively sought out government protection. For African Americans' efforts to obtain education: Heather Williams, *Self-Taught: African American Education in Slavery and Freedom* (Chapel Hill, NC, 2005); Hugh Davis, *"We Will Be Satisfied with Nothing Less": The African American Struggle for Equal Rights in the North during Reconstruction* (Ithaca, NY, 2011); and Davison M. Douglas, *Jim Crow Moves North: The Battle Over Northern School Segregation, 1865–1954* (New York, 2005).

on African Americans, in terms of where they could go, when, and how they could act.[13]

African Americans framed their claims to access using the rhetoric of rights and positioning themselves as citizens who should be treated like everyone else. In fact, it was difficult to express the issue in any other terms: Who, they asked, had a right to access public space and public accommodations if not the public? Many white Americans, moreover, experienced African Americans' claims in terms of rights. They took access to – and control over – public space for granted, much as they did other things denominated as rights in law. White southerners gritted their teeth as African Americans took over public streets and parks to celebrate the Fourth of July, Emancipation Day, and other events. They erupted in anger when they found themselves confronted on sidewalks by African Americans who refused to step aside and surrender the right of way. Popular conceptions ultimately made their way into legal arenas in these matters, much as they did with education. The Civil Rights Act of 1875 explicitly included access to public space as a right. "All persons within the jurisdiction of the United States," it stated, "shall be entitled to the full and equal enjoyment of the accommodations, advantages, facilities, and privileges of inns, public conveyances on land or water, theaters, and other places of public amusement." The U.S. Supreme Court ultimately declared the act unconstitutional, but cases involving access to public space continued to cast the issues in terms of civil rights – as Chapter 6 will discuss in more detail.[14]

The legal framework of rights, however, only extended so far. The Republican Party's commitment to property rights, which allowed for the wholesale appropriation of Indian lands, also derailed African Americans' efforts to obtain title to the lands that they had worked as slaves. Land, as former slaves saw it, provided

---

[13] C. Vann Woodward, *The Strange Career of Jim Crow* (New York, 1955) is the classic statement of the argument that segregation was created through law in the postwar era. Other scholars, however, have argued that postwar law formalized existing practices: Howard N. Rabinowitz, *Race Relations in the Urban South, 1865–1890* (New York, 1978).

[14] Civil Rights Act, 18 U.S. Statutes at Large, 335 (1875). Masur, *An Example for All the Land*.

the surest route to independence. Former slaves, wrote a Georgia planter, "will almost starve and go naked before they will work for a white man, if they can get a patch of ground to live on, and get from under his control." Not only did land provide the means for economic subsistence, but it also allowed African Americans to work for themselves, establish their own households, and live free of white supervision. That is why recent scholarship characterizes African Americans' desire for land as a means, not an end, as one part of a larger effort to control the terms of their labor. African Americans settled on abandoned lands throughout the South during the Civil War. In some instances, they did so with the permission of federal authorities, as on the coast of South Carolina and Georgia. In other instances, enslaved African Americans stayed put, working on the plantations where they lived, after their masters and their families fled in advance of Union troops. Those who worked land on their own during the Civil War hoped to formalize their claims afterward. Even African Americans who did not openly claim land still maintained a proprietary connection to it. Their logic echoed the labor theory of value of labor leaders in the urban North: they had rights to the land because it was their labor that had made it valuable and productive. As they saw it, their claims to landownership were stronger than those of their masters, who had stolen the labor of generations of people and then mounted a treasonous war against their own country. Surely the sanctity of property rights no longer applied in such circumstances.[15]

In fact, there was solid legal basis for African Americans' claims, not only in the Confiscation Acts, which allowed for the seizure of rebel property, but also preemption statutes, which secured settlers' title to federal lands on the basis of cultivation and improvement. The statutes "preempted" all other claims in favor of those of settlers who had moved in, worked the land, and added value through the application of their labor. Congressional Republicans,

---

[15] Quote from Foner, *Reconstruction*, p. 104. Willie Lee Rose, *Rehearsal for Reconstruction: The Port Royal Experiment* (New York, 1964); Julie Saville, *The Work of Reconstruction: From Slave to Wage Laborer in South Carolina, 1860–1870* (New York, 1994).

however, flatly refused to negate the property rights of Confederates in favor of the claims of African Americans. A group of African Americans from Edisto Island expressed the disappointment and outrage that so many other freedpeople felt when it became clear that they would not be able to claim the land they worked. "The government Haveing concluded to befriend Its late enemies and to neglect to observe the principles of common faith between Its self and us Its allies," they wrote, "now takes away from [us] all right to the soil [we] stand upon save such as [we] can get by again working for *your* late and [our] *all time ememies [sic]*." "This is not," they concluded, "the condition of really freemen."[16]

Landownership alone, however, would not have accomplished the kind of independence so many African Americans desired. In fact, the focus on freedpeople's economic circumstances in much of the current scholarship tends to obscure the underlying legal issues that made it impossible to achieve independence: the intractability of a legal order that pervaded every aspect of daily life in the slave states. Even had freedpeople received forty acres and a mule, they would have experienced difficulties working that property and maintaining ownership of it without fundamental changes in the legal order. Dismantling the existing legal order meant constant conflict over everything, all the time, even the shortcuts young children took on their way home from school.

African Americans in the states of the former Confederacy faced that challenge head on, mobilizing the legal system to change the dynamics of a legal order that was inseparable from the social order. In so doing, they followed established legal practices, in which local courts were charged with maintaining social order in their communities – keeping the peace. Before the Civil War, complaints ran the gamut: gambling, fighting, fornication, drinking, poaching, pilfering, prostitution, poor work habits, dilapidated fences, blocked roads, redolent latrines, adultery, domestic violence, and infanticide. In this area of law, all these matters were treated as disruptions of

---

[16] Committee of Freedmen on Edisto Island, South Carolina, to the Freedmen's Bureau Commissioner; the Commissioner's Reply; and the Committee to the President, October 1865, available at the Freedmen and Southern Society Project, http://www.history.umd.edu/Freedmen/Edisto%20petitions.htm. Syrett, *The Confiscation Acts*; Hamilton, *The Limits of Sovereignty*.

the social order, a breach of the peace, not violations of individual rights. Offenses of all kinds could qualify as a breach of the peace, even when against people, including slaves, who did not have rights necessary to access the legal system in their own names and who could not initiate legal proceedings on their own. But, given that local courts were bound to uphold a social order based in the slave system, they did not generally find transgressions against African Americans to constitute a breach of the peace.[17]

During and after the Civil War, African Americans interpolated rights into this system. They used their civil rights to obtain legal recognition of complaints that would have been ignored: they now had rights to access the legal system, and access it they did. The legal implications were wide reaching, as is evident in state and federal court cases in the late nineteenth and early twentieth centuries, which involved a wide variety of offenses, but which were appealed in terms of the individuals' rights of access to the legal system.

African Americans then used access to the system to initiate the substantive changes in their daily lives that civil rights and even political rights could not achieve. They did not just see the courts as a means of protecting their rights as individuals. They also made claims about the postemancipation social order in the context of the legal system: about economic justice, racial equality, and political democracy. Bella Newton's case, for instance, was not just about her ability to file charges. She wanted the courts to affirm her view of the social order, one in which white men like Alexander Noblin could no longer treat African Americans in the way he treated her children, simply because he was white and they were black. That pattern was duplicated, thousands of times in the late 1860s and 1870s, all over the South. In those places where it was possible for African Americans to access local courts, they did so. Where it was not, they made every effort to mobilize state and federal officials to intervene on their behalf. Their efforts spoke to the power of law in daily life. The legal system did not just protect individual rights; it was also a venue for defining and articulating collective conceptions of a just society. Like other southerners, African Americans understood the legal system in these terms and were familiar with

---

[17] Edwards, *The People and Their Peace.*

its workings, because those processes had been such an integral part of local community life during slavery. When they were enslaved, African Americans could only observe and endure the legal process that preserved the social order. After emancipation, they had every reason to think that they could assume more active roles in defining that order, even when their claims to individual rights were tenuous.[18]

The response of Reconstruction's opponents also suggests the importance of the legal system, particularly the local courts. Local courts did not just mediate violence; they also generated it, as southerners battled for control over local institutions. In some places, most notably New Orleans, they used local courts even more strategically, as part of a larger plan to foil the implementation of Reconstruction policies and to mount legal cases to challenge the Reconstruction Amendments.[19]

RECONSTRUCTION OF THE LEGAL ORDER
OUTSIDE THE FORMER CONFEDERACY

It has been common in the literature to separate the experiences of African Americans in the states of the former Confederacy from those of other Americans, as if Reconstruction was a regional affair primarily about race relations. A few historians, however, have drawn all Americans into a single narrative. As that work suggests, other groups of Americans took the principles of Reconstruction to heart, applied them to their own lives, and gave them interpretations strikingly similar to those of southern African Americans.[20]

---

[18] Laura F. Edwards, "Status without Rights: African Americans and the Tangled History of Law and Governance in the Nineteenth-Century U.S. South," *American Historical Review* 112 (2007): 365–93. Also see Downs, *Declarations of Dependence*.

[19] Jonathan M. Bryant, *How Curious a Land: Conflict and Change in Greene County, Georgia, 1850–1885* (Chapel Hill, NC, 1996); Michael A. Ross, "Obstructing Reconstruction: John Archibald Campbell and the Legal Campaign Against Louisiana's Republican Government, 1868–1873," *Civil War History* 49 (2003b): 235–53.

[20] Foner, *Reconstruction*. Also see Richardson, *West from Appomattox*; West, *The Last Indian War*.

The legal logic that positioned white men as the paradigmatic legal subjects also made it extremely difficult for women to claim civil and political rights. As wives, women lost their status as legal individuals and surrendered rights to their husbands. They could not enter into contracts, own property in their own names, claim their wages, assume custody of their children without court approval, or even control access to their own bodies, which were the sexual property of their husbands. Unmarried women did retain many civil rights, but not political rights. Even then, the legal disabilities attached to wives extended so deeply into the culture that they had become proscriptions on all women. It was assumed that women's nature was different from that of men: they were more religious, more moral, and more delicate; motivated by concern for their families, particularly their children, and not by economic interests or individual gain. They belonged in the private sphere of the household, not the coarse, public world of commerce and politics, a situation that limited all women's options. Such characterizations also hid the value of women's labor, rendering it an expression of love for their families and concern for others that should not be debased through monetization. Besides, the logic went, women did not need compensation because their primary economic support came from male relatives. Many women, however, needed to support themselves. Even married women needed to contribute to the support of their families, given that so few men at the time earned enough through their own labor to do it themselves. Yet the devaluation of women's labor extended into the workplace, where all women earned far less than men. Those gendered conceptions were as much about men as they were about women. More than that, men's legal status depended on the subordination of women. They held the civil and political rights necessary to fulfill their roles as heads of household, a position that also gave them rights over their wives and over all women to a lesser extent.[21]

Women's rights activists did try to alter that situation. The women's movement emerged in conversation with the abolition movement, with both advocating the end of slavery and the extension

---

[21] Boydston, *Home and Work*; Nancy F. Cott, *The Bonds of Womanhood: "Women's Sphere" in New England, 1780–1835* (New Haven, CT, 1977).

of full civil and political rights to all people, based on the principle of human equality. Many of the women involved assumed that the end of slavery would affirm that fundamental truth, resulting in the extension of rights to all women as well as African American men. Despite their involvement in the Union war effort, close ties to Republican legislators, and active lobbying on behalf of both women and African Americans, they were disappointed. Republican leaders announced their intention to exclude women from the legal changes of Reconstruction with the Fourteenth Amendment, which introduced gender into the U.S. Constitution for the first time in the clause that reduced a state's federal representation only if they restricted suffrage for men – and, by implication, allowed the restriction of suffrage for women. The Fifteenth Amendment then affirmed state laws disfranchising women by prohibiting the restriction of suffrage only on the basis of "race, color, or previous condition of servitude." Neither amendment addressed the issue of women's civil rights, the legal circumstances of which were not entirely parallel to those of African American men. In law, wives gave up their rights voluntarily when they entered into the legal contract of marriage. Unmarried women, in theory, did not lose their civil rights, narrowly construed as the rights to enter into contracts and control their property.[22]

Formal legal rights, be they civil or political, had never been the sole focus of the women's movement. Those who identified with abolition and the women's movement participated in a much wider array of social reform efforts. During and after the Civil War, black and white activists joined the Freedmen's Aid Movement, which sought to provide support for slavery's refugees. Some women moved into refugee camps and southern communities to set up schools, provide material relief, and advocate on behalf of black communities. Others worked tirelessly to raise money and political backing for such efforts. Women in the Freedmen's Aid Movement, for instance, applied a very different understanding of the problems that freedpeople faced, one that extended beyond formal legal equality. Instead, they argued that former slaves needed direct material assistance to establish independence. It was an approach

[22] DuBois, *Feminism and Suffrage.*

that women activists carried into their other reform work as well, from the labor movement to temperance, education, public health, poor relief, juvenile delinquency, and government accountability. The emphasis was on the material conditions of people's lives – on equality in a broader sense than just legal equality. While those efforts were not about the acquisition of rights, they often fell into the idiom of rights: of people's rights to basic standards of living.[23]

Women, moreover, did not necessarily see civil and political rights as a requirement for participation in debates about the social order. That presumption is, perhaps, the most striking in the actions of African American women in the South, like Bella Newton, who shed the legal bonds of slavery only to acquire all the legal disabilities of other free women. After emancipation, few of these women engaged in the legal system to claim civil and political rights for themselves, as women. Rather, they acted on the expectation that they, as women, could use the legal system to participate in the governance of their communities even if they did not have the same rights as men. They did so with the goal of creating a social order that reflected their interests and concerns. They used the legal system, for instance, to address a range of issues, including domestic concerns, which directly affected their lives. Like Bella Newton, they tried to protect their children and other family members. They also informed on annoying neighbors, testified in cases involving community conflicts, and prosecuted whites for all manner of physical abuse, including rape and sexual assault. And they even brought the courts into their marriages, with cases of spousal neglect and abuse as well as divorce. Scholars have tended to explain the willingness of formerly enslaved women to air their problems in terms of race: race not only made these women uniquely vulnerable by excluding them for the protections extended to white women, but also placed them outside cultural conventions that commanded white women to keep such matters private. Yet, at least in the South, African American women's use of the legal system was strikingly similar

---

[23] Carol Faulkner, *Women's Radical Reconstruction: The Freedmen's Aid Movement* (Philadelphia, 2003). For the variety of women's reform, see Julie Roy Jeffrey, *The Great Silent Army of Abolition: Ordinary Women and the Anti-Slavery Movement* (Chapel Hill, NC, 1998); Nancy A. Hewitt, *Women's Activism and Social Change: Rochester, New York, 1822–1872* (Ithaca, NY, 1984).

to those of white women of poor to modest means before the Civil War. Women, white and black, had expected the legal system to address the problems in their lives. More than that, they expected to be part of the larger job of both defining and maintaining the social order of their communities.[24]

Unlike women or African American men, white working men could claim the full array of civil and political rights. Yet they, too, gave those rights much more expansive interpretations than Republican leaders. Free labor, particularly the promise that all men had the right to enjoy the fruits of their labor, had particular resonance. For labor leaders, this right – which, in the hands of some Republican leaders, dwindled into the right to contract – became a broad mandate for measures that supported the dignity of labor. In the late 1860s, labor reformers advocated federal legislation to establish an eight-hour day for all workers. Limits on hours, they argued, were essential to give workers time for self-improvement and civic engagement. "Any system, social or political, which tends to keep the masses in ignorance, whether by unjust or oppressive laws, or by over-manual labor, is injurious alike to the interests of the state and the individual," declared the National Labor Congress of Workingmen of the United States at its 1866 meeting, which boasted attendance of sixty thousand. Workers also decried the inequitable distribution of property, which resulted from employers taking more than their share and leaving labor with the crumbs.[25]

Labor leaders recommended government action to rectify these problems. Their rhetoric cast the interests of labor as indistinguishable from the American people's interests: they *were* the American people, just as the Republican Party claimed during the Civil War. As citizens, they now looked to the federal government to uphold their interests. They also represented the interests of all labor as the same, regardless of race, a stance that reflected the principles of formal legal equality that marked Reconstruction-era policies. The inclusion of black workers on those terms obscured profound racial

[24] Edwards, *The People and Their Peace*, particularly pp. 100–202; Elsa Barkley Brown, "Negotiating and Transforming the Public Sphere: African American Political Life in the Transition from Slavery to Freedom," *Public Culture* 7 (1994): 107–26.

[25] Quoted in Richardson, *West from Appomattox*, p. 65.

differences – and animosities – between white and black workers, just as formal legal equality did in the legal system. But even if white workers did not wish to cooperate with black workers, particularly former slaves in the South, the efforts of white workers complemented those of African Americans in important ways. Labor gave much more expansive meanings to rights than those either in law or the minds of political leaders. They also identified the federal government, if not the courts, as an agent for broad social change.[26]

African Americans, laboring people, and women were, for the most part, unsuccessful in realizing their expansive view of rights and their transformative view of the legal system. Their claims constituted a substantive critique of narrow, legalistic conceptions of equality. But the political discourse turned against them, characterizing their arguments as the efforts of particular groups to obtain special consideration – as efforts to destroy the rights of other Americans, endangering the concept of legal equality.[27]

The backlash was particularly strong in the states of the former Confederacy, where the courts utterly failed in their traditional job of keeping the peace. Already strained to the breaking point by the internal conflicts of the war years, local legal venues could not handle, let alone reconcile, all the competing claims in their communities – largely because those claims represented contradictory conceptions of the social order. Nothing suggests the strain more than the pervasiveness of violence in the South. In fact, violence against African Americans by whites in that region was so ubiquitous that it is easy to miss the legal dynamics that generated it: as slavery collapsed, violence was the only way for whites to maintain a racial order once sanctioned by law. Alexander Noblin's violent response to William and Susan Newton might seem out of proportion to their offense. After all, they were only children crossing his land on the way home from school. But the offense was not that. It was that the members of the entire Newton family were no longer slaves. Bella Newton was working for wages, living in her own

---

[26] Montgomery, *Beyond Equality*.

[27] Richardson, *West from Appomattox*, pp. 39–120. Those political arguments echoed the federal courts' position on the protection of African Americans' individual rights; see ch. 6.

household, and making decisions about her life and those of her children. One of those decisions was that her children would attend school, instead of working for a white planter, as they would have done in slavery. All of that would have made many white southerners see red. Faced with a situation they could not countenance, but one that they could no longer avert through legal means, they turned to violence, the most extreme manifestation of the authority that all whites once held over all blacks in the slave system.[28]

Although often described in the scholarship as extralegal, white southerners' violence was connected to the legal transition underway in the region. White southerners hovered between two legal systems, one past and one present. Although forced to give up slavery, they held onto its legal order, which sanctioned white men's authority over all African Americans, even when it took violent forms. Clutching at the remnants of what they had, they refused to enter into the new legal order, unwilling to accept black men as equals in law. Alexander Noblin would not budge. His recalcitrance differed only in degree from that of other southerners, whose brutality routinely took much more extreme, organized forms.

Two race riots in 1866, one in Memphis and the other in New Orleans, signaled the onslaught of what was to come. Organized violence, through paramilitary groups, such as the Ku Klux Klan, had a legal as well as a political mission. Directly connected to the Democratic Party, which was opposed to all the changes instituted under Congressional Reconstruction and Republican rule, these

---

[28] For the centrality of violence to the social order of slavery, see Thavolia Glymph, *Out of the House of Bondage: The Transformation of the Plantation Household* (New York, 2008). The pervasiveness of violence was well documented at the time. See, for instance, 39th Cong., 1st Sess., House Report 101: Select Committee on the Memphis Riots; 40th Cong., 3rd Sess., House Miscellaneous Document 52: Condition of the Affairs in Georgia; 42nd Cong., 2nd Sess., House Report 22: Testimony Taken by the Joint Committee to Enquire into the Condition of Affairs in the Late Insurrectionary States (Ku Klux Klan Hearings); 43rd Cong., 2nd Sess., House Report 261: Condition of Affairs in the South (Louisiana); 43rd Cong., 2nd Sess., House Report 262: Affairs in Alabama; 43rd Cong. 2nd Sess., House Report 265: Vicksburg Troubles; 44th Cong., 1st Sess., Senate Report 527: Mississippi in 1875; 44th Cong., 2nd Sess., House Miscellaneous Document 31: Recent Election in South Carolina; 44th Cong., 2nd Sess., Senate Miscellaneous Document 45: Mississippi; 44th Cong., 2nd Sess., Senate Miscellaneous Document 48: South Carolina in 1876.

paramilitary groups did what they could to seize political power. They targeted white and black Republicans – anyone active or presumed to be active in the party, a fact that was easy to discern in the days before the secret ballot, when voters had to communicate their choices openly at the polls. They also singled out African Americans whose economic success challenged notions of racial inferiority that white Democrats embraced with the religious fervor of true believers. As recent scholarship has shown, however, violence was more than a means to keep African Americans from the polls or to punish them for their economic success. It also had more insidious legal implications. Whites specifically targeted black households, looting property, burning homes, destroying crops, and terrorizing entire families with ritualized forms of rape, torture, and murder. Such acts demonstrated the legal authority that all whites had enjoyed in the slave system. More than that, they struck at black households, which provided the legal basis for African American' independence. The point was clear: African Americans' rights meant nothing because legal authority belonged only to white men. In the absence of slavery, white southerners turned the legal framework that identified white men as paradigmatic legal individuals into a brief for white supremacy. One African American in South Carolina expressed the implications of the situation succinctly: "The Master he says we is all free, but it don't mean we is white."[29]

Violence overwhelmed African Americans' ambitious efforts to create a new legal order in the states of the former Confederacy, as Chapter 6 will discuss. But freedpeople in the South still left their imprint on the nation's legal order. They, like other Americans, saw possibilities in Reconstruction's legal principles that their leaders did not: as citizens of a nation "conceived in liberty, and dedicated to the proposition that all men are created equal," they not only defined their rights and the role of law broadly, but also looked to

---

[29] Quote from Lou Falkner Williams, *The Great South Carolina Ku Klux Klan Trials, 1871–1872* (Athens, GA, 2004), p. 2. Also see George C. Rable, *But There Was No Peace: The Role of Violence in the Politics of Reconstruction* (Athens, GA, 1984); Hannah Rosen, *Terror in the Heart of Freedom: Citizenship, Sexual Violence, and the Meaning of Race in the Postemancipation South* (Chapel Hill, NC, 2009); Allen W. Trelease, *White Terror: The Ku Klux Klan Conspiracy and Southern Reconstruction* (New York, 1971).

the legal system, particularly at the federal level, to support their efforts. The nation's political leaders failed to support these visions of the legal order, which were as much about economic justice as they were about formal civil and political rights. But the historiography's tendency to focus on Reconstruction's failures misses the stunning transformation of the law – which Chapter 6 will consider in more detail. That transformation owed as much to what ordinary people did with Reconstruction's legal principles as it did with the intentions and actions of the nation's political leaders.

6

The Power of Law and the Limits of Rights

The U.S. Supreme Court's decision in *Muller v. Oregon* (1908) is confusing. At issue was Oregon legislation that established a ten-hour day for women workers. Did the legislation represent a legitimate use of all states' traditional authority (its police power, in legal terminology) to look after the welfare of the general public? Or did it violate the individual rights of workers, who should be able to decide on the terms of their labor contracts and who might want to work more than ten hours a day? The U.S. Supreme Court had come down on the side of contractual rights in the past, most forcefully in *Lochner v. New York* (1905). Legal historians generally identify *Lochner* as the culmination of judicial decisions that mostly restricted Fourteenth Amendment rights to those involving the economic activities necessary for property accumulation: the bundle of rights needed to pursue one's livelihood. For people who had no choice but to work for someone else, that meant the right to enter into labor contracts – the right, simply, to work. In theory, workers were free to bargain with their employers as contractual equals, because the courts treated employers and even corporations as individuals in this area of law. In practice, most had absolutely no leverage and were forced to accept whatever terms their employers imposed.[1]

This reading of rights was not just limited, but also highly individualized, based as it was on the presumption that all individuals

---

[1] *Muller v. Oregon*, 208 U.S. 412 (1908); *Lochner v. New York*, 198 U.S. 45 (1905).

were fully equal and equally able to control their own fates. In law, individuals might be equal, in the sense that they had access to the same bundle of rights and could, in theory, use them for their own benefit. In practice, however, it was painfully obvious that equality did not describe the conditions of late-nineteenth-century America. Even so, this conception of rights led courts to strike down all kinds of legislation designed to address inequalities that people, particularly wage workers, faced in the real world: low wages, long hours, dangerous working conditions, and a host of other issues over which they had little control. To uphold such legislation, as the decision in *Lochner* put it, would have generated inequality by treating workers as "wards of state," instead of independent individuals. In *Muller*, however, the U.S. Supreme Court changed course, upholding Oregon's ten-hour day legislation.[2]

Why? One reason is that this case involved women, who fit awkwardly within the highly individualized conception of rights that had guided the courts' decisions in other cases. The discomfort of the justices in negotiating that situation is palpable in the circumlocutions of their decision. The opinion started out with the acknowledgment that much had changed in women's legal status over the course of the nineteenth century: "The current runs steadily and strongly in the direction of the emancipation of the wife" throughout the nation. "It is the law of Oregon that women, whether married or single, have equal contractual and personal rights with men," and "the policy ... is to place her upon the same footing as if she were a femme sole, not only with respect to her separate property, but as it affects her right to make binding contracts." The court then veered off in an entirely different direction, arguing that all women were, nonetheless, subordinate to all men by their very nature as women. "Woman has always been dependent upon man," the court maintained, because "woman's physical structure and the performance of maternal functions place her at a disadvantage in the struggle for subsistence." Given women's innate physical differences, they needed special protection from the state in some areas of their lives. The contrast with *Lochner* could not have been more dramatic. In *Lochner*, the U.S. Supreme Court had declared that the

---

[2] *Muller v. Oregon*; *Lochner v. New York*.

male bakers in question would have become "wards of the State" had their side prevailed. The female laundry workers of *Muller* were, essentially, "wards of the state," despite their possession of civil rights. Yet the court's roundabout restriction of women's rights nevertheless constituted a victory for women workers in the form of ten-hour day legislation, a long-time goal of the labor movement. It was something that workers had been unable to obtain on their own, precisely because their contractual rights had such limited power in practice.[3]

Historians have debated the implications of *Muller* for the status of women, the rights of workers, and the fate of legislation intended to protect the public interest. But *Muller* also captures broad legal dynamics that resulted directly from Reconstruction. The decision is representative of many others in both the state and federal courts that positioned the legal rights of individuals as a barrier to efforts by state and federal government to promote the public good. But that conceptual separation was diametrically opposed to popular notions of rights and the role of law. Many Americans saw absolutely no conflict between individual rights and government action – in fact, they considered individual rights and an activist legal order to be mutually reinforcing. Those popular conceptions, which produced powerful social movements in the late nineteenth and twentieth centuries, have been the focus of much of the scholarship outside of legal history. Concentrating on those social movements' goals and positioning the courts primarily as the obstacle to their realization, that historiography tends to draw a straight line from the struggles of the Reconstruction era to the various civil rights movements of the twentieth century. It is a compelling, heroic, and triumphal tale of tenacity in which justice ultimately prevails.

That approach, however, underestimates the power of law in shaping the terrain of American life. The Reconstruction Amendments and related legislation raised people's expectations about what individual rights could accomplish. Those amendments also altered the

---

[3] *Muller v. Oregon; Lochner v. New York*. Eileen Boris, *Home to Work: Motherhood and the Politics of Industrial Homework in the United States* (New York, 1994), pp. 21–122; Judith Baer, *The Chains of Protection: The Judicial Response to Women's Labor Legislation* (Westport, CT, 1978).

place of rights within the basic structure of the nation's legal order, by writing their protection into the U.S. Constitution, giving the federal government jurisdiction over them, and elevating them over other legal principles, particularly the role of state and local government in protecting the public welfare. The legal framework of individual rights, however, had definite limits. Rights, particularly civil rights, could accomplish only so much when it came to matters of social justice, even in their most expansive forms. Nor was the preservation of an individual's rights always synonymous with the public good. To be sure, the courts limited the transformative potential of rights. But popular conceptions could not escape the limitations of the existing legal framework either.

While the legal changes of Reconstruction extended the existing system to more people, it did not alter the logic that structured so much of American law. That logic not only sanctioned the denial of rights to the majority of the population, but also buttressed the inequalities of the status quo – inequalities that, if anything, became more pronounced as the nation's economy grew in the late nineteenth century. It was not possible, moreover, to tease out race from the rest of the law's workings. The legal logic that subordinated all people of color, all women, and all working people was so entwined with the law as to be nearly impossible to disentangle. Eliminating slavery without also pulling apart the configuration of other legal relationships – especially marriage and the labor relationship – left basic structures of inequality in place that ultimately undercut the legal status of all men of color as well. Reconstruction's legal limits did not just apply to the South; they were national in scope.

INSTITUTIONAL CONSTRAINTS

The policy changes of Reconstruction stretched the legal system to its breaking point. Already reeling from a war that taxed their legitimacy, state and local courts in the states of the former Confederacy were in no position to deal with the conflict of the postwar years. Reports of horrific violence kept pouring into the nation's capitol, filling up days of committee hearings and volumes of congressional reports. African Americans and white Republicans from the South repeatedly begged the federal government to step into the breach and to do more. Until recently, the scholarship has emphasized Congressional Republicans' failure to impose order on the South, chalking it up to their refusal to use the full force of federal authority. But, as recent scholarship in legal history has shown, Congressional Republicans did not just turn their backs on the situation. They confronted challenges that they simply could not overcome: not just armed mobs of white insurgents, but also the difficulties of mobilizing the federal government's new legal authority.

The notion that the federal courts could intervene in cases involving individual rights was a product of the Civil War era. "Removal," a concept that arose from the Habeas Corpus Act of 1863, allowed federal courts to intercede in state jurisdictions with a writ of *habeas corpus* and literally remove cases to federal courts in certain circumstances. Congressional Republicans applied that principle to the question of African Americans' legal status, embedded it in the 1866 Civil Rights Act, and then enshrined it in the Fourteenth and Fifteenth Amendments: all these measures permitted the removal of cases languishing in obstructionist state courts to federal courts. Subsequent legislation made removal easier to accomplish. The 1867 Habeas Corpus Act expanded federal power by transforming the concept of *habeas corpus* into an open-ended writ that gave federal officials the broad authority to intervene in cases being tried in a state court at any stage of the process. In response to widespread violence in the South, Congress then passed a series of acts between 1870 and 1872, meant to buttress the enforcement of the Fourteenth and Fifteenth Amendments – three of those passed in 1870 and 1871 are usually referred to as the Enforcement Acts or Force Acts (1870–1) and the one passed in the following session of Congress is known as the Ku Klux Force Act (1871). Those acts allowed the federal government to intervene directly against individuals who violated the civil and political rights of others. They also permitted military intervention to put down rebellions intended to deny citizens their rights.[4] President Ulysses S. Grant used these measures

---

[4] Habeas Corpus Act (1863); Habeas Corpus Act, 14 U.S. Statutes at Large 385 (1867); Enforcement Act, 16 U.S. Statutes at Large 140 (1870); Naturalization Law, 16 U.S. Statutes at Large 254 (1870); Enforcement Act, 16 U.S. Statutes at Large 433 (1871); The Ku Klux Klan Act, 17 U.S. Statutes at Large 13 (1871); Congressional Republicans then tried, but failed to pass yet another enforcement

in 1871 to send troops to South Carolina and to initiate federal prosecution of thousands of civil rights violations. He dispatched troops again in 1875, this time to Mississippi.

While powerful in principle, removal foundered in practice. The system essentially required the construction of a new federal agency and a new body of law – immediately and from whole cloth. The cases fell within the purview of the Department of Justice, the duties of which had been fairly limited before the Civil War. It had neither the institutional infrastructure nor the personnel to handle the load. Its handful of attorneys, who worked on their own without the assistance of an investigative agency, found themselves buried under an avalanche of complaints. Even if they could do the necessary background work, there was no way that federal district courts could ever get to all the cases. It was an impossible situation that left thousands of cases moldering on federal dockets, with no hope of seeing the inside of a courtroom. The scale of the conflict simply outpaced the ability of the federal courts to deal with it. More to the point, the federal effort was doomed to failure because, as one legal historian has put it, the legal process is not the best place to "combat rebellion and insurrection."[5]

Enforcement of the Reconstruction Amendments in the South also raised sticky legal issues about the use of federal power in the nation as a whole. Americans explained away the federal government's use of force against Indians in the West as a necessary means to subdue foreign elements. Indians were not American citizens. But white southerners still were – despite acts that, in other circumstances, constituted treason. The use of force necessary to bring these rebellious American citizens in line would have meant drastic changes in other parts of the United States as well. The Fourteenth and Fifteenth Amendments theoretically altered the legal status of everyone in the United States by extending federal authority over

---

act in 1875 that strengthened the previous legislation and explicitly prohibited conspiracies intended to subvert democratically elected state governments.

[5] Quote from Robert J. Kaczorowski, *The Politics of Judicial Interpretation: The Federal Courts, Department of Justice, and Civil Rights, 1866–1876* (New York, 1985), p. xv; see pp. 49–78 for a vivid description of the difficult circumstances under which federal officials operated.

questions that once belonged to the states as well as negating legal restrictions on African Americans in the North, just as they did in the South. Although subsequent legislation was intended to apply only to recalcitrant states in the former Confederacy, it set the precedent for federal intervention in other states. As such, Reconstruction-era measures opened up a series of troubling questions about the point as well as the extent of federal authority. Did the federal government operate at a comfortable remove from the lives of the American people, a distance that allowed it to affirm the nation's principles without having to delve into the details? Or did the federal government involve itself in the people's lives in a more direct way, one that necessitated choosing sides and deciding which Americans it would support? Measures that extended the federal government's ability to apply and enforce the principles of the Reconstruction Amendments foundered over these questions – questions that were as much about the role of federal power in the nation's legal order as they were about the commitment to racial equality.

Much of the scholarship on Reconstruction, particularly the scholarship outside legal history, has viewed enforcement solely as a matter of political will. Had Congressional Republicans wanted to, they could have simply forced rebellious white southerners into line and, thereby, realized the legal principles of their Reconstruction plan. But what this historiographical focus obscures is the role of the law. With its emphasis on the application of the law, rather than the law's substance, it imagines the law merely as an instrument controlled by political leaders. To be sure, the organized efforts to deny civil and political rights to African Americans and the federal government's failed response constituted an insurmountable barrier to the realization of racial equality. But the intransigence of white southerners and the fecklessness of white northerners were not the only problems. There were other, even more intractable challenges within the legal order. The law's underlying logic sustained profound inequalities, at odds with the kinds of legal equality that freedpeople and other Americans envisioned for themselves. When it came to these aspects of the legal order, the states of the former Confederacy had a great deal in common with the rest of the nation. In fact, the legal challenges of Reconstruction were not peculiarly southern; they were national in scope.

Historians usually characterize the Black Codes, enacted in 1865 and 1866 under President Johnson's Reconstruction plan, as a peculiarly southern attempt to resurrect the slave system. Those judgments reflect contemporary political rhetoric on the fallout between President Johnson and Congressional Republicans, who saw Johnson's Reconstruction plan as a crass attempt by a Confederate sympathizer to ignore the Union's victory. According to Johnson's detractors, the leaders of the former Confederacy exchanged a wink with Johnson and then passed the Thirteenth Amendment while they snuck slavery in through the back door. This interpretation stuck. In one sense, it was accurate. After all, the same delegates who passed the Black Codes also debated their secession ordinances and the Thirteenth Amendment as if they still had a choice in the matter.

But from the perspective of law, rather than politics, the distance between Congressional Reconstruction and the Black Codes was not as great as it might seem at first glance. At the close of the Civil War, only a minority of Americans actually exercised full civil and political rights. Restrictions in state and local laws placed most people somewhere on a very broad middle ground, removed from slavery on one side, but also distant from the full range of rights on the other side. No free woman of any race, married or single, could claim the full array of rights. Many men found themselves in a similar situation. Free blacks, in particular, had very limited rights: in fact, many states that remained in the Union had laws nearly identical to those in the Black Codes. In 1865, when the first Black Codes were passed, the citizenship of free blacks in the North also remained uncertain, clouded by contradictory laws within individual states and the U.S. Supreme Court's controversial decision in *Dred Scott*. Johnson's Reconstruction plan evaded all those questions by handing them back to the states, where they had always been dealt with heretofore. Drawing on the laws that had applied to free blacks in both the North and the South, former Confederates attempted to codify a new, extremely limited legal status for African Americans in their own states. In many ways, both the approach and the results revealed as much about the legal dynamics of race in the nation as it did about those in the South.

DOMESTIC DEPENDENCY AND RACE

The Black Codes also highlight the difficulty of separating slavery from other legal relationships of domestic subordination. Nowhere is that more apparent than in the Black Codes' handling of marriage. The Codes all mandated the legal marriage of formerly enslaved couples. As slaves, African Americans' marriages had not been recognized in law, and emancipation did not alter that. Some states simply declared couples then living together to be married, while others required registration as validation of those unions. Although saturated in the morality of the Victorian era, these policies were more about structure than sentiment. Like slavery, marriage extended so deeply into the legal order as to be nearly impossible to sort out without some rigorous pruning. Outside marriage, for instance, there were no legally recognized fathers. Without fathers, there were no legally recognized parents, because mothers had no formal rights to their children at this time. This situation posed serious problems for states, which depended on the legal bonds that tied families together and made fathers and husbands economically responsible for dependent wives and children. Children born outside legal marriages became wards of the state. Their economic support fell to counties, as did that of women who could not make ends meet on their own and whose extended families could not or would not provide for them. The last thing that conservative white lawmakers wanted was to acquire responsibility for formerly enslaved women and children. They thought freedpeople should take responsibility for their own family members. Given skepticism about African Americans' capacity for freedom, white lawmakers also thought that legal compulsion would be necessary to accomplish that assumption of responsibility. Marriage provided that compulsion, by placing families in a legal structure that made men into household heads, with enforceable, legal obligations to their dependents.[6]

In law, however, marriage conferred rights as well as responsibilities. Within the legal logic of household governance, marriage

---

[6] Laura F. Edwards, "'The Marriage Covenant Is at the Foundation of All Our Rights': The Politics of Slave Marriages in North Carolina after Emancipation," *Law and History Review* 14 (1996): 81–124.

was the legal institution that determined the distribution of civil and political rights, bestowing them on heads of household and denying them to dependents. Once African American men became household heads through marriage, they acquired a legal means for claiming civil and even political rights. In fact, that was how some radical Republicans saw the Thirteenth Amendment: with the elimination of slavery, African Americans assumed the same legal status as all other free men and women in law. The Black Codes slammed the door shut on that possibility with elaborate lists of legal restrictions that applied only to African Americans. Even though African Americans were now free, with legally recognized households of their own and all the attendant legal responsibilities, they could not claim the full range of rights that white southerners enjoyed. The Black Codes made sure that marriage gave African Americans only responsibilities, not rights.

Later federal legislation overturned the Black Codes' racial restrictions, but did not touch the logic of household governance. If anything, Congressional Republicans strengthened the legal principles that provided men (as husbands and heads of household) with rights while further distancing women (as wives and dependents) from them. Those presumptions were most apparent in the refusal to include women in the Reconstruction Amendments. At the time, debate focused on the extension of political rights, not civil rights. That was because a blanket extension of equal civil rights to women would have raised questions about the legal status of wives and also, therefore, of marriage. Aware of that situation, leaders in the women's movement focused on political rights, hoping that political leverage would eventually allow them to alter other aspects of women's legal status. Congressional Republicans balked, arguing that the extension of the vote to women was politically impossible and would only undermine efforts to obtain rights for African American men. But the excuse of political expediency spoke volumes about the realities of the legal order: granting civil and political rights to women was a much bigger leap than granting them to African American men because the law made it extremely difficult to place a woman, even an unmarried one, in the role of a rights-bearing individual, let alone a rights-bearing individual who could vote. Women were dependents within households, not independent individuals. They were intended to be women, not men.[7]

In addition, granting rights to women would have undermined the legal logic that supported their extension to African Americans. Under the Black Codes and afterward, freedpeople used men's legal status as husbands, fathers, and heads of household to claim other rights. Like the group of African Americans from Lincoln County, Tennessee, they argued that their position as men, with households to run, required the possession of civil and political rights: "We are recognized as men by the Constitution of the land: we only ask to be treated as such, and we will, in the future as in the past, be law abiding men." Republican leaders drew on the same logic, emphasizing African American men's manhood in justifying the extension of rights to them. Like white men, they maintained, African American men served as soldiers in the military, demonstrating their manhood and, by extension, their fitness for freedom. Now that African Americans were free and expected to take care of their families and represent their interests, they needed the civil and political rights, just like other men, to do so.[8]

This political rhetoric, which turned the legal rights of household heads into the rights of men, reinforced legal trends that detached individuals from the household, while still maintaining the inequalities sanctioned by household governance. In both formal law and popular legal culture, the emphasis moved from the household to the body, particularly in perceived physical differences between men and women. Rights – their conferral and their denial – resulted from individuals' nature as men and women, instead of their structural position within households. All men could, at least in theory, claim civil and political rights, regardless of their status as a household head. But insofar as women were not men, they were denied these rights.

One result was that all women came to be grouped together in a single category, downplaying the legal differences that had once

[7] Amy Dru Stanley, *From Bondage to Contract: Wage Labor, Marriage, and the Market in the Age of Slave Emancipation* (New York, 1998).

[8] Tennessee Freedmen to the Freedmen's Bureau Assistant Commissioner for Kentucky, Tennessee, and Northern Alabama. Bercaw, *Gendered Freedoms*, particularly pp. 158–87; Edwards, *Gendered Strife and Confusion*, particularly pp. 184–254.

separated married women (who surrendered rights at marriage) and unmarried women (who could still claim some rights). Those changes unfolded slowly over the course of the nineteenth century, state by state. The extent of change was evident by the time of *Muller v. Oregon*, which referred to the legal changes that now granted married women the property rights of unmarried women and men: rights to enter into contracts, own property in their names, and keep their own wages. Those changes applied to married women, diminishing the significance of marriage in defining women's legal status.[9]

Equality among women, however, did not make them equal to men. In this sense, the logic of gender simply expressed the central elements of household governance in different terms. In law, women's differences from men inevitably translated into inequality, as Myra Bradwell discovered when she applied for admission to the bar in the state of Illinois in the 1870s. Bradwell played an influential role in Illinois legal circles as editor of the *Chicago Legal News*, the publication on which many practicing lawyers depended to keep current on the law. It was, then, deeply ironic when the Illinois state legislature – filled with lawyers who read her publication – refused to consider her application to the bar. Not one to be cowed, Bradwell challenged the decision, arguing that it violated her Fourteenth Amendment rights. She also made creative use of that amendment. She admitted that the opportunity to apply to the bar was not, in itself, a right. Even so, it was centrally connected to her right to pursue her livelihood and her property interests. So when the legislature refused to consider her application, they had denied rights granted as a matter of course to other (male) citizens. In *Bradwell v. Illinois* (1873), the U.S. Supreme Court rejected the first part of the argument, which focused on what qualified as a protected right in the Fourteenth Amendment, thereby evading the second part, which dealt with amendment's application to women. One of the justices, however, could not resist opining on the subject of women's status, even though there was no need to do so.

---

[9] *Muller v. Oregon.* For an apt summary of married women's property rights, see Welke, *Law and Borders of Belonging in the Long Nineteenth Century*, pp. 46–7.

"The natural and proper timidity and delicacy which belongs to the female sex evidently unfits it for many of the occupations of civil life," wrote Justice Joseph P. Bradley in a particularly infamous passage: "The paramount destiny and mission of women are to fulfill the noble and benign offices of wife and mother. This is the law of the Creator."[10]

Those sections on women, while unnecessary to the decision, did engage Bradwell's claim that she was entitled to the privileges and immunities protected by the Fourteenth Amendment. Where she was claiming equality to other citizens, the passages that emphasized women's innate differences from men set up a circular argument that also implied women's exclusion from the rights of citizenship: women were different by nature than men; men were citizens with claims to full civil and political rights; therefore, the rights guaranteed to all citizens by the Fourteenth Amendment did not necessarily extend to women. In fact, Justice Bradley's passages on women's status are so provocative that *Bradwell v. Illinois* is often misremembered as a decision about women's relationship to the Fourteenth Amendment, not the amendment's privileges and immunities clause. In that sense, *Bradwell* also signaled what was to come. Invocations of gender difference as a means to sanction legal restrictions on women became an established feature of law by the end of the nineteenth century. Legitimating women's inequality through nature – be it by the hand of God or the workings of natural selection – also conveniently placed the issue beyond the ken of mere humans. If anything, it made the possibility of change that much more remote.[11]

Gender difference also moved authority over women from individual male household heads to the state. Those elements were on full display in *Muller v. Oregon*, which made women fit objects for state protection because of their physical inferiority to men. "By

[10] *Bradwell v. Illinois*, 83 U.S. 130 (1873).
[11] Ibid. Joan Hoff, *Law, Gender, and Injustice: A Legal History of U.S. Women* (New York, 1991), pp. 151–91. Myra Bradwell's case, however, also suggests countervailing political currents, giving women the same rights as men without acknowledging the particularities of structural inequalities that they faced as women; Illinois allowed women admission to the bar within a year of the U.S. Supreme Court's decision.

abundant testimony of the medical fraternity," the justices wrote in *Muller*, it is clear that "continuance for a long time on her feet at work, repeating this from day to day, tends to injurious effects upon the body." The state, moreover, had an interest in protecting women, because they were the mothers of the future generation: "as healthy mothers are essential to vigorous offspring, the physical well-being of woman becomes an object of public interest." Not all state oversight disadvantaged women. The terms of some protective legislation, such as Oregon's ten-hour day, were formulated in consultation with labor leaders and reflected the interests of working people. But the notion that women required public protection invited unwelcome intrusion as well. As historians of twentieth-century public policy have argued, the social safety net bears the imprint of such assumptions, with separate, unequal tracks for men and women. Male wage earners received unemployment insurance and Social Security in the form of direct payments, which they controlled. Women, as wives and mothers, received various forms of welfare, with miserly benefits that came with close, continual surveillance of their lives.[12]

It might seem that the rights of African American men and the rights of women were entirely separate issues, given the immediate fallout from Congressional Republicans' decision to exclude women from the rights protected by the Reconstruction Amendments. The women's movement split in two, with one side supporting racial equality for African American men and the other criticizing those efforts. The critics, most of whom were white, expressed their dissatisfaction in overtly racial terms, using negative characterizations of African Americans. They did so to question the logic that enshrined manhood as the standard for claiming civil and political rights. Why should civil and political rights be the prerogative of men, simply because they were men? What made men more deserving of those rights and more capable of exercising them than women? Specifically, why could poor, ignorant black men of questionable

---

[12] Alice Kessler-Harris, *In Pursuit of Equity: Women, Men, and the Quest for Economic Citizenship in 20th-Century America* (New York, 2001); Suzanne Mettler, *Dividing Citizens: Gender and Federalism in New Deal Public Policy* (Ithaca, NY, 1998).

morals exercise rights more responsibly than wealthy, educated, respectable white women? The content of their rhetoric drew on and reinforced deeply rooted racial biases that justified the denial of rights in terms of race. That racial strain continued to mark the feminist movement in the late nineteenth and early twentieth centuries, not only severing questions of gender from race but also casting gender inequality in racial terms and racial inequality in gendered terms by placing white women and African American men in opposition to each other.[13]

The racial biases of white feminists also inflected the policies that guaranteed federal protection of African American men's civil and political equality. To be sure, radical Republicans supported the extension of rights to African American men because they rejected the notion that race determined human capacity or the content of individual character. But they were in the minority. Most white people in the nation believed that race mattered a great deal and made all African Americans innately inferior to all whites. How they acted on those ideas, however, differed. Where conservative whites in the former Confederacy believed that laws were necessary to single out African Americans and keep them in their place, whites elsewhere in the country thought the situation would take care of itself. Even the elimination of racial distinctions in law would not result in actual equality between the races, because nothing would alter African Americans' racial destiny. They would sink to the lowest segments of society, where existing laws would be sufficient to keep them in line.[14]

---

[13] Faye E. Dudden, *Fighting Chance: The Struggle Over Women Suffrage and Black Suffrage in Reconstruction America* (New York, 2011); Louise Newman, *White Women's Rights: The Racial Origins of Feminism in the United States* (New York, 1999); Marjorie Julian Spruill, *New Women of the New South: The Leaders of the Woman Suffrage Movement in the Southern States* (New York, 1993). Other white women, however, did reach across the color line, see Feimster, *Southern Horrors*; Jacquelyn Dowd Hall, *Revolt against Chivalry: Jessie Daniel Ames and the Women's Campaign against Lynching* (New York, 1979).

[14] Heather Cox Richardson, *The Death of Reconstruction: Race, Labor, and Politics in the Post–Civil War North* (Cambridge, MA, 2001); Leslie A. Schwalm, *Emancipation's Diaspora: Race and Reconstruction in the Upper Midwest* (Chapel Hill, NC, 2009).

Such racial sentiments lay just beneath the surface of federal policies, which were framed with the assumption that access to the legal system and the ballot box would address the legal status of former slaves. These notions acquired legal resonance in the federal courts, where, ironically, the application of a narrow, individualized construction of rights perpetuated exactly the kinds of racial restrictions that the extension of rights was intended to rectify. That was the case even in the 1870s, when federal judges supported the Justice Department's efforts to prosecute violations of the Fourteenth and Fifteenth Amendments. Federal prosecutors approached each violation as a case unto itself, instead of grouping them together or applying the findings in one case to other similar cases. The framework of individual rights, which allowed for federal intervention, individualized problems that were in fact systemic. The problem was an entire population of white southerners committed to white supremacy, not the wrong-headed acts of a few errant individuals. Moreover, ensuring compliance was difficult. The various Enforcement Acts allowed for federal intervention in moments of acute crisis. Federal action under those acts did successfully rout out Klan violence in some areas, notably in the South Carolina upcountry in the early 1870s. But those dramatic eruptions were symptomatic of a chronic condition that afflicted most of the former Confederacy. The federal government had neither the means nor the manpower necessary to monitor, let alone cure, that infirmity. As a result, victory in one case neither altered the circumstances that produced such egregious violations of civil and political rights nor repaired the broken state systems that required continual federal intervention.

The federal courts then further constrained enforcement efforts by limiting the range of rights that fell within the federal government's purview. In fact, conventional historiographical wisdom has laid much of the blame for Reconstruction's failure at the feet of the U.S. Supreme Court for this reason. The Court's decisions, historians have argued, represented nothing less than the conscious abandonment of African Americans to conservative whites intent on stripping them of their newly acquired civil and political rights. Recent scholarship, however, has moderated those conclusions, arguing that the Court was not as hostile to African Americans' rights as previous scholarship suggests, particularly in the area of voting rights, where it left significant protections in place. Throughout the late nineteenth century, however, the Court upheld a narrow, individualized view of civil rights, one at odds with the aspirations of many Americans. While it upheld federal enforcement, the Court's decisions did nothing to make an already difficult job any easier.[15]

One of the first, key cases involved a group of white butchers in New Orleans, who argued that regulations on slaughter houses abridged their Fourteenth Amendment rights by denying them privileges and immunities – in this case, the right to pursue their livelihood – that other citizens enjoyed. In the *Slaughter-House Cases* (1873), the U.S. Supreme Court decided against the butchers, placing the rights that they claimed within the purview of the states, not the federal government. The economic concerns of a group of disgruntled butchers might seem unrelated to the civil rights of African Americans. But they were – in more than one respect. The cases were part of a systematic effort by Democrats to undercut Republican rule and Reconstruction policies in New Orleans. They saw these cases as a direct challenge to the Fourteenth Amendment. In that respect, their efforts failed. In the *Slaughter-House Cases*, the U.S. Supreme Court explicitly affirmed the Fourteenth Amendment's applicability to the rights of African Americans.[16]

But what the decision gave with one hand, it took away with the other. In 1876, the U.S. Supreme Court referenced the *Slaughter-House Cases* in its decision in *United States v. Cruikshank* (1876), which made it far more difficult for the federal government to prosecute violations of African Americans' civil and political rights.

---

[15] Pamela Brandwein, *Rethinking the Judicial Settlement of Reconstruction* (New York, 2011). Brandwein argues that the U.S. Supreme Court did not change direction and abandon the principle of supporting African Americans' rights until the late 1880s, when Melville W. Fuller became Chief Justice. Also see G. Edward White, "The Origins of Civil Rights in America" (April 15, 2013), *Case Western Reserve Law Review*, forthcoming, Virginia Public Law and Legal Theory Research Paper No. 2013–03, available at SSRN: http://ssrn.com/abstract=2251425. For cases supporting African Americans' political rights, see, e.g., *Ex Parte Siebold*, 100 U.S. 371 (1879); *Neal v. Delaware*, 103 U.S. 370 (1880); and *Ex Parte Yarbrough*, 110 U.S. 651 (1884).

[16] *Slaughter-House Cases*, 83 U.S. 36 (1873). Michael A. Ross, "Justice Miller's Reconstruction: The Slaughter House Cases, Health Codes, and Civil Rights in New Orleans, 1861–1873," *Journal of Southern History* 64 (1998): 649–76.

Cruikshank resulted from the federal government's prosecution of white vigilantes in Colfax, Louisiana. Mired in fraud, intimidation, and violence, the Louisiana election of 1872 produced no clear outcome. The federal government stepped in to sort things out at the state level. But some local areas were still in a state of upheaval well into 1873. In Colfax, uncertainty exploded into violence on Easter of that year, when a white mob attacked local African Americans, who had gathered at the courthouse to prevent a takeover by the Democratic Party. Although some of the African Americans were armed, they were soon overwhelmed. There is no clear reckoning of the death toll, but it is estimated that the mob killed between 60 and 150 African Americans. Federal prosecutors did what they could to identify, charge, and convict the white vigilantes. The defendants then promptly and unrepentantly turned around and appealed.[17]

In *Cruikshank*, the U.S. Supreme Court picked up its narrow conception of federal jurisdiction from the *Slaughter-House Cases*, applied it to a case involving African Americans' rights, and overturned the convictions of the white vigilantes. As the court argued, the federal government could not intervene in states to enforce rights granted at the federal level, particularly those enumerated in the Bill of Rights, such as the right of assembly – obviously an important issue in Colfax. The federal government could intervene if race were proved to be a motive; but that was difficult to prove. Ultimately, the case made it even more difficult for the federal government to intervene when individuals violated the rights of other individuals, which the court determined to be the case in the Colfax massacre. The federal government's authority was limited to state actions that singled out African Americans and denied them rights that others could claim.[18]

The U.S. Supreme Court built upon this logic in the *Civil Rights Cases* (1883). In addition to striking down the Civil Rights Act

[17] Leanna Keith, *The Colfax Massacre: The Untold Story of Black Power, White Terror, and the Death of Reconstruction* (New York, 2008); Charles Lane, *The Day Freedom Died: The Colfax Massacre, the Supreme Court, and the Betrayal of Reconstruction* (New York, 2008).

[18] *United States v. Cruikshank*, 92 U.S. 542 (1876). Also see *United States v. Reese*, 92 U.S. 214 (1876). Ronald M. Labbé and Jonathan Lurie. *The Slaughterhouse Cases: Regulation, Reconstruction, and the Fourteenth Amendment* (Lawrence, KS, 2003).

of 1875 – which defined access to jury service as well as public accommodations and transportation as protected rights under the Fourteenth Amendment – the *Civil Rights Cases* promulgated the principle that federal courts could only consider the letter of state law, not its results. As long as state law did not explicitly differentiate on the basis of race there was no reason for federal intervention. In fact, as the court saw it in the *Civil Rights Cases*, aggressive federal intervention to protect African Americans' exercise of rights – however they might be defined – produced inequality, not equality. It amounted to special treatment at odds with the legal principle that all individuals were equal in the eyes of the law. "When a man has emerged from slavery, and by the aid of beneficent legislation has shaken off the inseparable concomitants of that state," wrote Justice Bradley for the court's majority, "there must be some stage in the progress of his elevation when he takes the rank of a mere citizen, and ceases to be the special favorite of the laws, and when his rights as a citizen, or a man, are to be protected in the ordinary modes by which other men's rights are protected." The rights of the individual took precedence over obvious social inequalities that federal officials sought to address. The *Civil Rights Cases* affirmed in federal law what was already a legal reality in many states. In 1876, as part of the settlement in the disputed presidential election of that year, national political leaders agreed to withdraw the federal government from the Reconstruction process and return authority over questions of civil and political rights to the states. Dedicated Republican political leaders and federal attorneys fought a rearguard action against the implications of "home rule," but the *Civil Rights Cases* made an already difficult job nearly impossible. The decision now codified the racial inequalities that had long defined the nation's legal order.[19]

That same narrow, highly individualized interpretation of rights also allowed legal segregation to flourish. The *Civil Rights Cases* set the stage by striking down provisions of the 1875 Civil Rights Act that placed equal access to public transport and other accommodations within the category of civil rights. The practice of segregation had a certain legal ambiguity, because it involved

---

[19] *Civil Rights Cases*, 109 U.S. 3 (1883); quote on 61.

private as well as public property and issues traditionally defined as social rights, which were considered best left to local areas and individuals. During and after Reconstruction, conservative white Democrats also began codifying social practices, writing segregation into law, first in local ordinances and ultimately in state law as well. In response, the Civil Rights Act guaranteed federal protection to a range of social rights, elevating them to the same status as other civil rights.[20]

African Americans continued to challenge segregation after the *Civil Rights Cases*, mounting a series of cases that culminated in *Plessy v. Ferguson* (1898). *Plessy* has achieved iconic status in the scholarship, largely at the expense of the cases leading up to it and the existing legislation and legal practice that it merely affirmed. The most well-known portion of the decision, the "separate but equal" doctrine, held that the separation of the races did not necessarily imply inequality or a violation of Fourteenth Amendment rights. That finding rested on the court's view of segregation as a matter of social rights, not civil rights. States, localities, and individuals – not the federal government – maintained authority over social rights, and could handle them as they wished.[21]

Given the courts' narrow definition of civil rights, however, social rights were increasingly important in defining the substance of race relations. *Plessy* thus solidified the states' authority over the dynamics of race. *Plessy* also invoked the long-standing legal rubric that gave household heads authority over their domestic dependents and their private property, free from outside interference. In *Plessy*, however, states assumed the role of household head, which oversaw their domestic realms and did what was necessary to keep their dependents from squabbling. In the South, states were empowered to enact measures that diminished social disorder by keeping whites and blacks apart. As such, the language in *Plessy* returned African Americans to a position similar to the domestic dependency of slaves; although this time they were the metaphoric dependents of Democratic officeholders in state government, instead of the actual dependents of individual slaveholders. African Americans had rights

---

[20] Ibid.
[21] *Plessy v. Ferguson*, 163 U.S. 537 (1896).

in theory, but paradoxically, those rights were so sacrosanct that the federal government could not intervene to support them without endangering them. Practically, they had no recourse to contest their states' efforts to restrict those rights. It placed all African Americans in a position similar to that of women: as fit objects of state regulations that restricted their rights in the name of the public good.[22]

LABOR AND PRIVATE PROPERTY

The failure of Reconstruction policies to acknowledge, let alone address, the legal status of wage laborers magnified the vulnerabilities of both African Americans and women in law. In fact, labor law constituted another key link between Congressional Reconstruction and the Black Codes. The Black Codes framed these restrictions in terms of race, with the intent of forcing free African Americans into agricultural wage labor, supervised by whites. Contemporary critics and later historians rightly saw these laws as creating a labor relation akin to slavery. To be sure, the restrictions on black workers moved them very close to the position of slaves. They also faced constraints that white workers did not. Yet the laws were not just a throwback to slavery. In many instances, they restated existing laws that already applied to free white laborers. Like the Black Codes, existing laws cast the labor relationship as an unequal relationship between "master" and "servant." Employees surrendered rights just by entering into the wage contract: they could not leave until the end of the contract, could forfeit all their wages and face criminal penalties if they left, and had virtually no legal recourse in conflicts with their employers. The terms of the contract could limit workers' rights even further. Employers wrote in restrictions regulating their employees' dress, place of residence, hours of labor, recreation, and their demeanor. Other than refusing the work, which carried the possibility of vagrancy charges, there was nothing workers could do about the terms imposed on them by their employers. Some states intentionally extended the application of labor legislation beyond

[22] For the complicated connections between gender and racial segregation, particularly on the railway, see Barbara Young Welke, *Recasting American Liberty: Gender, Race, Law, and the Railroad Revolution, 1865–1920* (New York, 2001), pp. 249–375.

African Americans by passing a separate set of laws that applied to all wage workers. But even legislation framed in racial terms did not negate existing laws that already applied to whites. In the perverse logic of the time, such duplication was legally necessary because the Black Codes categorized freed slaves as a separate category of people, governed by a different set of laws.[23]

Subsequent federal policies prohibited restrictions that applied only to African American workers. But the inequalities built into labor relations in southern law never drew the fire or the attention that racial inequalities did, largely because they fit so well with the Republican Party's vision of free labor. In fact, the elimination of racial distinctions had the effect of extending those inequalities in labor law to all workers. The limitations begun by the Black Codes continued under Republican regimes in the former Confederate states, although Republicans did infuse the labor relationship with some of the progressive aspects of northern free labor ideology. Most states, for instance, strengthened workers' ability to collect their wages through laborers' lien laws. But Republicans did not change the hierarchical structure of the labor relationship. Quite the opposite. Laborers' lien laws generally restrained workers' mobility and their right to determine the terms of the labor relationship by specifying that the lien applied only if the laborer had worked the contract's full term and fulfilled its other specifications. A few states, South Carolina among them, granted laborers' liens without such restrictions and established procedures for mediating contract disputes. This legislation allowed workers to bring their complaints to mediators who could force employers to meet contractual obligations and made labor-related issues a matter of public debate. Even more than laborers' liens, contract mediation held the potential for remaking labor relations by allowing workers legal recourse. Still, the effects were limited because the mediation process affirmed the very inequalities that had subordinated laborers as domestic dependents. Laborers brought themselves to white,

---

[23] Laura F. Edwards, "The Problem of Dependency: African Americans, Labor Relations, and the Law in the Nineteenth-Century South," *Agricultural History* 72 (1998): 313–40. Historians generally consider the implications of the Black Codes for African Americans, instead of seeing them as part of a larger body of laws that applied to both whites and blacks.

elite mediators at great personal risk, facing fines and imprisonment if they were judged to have broken their contracts' provisions. At a time when contracts regularly demanded such things as obedience and respect from workers, the burden of proof clearly rested with the workers.[24]

Under Republican rule, the states of the former Confederacy also expanded the category of common labor to include "sharecroppers." During the antebellum period, no southern state except North Carolina recognized a distinction between sharecroppers and renters. All were tenants, who retained legal rights over their labor and its product when they rented land. Even in North Carolina, where the law placed sharecroppers under the direct supervision of their landlords and denied them property rights in the goods they produced, this legal definition was not always observed. But such independence, whether legal or customary, became problematic for landlords after emancipation. White planters first assumed that former slaves would work for them as wage laborers. Then credit shortages, poor crops, and the resistance of freedpeople closed off this possibility. As African American laborers began to work for a share of the crop on specific plots of land, the courts denied them the legal rights granted tenants, turned them into sharecroppers, and lumped them into the same category as common laborers. Although sharecroppers might exercise some authority over their labor and its product, in practice they had no legally established rights to either.[25]

While particularly extreme, the restrictions in southern labor law were not completely out of line with the direction of labor relations in the nation as a whole. Throughout the United States, more people entered the ranks of wage labor, which became a permanent status, instead of a stage in the life cycle. They sold their labor and received wages for it, but had no claim on the products of their labor. With few options, they were forced to sign contracts that demanded the surrender of a range of rights to their employers and placed them in dangerous conditions over which they had little control. Workers

---

[24] Gerald David Jaynes, *Branches without Roots: Genesis of the Black Working Class in the American South, 1862–1882* (New York, 1986).

[25] Harold D. Woodman, *New South, New Law: The Legal Foundations of Credit and Labor Relations in the Postbellum Agricultural South* (Baton Rouge, LA, 1995).

registered their dissatisfaction in a series of strikes that rocked the North and Midwest during the last decades of the nineteenth century. Beginning in the late 1870s, labor unrest not only overlapped with Reconstruction in the South but also picked up on issues central there, namely laborers' control over the work process and the fruits of their labor.

Individual rights, as defined by the courts, prevented people from doing anything about the issues that actually mattered to them in their lives as workers. Before the Civil War, workers' collective organizations made little headway in a legal order in which the individual was the paradigmatic subject and property rights were paramount. The courts treated unions as criminal conspiracies: no better than gangs of thugs who targeted an unsuspecting mark. After the war, the laws loosened up, permitting workers to unionize, as long as they engaged in legal activities. With legal recognition, however, came legal scrutiny, most of which did not favor the goals of workers. In particular, the courts left the legal bias against collective action in place, which resulted in an extremely narrow view of the legal activities in which unions could engage. Strikes, even public protests, were not deemed legal. Further restrictions came through state legislatures, with measures that targeted labor leaders with various prohibitions, including speech or actions of any kind that questioned existing order.

The Fourteenth Amendment also worked against laborers. In the 1870s, the U.S. Supreme Court dismissed claims that the Fourteenth Amendment protected economic rights, notably in the *Slaughter-House Cases* and *Bradwell v. Illinois*. Both affirmed the authority of states to regulate in the public interest, even if that meant restricting rights. State and local governments, for instance, had traditionally regulated the slaughterhouses where butchers worked, because of the health risks they posed. If located upstream or within the city limits, the offal and other waste could contaminate the city's water supply, spreading disease and death. But the butchers in New Orleans felt particularly aggrieved: they were white, mostly Democratic butchers with strong backing from the city's Democratic leadership, who all felt that Republican rule needed to be overturned. So they reached for the laws of their political opponents, using the Fourteenth Amendment to protect what they saw as their right – their right to pursue a livelihood as others could. Although the legal arguments in the *Slaughter-House Cases* were different from those in *Bradwell v. Illinois*, there were distinct parallels. Like the butchers, Myra Bradwell framed access to economic opportunities as a right protected by the Fourteenth Amendment. The court rejected both claims.[26]

Once opened, however, the door of property rights could not be closed. At the very moment when the courts made it more difficult to prosecute violations of African Americans' civil and political rights, they started hearing a range of cases involving economic claims like those of the butchers and Bradwell. In these cases, the U.S. Supreme Court extended the Fourteenth Amendment to the protection of Americans' right to pursue their livelihoods, an individual right that also limited states' traditional rights to regulate in the public interest. According to the courts, state legislatures could no longer restrict the economic rights of individuals to promote policies that advanced the collective interests of the public. Some of the initial cases involved farmers, who had more political leverage than wage workers to take on the economic powers of the late nineteenth century. Farmers, particularly in the West and Midwest, depended on grain elevators to store their crops and on railroads to get them to market. But the capital-intensive nature of these services and the fact that farms were so widely dispersed meant that there was no competition. In any given area, there was only one railroad line and only one grain elevator. The owners could charge what they wanted – and they did. Traditionally, local and state government had regulated these kinds of businesses, for the same reasons they had regulated slaughterhouses. Although privately owned, businesses that provided services the public could not do without were considered fit subjects of government regulation. Farmers successfully pressured state legislatures to do just that. The courts, however, slowly whittled away at such legislation on the grounds that public regulation interfered with the operators' rights, under the Fourteenth Amendment, to pursue their

---

[26] *Slaughter-House Cases; Bradwell v. Illinois.* For the local dynamics involved in the case, see Ross, "Justice Miller's Reconstruction."

livelihoods and to substantive due process. The rights of property owners took precedence, in law, over the interests of the public.[27]

The logic of those rulings also accentuated employers' traditional legal authority over their workers by solidifying the notion of the workplace – including everything that went on there or that was connected to it – as the employers' private property. Then they connected those property rights to the Fourteenth Amendment, freeing them from the regulatory power of the states. Workers, by contrast, maintained that they deserved a say in these matters: that their knowledge about manufacturing processes should not be summarily dismissed; that those processes should not elevate profit above their safety; and that the profits derived from their labor should be more evenly distributed. Their labor, as workers saw it, gave them a stake in the workplace.[28]

While many Americans found workers' claims problematic, they did not see workplaces as wholly private spaces either. Reports of the dire living conditions in urban slums and the appalling working conditions in the nation's factories fueled a sense of outrage and crisis. The waves of labor unrest that rocked the country in the years following the Civil War added to that situation. The result was reform legislation that sought to ameliorate the worst of these problems: legislation to limit working hours, establish a minimum wage, create safety standards, and prohibit practices that kept workers tied to their employers, such as payment in scrip redeemable only at company stores with inflated prices that kept workers in debt and unable to quit. Legislation, its proponents argued, represented

---

[27] See, e.g., *Munn v. Illinois*, 94 U.S. 113 (1877); *Mugler v. Kansas*, 123 U.S. 623 (1887); *Railway v. Minnesota*, 134 U.S. 138 (1890). *Munn* affirmed states' rights to regulate businesses that dealt with the public interest, but placed limits on the extent of state regulation in the sense that what constituted the public interest was now in the federal courts' purview. *Mugler* went further, giving federal courts more power to scrutinize state regulations and allowing for such regulation only if it actually had a relationship to public health, safety, or morals. *Minnesota* eliminated the possibility for the kind of regulation sanctioned in *Munn*, by characterizing legislative regulation of railroad freight rates as a violation of Fourteenth Amendment rights.

[28] David Brody, *Workers in Industrial America: Essays on the Twentieth Century Struggle* (New York, 1980); David Montgomery, *Workers' Control in America: Studies in the History of Work, Technology, and Labor Struggles* (New York, 1979).

a traditional, accepted use of police power. The states regulated for the public interest: to protect workers' lives as well as the health and safety of the general populace. The courts, however, routinely struck down those measures as either a violation of employers' property rights or of workers' rights to contract – although there were exceptions, which only showed how contentious the issues were. Individual rights defined the public good; no further intervention was necessary.

This conception of rights also enveloped Indians, who entered the post–Civil War era with no recognized rights whatsoever. They had their own conceptions of how they would like to live their lives, conceptions that did not involve the kind of individual rights that were so central to the American legal order. Although sympathetic federal officials often framed those claims in the language of rights, Indians had neither rights to their cultural traditions nor the legal means of maintaining them in the face of overwhelming federal force.[29]

After the Civil War, federal officials abandoned the treaty system, particularly its recognition of Indian sovereignty, and began imposing conditions on Indian tribes instead. At issue was culture as well as land. The Bureau of Indian Affairs began an aggressive campaign designed to turn Indians into Americans. Moving tribes off their lands or onto tiny reservations eliminated the basis of traditional, communal means of subsistence. Then the interposition of bureau officials into the daily lives of Indians further undermined the traditional forms of tribal governance. Bureau officials imposed American economic, cultural, and social practices, encouraging the division of tribal land into individual lots, conversion to Christianity, and the adoption of American habits of dress, consumption, and interaction. Mission schools scooped up small children in an effort to hasten the process, raising them up as Americans, not Indians.[30]

[29] Sidney I. Harring, *Crow Dog's Case: American Indian Sovereignty, Tribal Law, and United States Law in the Nineteenth Century* (New York, 1994).

[30] West, *The Last Indian War*; Frederick E. Hoxie, *A Final Promise: The Campaign to Assimilate the Indians, 1880–1920* (Lincoln, NE, 1984). For the cultural gulf between these policies and Indian culture, see Emily Greenwald, *Reconfiguring the Reservation: The Nez Perces, Jicarilla Apaches, and the Dawes Act* (Albuquerque, NM, 2002).

Those efforts culminated in the Dawes Act (1887), which formally ended tribal governance. The act divided up tribal land, distributed it as private property to individuals who could prove tribal membership, and declared those property owners to be American citizens. Unintentionally underscoring the importance of property in the nation's legal order, the effect of the Dawes Act was the loss of more than two-thirds of tribal lands: from 138 million acres in 1871 to 48 million acres by 1934. The rights of American citizenship, however, meant little to Indians who never wanted to be Americans or claim rights in the first place. The process by which they acquired those rights, moreover, made it clear that equality – in any meaningful sense – was a legal fiction.[31]

The parallels between the legal status of workers, women, African Americans, and Indians are striking. As individuals, all these people could claim civil, if not political rights. But no one in America was the ideal legal individual, self-interested, unencumbered, and fully empowered. Everyone was folded into other legal relationships, many of which made it difficult to access their rights, let alone exercise them to advance their interests or improve their lives. The individualized view of rights embraced by the courts and political leaders in the late nineteenth century ignored the social context that described actual Americans' lives. It also ignored the sources of the problems with which so many Americans struggled. No matter how empowered, individuals could not find their way through the profound structural inequalities that characterized the late nineteenth century: white supremacy, the systemic subordination of women, and an ever-widening chasm between the rich and the poor. Such inequalities required collective solutions. Yet the era's individualized definition of rights made it extremely difficult for the American people to harness the federal government's power to realize collective visions of social change. That individualized definition was at odds with those held by many of the American people. It promised equality in law but delivered inequality in practice.

---

[31] The General Allotment Act of 1887 (Dawes Act), 24 U.S. Statutes at Large 388 (1887). Kevin Bruyneel, "Challenging American Boundaries: Indigenous People and the 'Gift' of U.S. Citizenship," *Studies in American Political Development* 18 (2004): 130–43.

Conclusion

When historians write about the Civil War and Reconstruction, their attention is usually engaged elsewhere. For better or worse, studies of the period also serve as a way to evaluate the nation's core values: What does the United States stand for?

The demands of the present weigh so heavily on this particular period that the literature veers wildly between hope and despair, a situation that says as much about historians' concerns with law and government now as it does about their involvement in the past. The historians of the Dunning School established the precedent, characterizing Reconstruction as a repudiation of national ideals that required a violent "redemption" to reclaim government. Recently, the literature has taken a more optimistic tone, with historians tending to approach Reconstruction in terms of its possibilities. Notes of despair, however, punctuate these studies, with historians faulting the nation's failure to achieve the very principles that the Dunning School saw as problematic: instead of going too far, the nation did not go – and still has not gone – far enough in writing its ideals into its governing structure.

Although the historiographical conclusions are different than they were in the early twentieth century, the conceptual frame is not. That conceptual frame explains national development, primarily, in terms of the laws and institutions of the federal government. Historians of the Dunning School set the standard by conflating questions about the nation's character with those about the federal government, as if the two were one and the same. As these historians saw it, the problem with Reconstruction was that the federal government overstepped its authority. Responding to those arguments, subsequent scholarship has continued to engage questions about federal authority, its use, and its development. Even scholarship that does not focus on the federal level is still shaped by a set of assumptions that tends to characterize the federal government as the embodiment of the nation and its ideals.

The federal government, however, is not necessarily the same thing as the nation, which is an imagined entity, the construction and meanings of which have been anything but stable.[1] More specifically, the conflation of the federal government with the nation oversimplifies governance within the nation. That is particularly true in the mid-nineteenth century, when governance took place through an array of institutions: those that were relatively private, such as households, churches, and communities as well as those that were formally public, such as local, state, and federal governments in their judicial, legislative, and administrative forms. Extending conceptions of governance to capture this wide array of institutions not only is true to the context of the time, but also captures the full range of practices that actually shaped the nation's governing system. This broader conception of governance also recasts characterizations of the nation, by shifting the focus away from the federal government to the state and local level and from a singular national identity to an inherently contested one. From this perspective, the story of the nation is one of ongoing conflict that mirrored the American people's aspirations in all their contradictory possibilities.

Those aspirations and all their contradictory possibilities are central to the history of the Civil War and Reconstruction, which reflects nothing so much as the unresolved tensions that have always defined the nation. To the extent that national legal principles emerged during Reconstruction, they owed as much to the various efforts of diverse groups of people working in localized contexts as they did to federal policy. Federal policy, moreover, assumed the form that it did in large part because of ordinary Americans who not only combined notions of individual rights with collective

---

[1] I am borrowing from Benedict Anderson, *Imagined Communities: Reflections on the Origins and Spread of Nationalism* (London, 1983).

conceptions of a just society, but also brought expectations of an activist government to their interactions with the federal level.

In the decades following Reconstruction, federal courts struck down those claims, characterizing them as the efforts of particular groups to obtain special consideration, destroy the rights of individuals, and endanger the very concept of equality. But even though these expansive views of rights were unsuccessful at the time, they became firmly embedded in the legal order of the emerging nation – a legal order in which individual rights became firmly linked to conceptions of social justice. That link carries its own problems. But to miss the historical dynamics that created it is to misconstrue the importance of legal change in the Reconstruction period. Those changes allowed the aspirations of diverse groups of Americans to move into the realm of federal law and to acquire the status of universal legal principles. While those aspirations expressed the unique values of particular groups of Americans, they were also deeply rooted in existing governing practices, which had long described local and, to a certain extent, state governance. What was new was their appearance at the federal level.

One result of this new interaction between the American people and their federal government was that individual rights were remade, not just extended. Another was the demand that the federal government should embody the ideals of the nation in a more active way: it should act on those ideals to achieve social justice. Those expectations could only result in conflict, because there was no consensus among the American people about what constituted a just society. Yet those aspirational visions of rights and social justice guided the nation's development and, ultimately, our own expectations about what the nation should be. They also supported the notion – one that still guides the historiography today – that the federal government should represent the nation: a nation defined through its people.

Bibliographic Essay

This book brings together several strands of the historiography: legal history, political history, southern history, African American history, women's history, and labor history.

Traditionally, legal and political histories of the Civil War and Reconstruction have tended to focus on federal policies, both in the Union and the Confederacy. The distinction between the two fields has not always been clear, particularly in the scholarship of the late nineteenth and early twentieth centuries. But legal historians have tended to emphasize the institutional development of law and government, while political historians have tended to subordinate law and policy to the political process, seeing them primarily as the outcomes of those negotiations in which they are most interested, rather than the primary subject of study. Much of this scholarship has treated the Civil War and Reconstruction as a unit, linking Union policies of the war years to those of Reconstruction.

The legal and political history from the late nineteenth and early twentieth centuries has been incredibly influential in shaping the basic questions that still inform the historiography of the period. It also reflects the politics of the time, with its emphasis on sectional reconciliation, rejection of federal authority, and sympathy for the states of the former Confederacy. The most well known is William Archibald Dunning, *Essays on the Civil War and Reconstruction and Related Topics* (New York, 1898) and *Reconstruction, Political and Economic, 1865–1877* (New York, 1907). Dunning's students produced a body of work that did for the states what Dunning had done at the national level, producing histories of the Civil War and

Reconstruction for all the states of the former Confederacy. Also see John William Burgess, *Reconstruction and the Constitution, 1866–1876* (New York, 1902) and James Ford Rhodes, *History of the United States from the Compromise of 1850 to the Final Restoration of Home Rule at the South in 1877, 7 Vols.* (New York, 1893–1906). This body of literature tends to connect law to politics and society, rather than separating out legal issues, a situation that reflects the primacy of political history in the newly professionalized discipline of history at that time.

Historians of the Progressive Era broke ranks with the ideological frame of the Dunning School, emphasizing economic differences between the sections and characterizing the war as an inevitable conflict, rather than an avoidable tragedy between two essentially similar regions of the country. In legal history, the work of James G. Randall, particularly *Constitutional Problems under Lincoln* (New York, 1926), is often seen as turning point because it deals with the complications of the Lincoln administration's policies, instead of simply condemning them. Progressive historians, however, still maintained a critical stance toward Republican policies. See Howard K. Beale, *The Critical Year: A Study of Andrew Johnson and Reconstruction* (New York, 1930); Charles A. Beard and Mary R. Beard, *The Rise of American Civilization, 2 Vols.* (New York, 1927); Claude Bowers, *The Tragic Era: The Revolution after Lincoln* (Cambridge, MA, 1929); and Arthur Charles Cole, *The Irrepressible Conflict, 1850–1865* (New York, 1934).

In political history, revisionists of the 1930s and 1940s deemphasized sectional differences to focus on the failure of institutions in explaining the causes of the Civil War and the outcome of the resulting policies. The early revisionists also broke decisively from earlier scholarship in adopting a more positive view of Republicans' goals, particularly their efforts to achieve civil and political equality for African Americans. Even so, they still characterized the Civil War and Reconstruction in terms of failure, although the emphasis was increasingly on the execution, not the conception of Republican policies. See Avery Craven, *The Repressible Conflict 1830–1861* (Baton Rouge, LA, 1939); James G. Randall, *Lincoln the President, 4 Vols.* (New York, 1945–55); and David M. Potter, *The Impending Crisis 1848–1861* (New York, 1976).

The distinction between political history and legal history began to emerge clearly in the early revisionist scholarship. In political history, the next generation of revisionist scholars brought back the irrepressible conflict, without the sharp economic determinism of the Progressive Era, with more emphasis on ideology, and with a wider variety of topical frames. Their emphasis on sectional differences played into analyses that cast Republican policies – particularly those that extended federal authority and were favorable to racial equality – as positive extensions of national values. This body of scholarship also tended to focus on the failure to realize those values, reflecting the politics of the post–World War II era, particularly the civil rights movement. See Michael Les Benedict, *A Compromise of Principle: Congressional Republicans and Reconstruction, 1863–1869* (New York, 1974); LaWanda Cox and John H. Cox, *Politics, Principle, and Prejudice, 1865–1866: Dilemma of Reconstruction America* (New York, 1963); William W. Freehling, *The Road to Disunion*, 2 Vols. (New York, 1990–2007); Eric Foner, *Free Soil, Free Labor, Free Men: The Ideology of the Republican Party before the Civil War* (New York, 1970); Eugene D. Genovese, *The Political Economy of Slavery: Studies in the Economy and Society of the Old South* (New York, 1965); Peyton McCrary, *Abraham Lincoln and Reconstruction: The Louisiana Experiment* (Princeton, NJ, 1978); James M. McPherson, *Battle Cry of Freedom: The Civil War Era* (New York, 1998); David Montgomery, *Beyond Equality: Labor and the Radical Republicans, 1862–1872* (New York, 1967); Kenneth M. Stampp, *The Era of Reconstruction, 1865–1877* (New York, 1965); and Hans L. Trefousse, *The Radical Republicans: Lincoln's Vanguard for Racial Justice* (New York, 1969).

The scholarship in legal history has followed a similar trajectory in terms of the emphasis on sectional differences, the positive aspects of Republican policies, and the failure in achieving the underlying principles of those policies. But, unlike political historians, legal historians focused more on the application and implementation of new policies and law than on the dynamics involved in their initial formulation. Their emphasis tended to be on federal policy, with analyses that explored events at the national level, rather than on domestic conditions within the South, where those policies were directed (at least initially). As a result, the scholarship tends to focus on the development of law within national institutions, not in the lives of the people whom the laws were intended to serve. See, for instance, Bruce Ackerman, *We the People, Vol. 2: Transformations* (Cambridge, MA, 1998); Herman Belz, *Abraham Lincoln, Constitutionalism, and Equal Rights in the Civil War* (New York, 1998); Harold M. Hyman, *A More Perfect Union: The Impact of the Civil War and Reconstruction on the Constitution* (New York, 1973); Harold M. Hyman and William M. Wiecek, *Equal Justice under Law: Constitutional Development, 1835–1875* (New York, 1982); David E. Kyvig, *Explicit and Authentic Acts: Amending the U.S. Constitution, 1776–1995* (Lawrence, KS, 1996); Mark E. Neely, *The Last Best Hope of Earth: Abraham Lincoln and the Promise of America* (Cambridge, MA, 1983) and *Lincoln and the Triumph of the Nation: Constitutional Conflict in the American Civil War* (Chapel Hill, NC, 2011); William E. Nelson, *The Fourteenth Amendment: From Political Principle to Judicial Doctrine* (Cambridge, MA, 1988); and Phillip S. Paludan, *A Covenant with Death: The Constitution, Law, and Equality in the Civil War Era* (Urbana, IL, 1975).

While focusing on the same issues, recent work in legal history roots legal change and political debates in social context, revealing new complexities and contingencies in their formulation and, particularly, their implementation. See, for instance, Richard Franklin Bensel, *Yankee Leviathan: The Origins of Central State Authority in America, 1859–1877* (Cambridge, MA, 1990); Pamela Brandwein, *Rethinking the Judicial Settlement of Reconstruction* (New York, 2011); Charles W. Calhoun, *Conceiving a New Republic: The Republican Party and the Southern Question, 1869–1900* (Lawrence, KS, 2006); Paul A. Cimbala, *Under the Guardianship of the Nation: The Freedmen's Bureau and the Reconstruction of Georgia, 1865–1870* (Athens, GA, 1997); Robert Goldman, *Reconstruction and Black Suffrage: Losing the Vote in Reese and Cruikshank* (Lawrence, KS, 2001b) and *A Free Ballot and a Fair Count: The Department of Justice and the Enforcement of the Voting Rights Act in the South, 1877–1893* (New York, 2001a); Robert J. Kaczorowski, *The Politics of Judicial Interpretation: The Federal Courts, Department of Justice, and Civil Rights, 1866–1876* (New York, 1985); Michael A. Ross, *Justice of Shattered Dreams: Samuel*

Miller Freeman and the Supreme Court during the Civil War Era (Baton Rouge, LA, 2003); Michael Vorenburg, *Final Freedom: The Civil War, the Abolition of Slavery, and the Thirteenth Amendment* (New York, 2001); Xi Wang, *The Trial of Democracy: Black Suffrage and Northern Republicans, 1860–1910* (Athens, GA, 1997); and Lou Falkner Williams, *The Great South Carolina Ku Klux Klan Trials, 1871–1872* (Athens, GA, 2004).

Other recent strands of legal history explore questions of inequality – the fundamental question that drove the policies of the era – with a broader lens, one that links questions of racial inequality to gender, class, and other issues. For a sweeping view of the issues of race and inequality in America that roots the law in a broad social, economic, and political context, see Christopher L. Tomlins, *Freedom Bound: Law, Labor, and Civic Identity in Colonizing English America, 1580–1865* (New York, 2010). Also see Amy Dru Stanley, *From Bondage to Contract: Wage Labor, Marriage, and the Market in the Age of Slave Emancipation* (New York, 1998); and Barbara Young Welke, *Recasting American Liberty: Gender, Race, Law, and the Railroad Revolution, 1865–1920* (New York, 2001) and *Law and the Borders of Belonging in the Long Nineteenth Century United States* (New York, 2010).

In many ways, Confederate history *was* U.S. history in the scholarship of the Dunning School and the Progressives, given the bias against Republican policies and the clear support for white supremacy. The Confederacy, however, also has its own historiography, which focuses inward on the politics and policies that founded the nation and then led to its demise. Initially, the emphasis was on the policies of the Confederate federal government. For classic statements, see Frank L. Owsley, *State Rights in the Confederacy* (Chicago, 1925) and *The Collapse of the Confederacy* (Washington, DC, 1937). The concern with explanations of the Confederacy's defeat is still evident in the current literature, which explores the Confederacy's efforts to mobilize for war and emphasizes both the modernizing effects of its policies on the economy and the centralization of authority in the Confederate federal government. See, for example, William C. Davis, *Jefferson Davis: A Man and His Hour* (New York, 1991); Clement Eaton, *Jefferson Davis* (New York, 1977); Emory M. Thomas, *The Confederacy as a Revolutionary*

Experience (Englewood Cliffs, NJ, 1970); and Frank Everson Vandiver, *Jefferson Davis and the Confederate State: An Inaugural Lecture Delivered before the University of Oxford on 26 February 1964* (Oxford, 1964). Also see Bensel, *Yankee Leviathan*, although the book comes to the subject through the scholarship on the development of the nation state, not the Confederate experience. Scholarship on the effectiveness of Confederate policies in waging war addresses another historiographical concern, in assessing the Confederate government's commitment to its principles of states' rights and individual liberty. See Mark E. Neely Jr., *Southern Rights: Political Prisoners and the Myth of Confederate Constitutionalism* (Charlottesville, VA, 1999); Marshall L. DeRosa, *The Confederate Constitution of 1861: An Inquiry into American Constitutionalism* (Columbia, MO, 1991); and Charles Robert Lee, *The Confederate Constitutions* (Chapel Hill, NC, 1963).

With the influence of revisionist scholarship and the rise of social history after World War II, historians of the Confederacy turned to conditions on the home front, focusing more on the impact of Confederate policies on the ground. In social and cultural histories, one key line of inquiry casts questions about Confederate defeat in terms of nationalism, focusing particularly on the Confederate people's will to win. See Richard E. Berringer, Herman Hattaway, Archer Jones, and William N. Still, *Why the South Lost the Civil War* (Athens, GA, 1986); Drew Gilpin Faust, *The Creation of Confederate Nationalism: Ideology and Identity in the Civil War South* (Baton Rouge, LA, 1990); Gary W. Gallagher, *Confederate War: How Popular Will, Nationalism, and Military Strategy Could Not Stave Off Defeat* (Cambridge, MA, 1997); Bruce C. Levine, *The Fall of the House of Dixie: The Civil War and the Social Revolution That Transformed the South* (New York, 2013); George C. Rable, *Civil Wars: Women and The Crisis of Southern Nationalism* (Urbana, IL, 1989); Anne S. Rubin, *A Shattered Nation: The Rise and Fall of the Confederacy, 1861–1868* (Chapel Hill, NC, 2005); and Paul Quigley, *Shifting Grounds: Nationalism and the American South, 1848–1865* (New York, 2012).

Other strands of this literature focus on the failure of Confederate policies in meeting the needs of the people. Although not specifically about legal issues, this work suggests vast differences among whites in the region, differences that ultimately shaped law and government not only within the Confederacy, but also at the state level after Reconstruction. Classic statements are E. Merton Coulter, *The Confederate States of America, 1861–1865* (Baton Rouge, LA, 1950); Emory M. Thomas, *The Confederacy as a Revolutionary Experience* and *The Confederate Nation, 1861–1865* (New York, 1979). Influenced by social history and the legacy of C. Vann Woodward's *Origins of the New South, 1877–1913* (Baton Rouge, LA, 1951), recent work considers class divisions and political conflict among white southerners both before and after the Civil War. See Daniel W. Crofts, *Reluctant Confederates: Upper South Unionists in the Secession Crisis* (Chapel Hill, NC, 1989); Wayne K. Durrill, *War of Another Kind: A Southern Community in the Great Rebellion* (New York, 1990); Paul D. Escott, *The Confederacy: The Slaveholders' Failed Venture* (Santa Barbara, CA, 2010); Drew Gilpin Faust, *Mothers of Invention: Women of the Slaveholding South in the American Civil War* (Chapel Hill, NC, 1996); Steven Hahn, *The Roots of Southern Populism: Yeoman Farmers and the Transformation of the Georgia Upcountry, 1850–1890* (New York, 1983); and Armstead Robinson, "Beyond the Realm of Social Consensus: New Meanings of Reconstruction for American History," *Journal of American History* 68 (1981): 276–97.

A related body of scholarship considers the development of sharecropping after the Civil War, tracing the legal and economic development of an institution that defined the region's poverty for white as well as black southerners: Roger L. Ransom and Richard Sutch, *One Kind of Freedom: The Economic Consequences of Emancipation* (New York, 1977); Jonathan Weiner, "AHR Forum: Class Structure and Economic Development in the American South, 1865–1955," *American Historical Review* 84 (1979): 970–1006; and Harold D. Woodman, *New South, New Law: The Legal Foundations of Credit and Labor Relations in the Postbellum Agricultural South* (Baton Rouge, LA, 1995).

The influence of social history also encouraged scholarship that focused on the experiences of African Americans in the South and placed them at the center of narratives on the Civil War and Reconstruction. The work of the Freedmen and Southern Society

Project, based at the University of Maryland, has been particularly influential in this regard. The project's volumes have made the rich documentary record of the period accessible. They also have provided a compelling interpretative framework that places African Americans within the wider historiography of southern history by integrating questions about the South's transition to capitalist production into a narrative traditionally concerned with the connection between race and civil and political rights. For early pivotal work in the series, see Ira Berlin, Joseph P. Reidy, and Leslie S. Rowland, eds., *Freedom: A Documentary History of Emancipation, 1861–1867*, Series 2: *The Black Military Experience* (New York, 1982); Ira Berlin, Barbara J. Fields, Thavolia Glymph, Joseph P. Reidy, and Leslie S. Rowland, eds., *Freedom: A Documentary History of Emancipation, 1861–1867*, Series 1, Vol. 1: *The Destruction of Slavery* (New York, 1985); and Ira Berlin, Stephen F. Miller, and Leslie S. Rowland, eds. "Afro-American Families in the Transition from Slavery to Freedom," *Radical History Review* 42 (1988): 89–121. For related scholarship, see Barbara J. Fields, *Slavery and Freedom on the Middle Ground: Maryland during the Nineteenth Century* (New Haven, CT, 1985); Eric Foner, *Nothing but Freedom: Emancipation and Its Legacy* (Baton Rouge, LA, 1983); Steven Hahn, *A Nation under Our Feet: Black Political Struggles in the Rural South from Slavery to the Great Migration* (Cambridge, MA, 2003); Susan E. O'Donovan, *Becoming Free in the Cotton South* (Cambridge, MA, 2007); Joseph P. Reidy, *From Slavery to Agrarian Capitalism in the Cotton Plantation South: Central Georgia, 1800–1880* (Chapel Hill, NC, 1992); John C. Rodrigue, *Reconstruction in the Cane Fields: From Slavery to Free Labor in Louisiana's Sugar Parishes, 1862–1880* (Baton Rouge, LA, 2001); Julie Saville, *The Work of Reconstruction: From Slave to Wage Laborer in South Carolina, 1860–1870* (New York, 1994); and Leslie A. Schwalm, *A Hard Fight for We: Women's Transition from Slavery to Freedom in South Carolina* (Urbana, IL, 1997). This scholarship is influenced by comparative approaches to emancipation, which also emphasizes freedpersons' political agency and labor relations. See, for instance, Thomas C. Holt, *The Problem of Freedom: Race, Labor, and Politics in Jamaica and Britain* (Baltimore, 1992). This body of work also owes an intellectual debt to W. E. B. DuBois's *Black*

Reconstruction: An Essay Toward a History of the Part Which Black Folk Played in the Attempt to Reconstruct Democracy in America, 1860–1880 (New York, 1935).

One important implication of recent scholarship in African American history has been the recovery and analysis of African Americans' use of law in a variety of forums, including the federal army, the Freedmen's Bureau, and state and local courts. See Nancy D. Bercaw, *Gendered Freedoms: Race, Rights, and the Politics of Household in the Delta, 1861–1875* (Gainesville, FL, 2003); Laura F. Edwards, *Gendered Strife and Confusion: The Political Culture of Reconstruction* (Urbana, IL, 1997); Noralee Frankel, *Freedom's Women: Black Women and Families in Civil War Era Mississippi* (Bloomington, IN, 1999); Dylan Penningroth, *The Claims of Kinfolk: African American Property and Community in the Nineteenth-Century South* (Chapel Hill, NC, 2003); Hannah Rosen, *Terror in the Heart of Freedom: Citizenship, Sexual Violence, and the Meaning of Race in the Postemancipation South* (Chapel Hill, NC, 2009); and Diane Miller Sommerville, *Rape and Race in the Nineteenth-Century South* (Chapel Hill, NC, 2004). This body of work tends to rely on legal records for its evidentiary base, but considers the dynamics in those documents as expressions of social, economic, and even political culture, not of law and legal culture. There are exceptions, and recent scholarship is beginning to consider the law as a subject of study, not just a source for information about African Americans: Jonathan M. Bryant, *How Curious a Land: Conflict and Change in Greene County, Georgia, 1850–1885* (Chapel Hill, NC, 1996) and Kate Masur, *An Example for All the Land: Emancipation and the Struggle Over Equality in Washington, D.C.* (Chapel Hill, NC, 2010). In its emphasis on African Americans' use of law, such work is related to but distinct from scholarship in southern legal history, which tends to focus on the institutional development of law and which also tends to focus on either slave law or the implications of racial restrictions after Reconstruction. See, for instance, Edward L. Ayers, *Vengeance and Justice: Crime and Punishment in the Nineteenth-Century American South* (New York, 1984) and Christopher Waldrep, *Roots of Disorder: Race and Criminal Justice in the American South, 1817–80* (Urbana, IL, 1998).

These new directions in southern history, particularly the focus on the experiences of African Americans, have reshaped the history of the Civil War and Reconstruction by placing the emphasis on people's interactions with federal policies. That approach allowed for new kinds of histories that united social history with both legal and political histories, although much of the scholarship tends to highlight social and political history, treating law less as a subject in its own right and more as an instrument to achieve particular social and political ends. Perhaps the best examples are Eric Foner's *The Fiery Trial: Abraham Lincoln and American Slavery* (New York, 2010) and *Reconstruction: America's Unfinished Revolution* (New York, 1988), which both not only combine the traditional emphasis of legal and political history with social history but also place the literature on the South and the North in dialogue, largely through the inclusion on African Americans.

Recent work has extended the geographic and topical base, calling for a full integration of western history and Indian history into the history of Reconstruction. For Indian history, see Stuart Banner, *How the Indians Lost Their Land: Law and Power on the Frontier* (Cambridge, MA, 2005); David A. Chang, *The Color of Land: Race, Nation, and the Politics of Land Ownership in 1832–1929* (Chapel Hill, NC, 2010); Tim Alan Garrison, *The Legal Ideology of Removal: The Southern Judiciary and the Sovereignty of Native American Nations* (Athens, GA, 2002); Emily Greenwald, *Reconfiguring the Reservation: The Nez Perces, Jicarilla Apaches, and the Dawes Act* (Albuquerque, NM, 2002); Sidney I. Harring, *Crow Dog's Case: American Indian Sovereignty, Tribal Law, and United States Law in the Nineteenth Century* (New York, 1994); Frederick E. Hoxie, *A Final Promise: The Campaign to Assimilate the Indians, 1880–1920* (Lincoln, NE, 1984); and Maria Montoya, *Translating Property: The Maxwell Land Grant and the Conflict over Land in the American West, 1840–1900* (Berkeley, 2002). For the importance of the history of the West more broadly, see Adam Arenson, *The Great Heart of the Republic: St. Louis and the Cultural Civil War* (Cambridge, MA, 2011); Eugene Berwanger, *The West and Reconstruction* (Urbana, IL, 1981); Alvin M. Josephy, *The Civil War in the American West* (New York, 1991); Heather Cox Richardson, *West from Appomattox: The Reconstruction of*

America after the Civil War (New Haven, CT, 2007); Stacey Smith, *Freedom's Frontier: California and the Struggle over Unfree Labor, Emancipation, and Reconstruction* (Chapel Hill, NC, 2013); and Elliott West, *The Last Indian War: The Nez Perce Story* (New York, 2009).

The turn to gender in women's history has produced work that emphasizes connections among forms of legal inequality that historians once treated separately, highlighting similarities among race, class, and gender and positing new ways of understanding the experiences of men and women of both races in this period. By placing women at the center of the analysis, this body of scholarship also challenges traditional narratives that emphasize the expansion and then retraction of civil and political rights in this period. In particular, see Peter W. Bardaglio, *Reconstructing the Household: Families, Sex, and the Law in the Nineteenth-Century South* (Chapel Hill, NC, 1995); Nancy Cott, *Public Vows: A History of Marriage and the Nation* (Cambridge, MA, 2000); Edwards, *Gendered Strife and Confusion*; Stanley, *From Bondage to Contract*; and Welke, *Recasting American Liberty* and *Law and the Borders of Belonging*.

Also influential is the scholarship that highlights women's efforts to engage in questions of governance. Traditionally, the scholarship has focused on the acquisition of civil and political rights and women's exclusion from them, a line of inquiry that is still current within the historiography: Nancy Isenberg, *Sex and Citizenship in Antebellum America* (Chapel Hill, NC, 1998); Linda K. Kerber, *No Constitutional Right to be Ladies: Women and the Obligations of Citizenship* (New York, 1998); Mary P. Ryan, *Civic Wars: Democracy and Public Life in the American City during the Nineteenth Century* (Berkeley, CA, 1997); and Rosemary Zagarri, *Revolutionary Backlash: Women and Politics in the Early American Republic* (Philadelphia, 2007).

Another line of scholarship highlights women's legal agency, as women and dependents, despite the denial of those rights. This body of scholarship not only emphasizes women's active engagement in law, but also explores the development of the laws and their implications for women's legal status: Laura F. Edwards, *The People and Their Peace: Legal Culture and the Transformation of Inequality in the Post-Revolutionary South* (Chapel Hill, NC, 2009); Hendrik

Hartog, *Man and Wife in America: A History* (Cambridge, MA, 2000); and Michael Grossberg, *Governing the Hearth: Law and the Family in Nineteenth-Century America* (Chapel Hill, NC, 1985) and *A Judgment for Solomon: The d'Hauteville Case and Legal Experience in Antebellum America* (New York, 1996).

Recent scholarship has emphasized the active participation of southern women – white and black – in the events of the Civil War and Reconstruction. Much of this scholarship assumes women's engagement in questions of governance, although the analyses do not always cast the issue in that way: Bercaw, *Gendered Freedoms*; Victoria E. Bynum, *Unruly Women: The Politics of Social and Sexual Control in the Old South* (Chapel Hill, NC, 1992); Jacqueline Glass Campbell, *When Sherman Marched North from the Sea: Resistance on the Confederate Home Front* (Chapel Hill, NC, 2003); Laura F. Edwards, *Scarlett Doesn't Live Here Anymore: Southern Women and the Civil War Era* (Urbana, IL, 2000); Drew Gilpin Faust, *Mothers of Invention: Women of the Slaveholding South in the American Civil War* (Chapel Hill, NC, 2004); Thavolia Glymph, *Out of the House of Bondage: The Transformation of the Plantation Household* (New York, 2008); and Stephanie McCurry, *Confederate Reckonings: Power and Politics in the Civil War South* (Cambridge, MA, 2010). The scholarship tends to follow established questions in the historiography about how much women's lives changed as a result of the Civil War: where elements of the historiography have suggested that women's lives did not change that much, other scholarship identifies the crisis of the Civil War as the reason that white southern women, in particular, took on new roles.

The scholarship on northern white women's activism reveals both the broad nature of women's activism and the important – often problematic – connections between efforts to achieve racial and gender equality. See, for instance, Ellen Carol DuBois, *Feminism and Suffrage: The Emergence of an Independent Women's Movement in America, 1848–1869* (Ithaca, NY, 1978); Carol Faulkner, *Women's Radical Reconstruction: The Freedmen's Aid Movement* (Philadelphia, 2004); Nancy A. Hewitt, *Women's Activism and Social Change: Rochester, New York, 1822–1872* (Ithaca, NY, 1984); Julie Roy Jeffrey, *The Great Silent Army of Abolitionism: Ordinary Women in the Anti-Slavery Movement* (Chapel Hill, NC,

1998); Louise Michele Newman, *White Women's Rights: The Racial Origins of Feminism in the United States* (New York, 1999); and Mary P. Ryan, *Cradle of the Middle Class: The Family in Oneida County, New York, 1790–1865* (New York, 1981).

The status of working people and the labor movement has long been associated with the historiography on the Civil War and Reconstruction. See Eric Foner, *Free Soil, Free Labor, Free Men* and David Montgomery, *Beyond Equality*. Recent work in labor history has highlighted the inequalities inherent within the concept of free labor before and after the Civil War. The emphasis on the limitations of laborers' legal rights also suggests the parallels between the legal status of working-class men and other subordinated groups, namely African Americans and women. See William E. Forbath, "The Ambiguities of Free Labor: Labor and the Law in the Gilded Age," *Wisconsin Law Review* 4 (1985): 767–817; Cindy Hahamovitch, *The Fruits of Their Labor: Atlantic Coast Farmworkers and the Making of Migrant Poverty, 1870–1945* (Chapel Hill, NC, 1997); Alex Lichtenstein, *Twice the Work of Free Labor: The Political Economy of Convict Labor in the New South* (New York, 1996); Gunther Peck, *Reinventing Free Labor: Padrones and Immigrant Workers in the North American West, 1880–1930* (Cambridge, 2000); Robert J. Steinfeld, *The Invention of Free Labor: The Employment Relation in English and American Law and Culture, 1350–1870* (Chapel Hill, NC, 1991); Steinfeld, *Coercion, Contract, and Free Labor in the Nineteenth Century* (New York, 2001); and Christopher L. Tomlins, *Law, Labor, and Ideology in the Early American Republic* (New York, 1993). Other work makes explicit connections between class and gender in the problematic place of wage laborers outside the South. See, for instance, Eileen Boris, *Home to Work: Motherhood and the Politics of Industrial Homework in the United States* (New York, 1994); Jeanne Boydston, *Home and Work: Housework, Wages, and the Ideology of Labor in the Early Republic* (New York, 1990); and Stanley, *From Bondage to Contract.*

Bibliography

Ackerman, Bruce. *We the People, Vol. 2: Transformations*. Cambridge, MA, 1998.

Arenson, Adam. *The Great Heart of the Republic: St. Louis and the Cultural Civil War*. Cambridge, MA, 2011.

Ayers, Edward L. *Vengeance and Justice: Crime and Punishment in the Nineteenth-Century American South*. New York, 1984.

Aynes, Richard L. "On Misreading John Bingham and the Fourteenth Amendment." *Yale Law Journal* 107 (1993): 57–104.

Baer, Judith. *The Chains of Protection: The Judicial Response to Women's Labor Legislation*. Westport, CT, 1978.

Banner, Stuart. *How the Indians Lost Their Land: Law and Power on the Frontier*. Cambridge, MA, 2005.

Bardaglio, Peter Winthrop. *Reconstructing the Household: Families, Sex, and the Law in the Nineteenth-Century South*. Chapel Hill, NC, 1995.

Beale, Howard K. *The Critical Year: A Study of Andrew Johnson and Reconstruction*. New York, 1930.

Beard, Charles A. and Mary R. Beard. *The Rise of American Civilization, 2 Vols*. New York, 1927.

Belz, Herman. *Reconstructing the Union: Theory and Policy during the Civil War*. Ithaca, NY, 1969.

Abraham Lincoln, Constitutionalism, and Equal Rights in the Civil War. New York, 1998.

Benedict, Michael Les. *A Compromise of Principle: Congressional Republicans and Reconstruction, 1863–1869*. New York, 1974.

Bensel, Richard Franklin. "Southern Leviathan: The Development of Central State Authority in the Confederate States of America." *Studies in American Political Development* 2 (1987): 68–136.

Yankee Leviathan: The Origins of Central State Authority in America 1859–1877. New York, 1990.

Bercaw, Nancy D. *Gendered Freedoms: Race, Rights, and the Politics of Household in the Delta, 1861–1875*. Gainesville, FL, 2003.

Berlin, Ira, Stephen F. Miller, and Leslie S. Rowland, eds. "Afro-American Families in the Transition from Slavery to Freedom." *Radical History Review* 42 (1988): 89–121.

Berlin, Ira, Joseph P. Reidy, and Leslie S. Rowland, eds. *Freedom: A Documentary History of Emancipation, 1861–1867*. Series 2: *The Black Military Experience*. New York, 1982.

Berlin, Ira, Steven F. Miller, Joseph P. Reidy, and Leslie S. Rowland, eds. *Freedom: A Documentary History of Emancipation, 1861–1867*. Series 1, Vol. 2: *The Wartime Genesis of Free Labor: The Upper South*. New York, 1993.

Berlin, Ira, Barbara J. Fields, Thavolia Glymph, Joseph P. Reidy, and Leslie S. Rowland, eds. *Freedom: A Documentary History of Emancipation, 1861–1867*. Series 1, Vol. 1: *The Destruction of Slavery*. New York, 1985.

Berlin, Ira, Thavolia Glymph, Steven F. Miller, Joseph P. Reidy, Leslie S. Rowland, and Julie Saville, eds. *Freedom: A Documentary History of Emancipation, 1861–1867*. Series 1, Vol. 3: *The Wartime Genesis of Free Labor: The Lower South*. New York, 1990.

Bernstein, Iver. *The New York City Draft Riots: Their Significance for American Society and Politics in the Age of the Civil War*. New York, 1990.

Berringer, Richard E, Herman Hattaway, Archer Jones, and William N. Still. *Why the South Lost the Civil War*. Athens, GA, 1986.

Berwanger, Eugene. *The West and Reconstruction*. Urbana, IL, 1981.

Black, Robert C. *Railroads of the Confederacy*. Chapel Hill, NC, 1952.

Blair, William Alan. *Virginia's Private War: Feeding Body and Soul in the Confederacy, 1861–1865*. New York, 1998.

Boman, Dennis K. *Lincoln and Citizens' Rights in Civil War Missouri: Balancing Freedom and Security*. Baton Rouge, LA, 2011.

Boris, Eileen. *Home to Work: Motherhood and the Politics of Industrial Homework in the United States*. New York, 1994.

Bowers, Claude. *The Tragic Era: The Revolution after Lincoln*. Cambridge, MA, 1929.

Boydston, Jeanne. *Home and Work: Housework, Wages, and the Ideology of Labor in the Early Republic*. New York, 1990.

Brandwein, Pamela. *Rethinking the Judicial Settlement of Reconstruction*. New York, 2011.

Brody, David. *Workers in Industrial America: Essays on the Twentieth Century Struggle*. New York, 1980.

Brown, Elsa Barkley. "Negotiating and Transforming the Public Sphere: African American Political Life in the Transition from Slavery to Freedom." *Public Culture* 7 (1994): 107–26.

Bruyneel, Kevin. "Challenging American Boundaries: Indigenous People and the 'Gift' of U.S. Citizenship." *Studies in American Political Development* 18 (2004): 130–43.

Bryant, Jonathan M. *How Curious a Land: Conflict and Change in Greene County, Georgia, 1850–1885.* Chapel Hill, NC, 1996.

Burgess, John W. *Reconstruction and the Constitution, 1866–1876.* New York, 1902.

Bynum, Victoria E. *Unruly Women: The Politics of Social and Sexual Control in the Old South.* Chapel Hill, NC, 1992.

 The Free State of Jones: Mississippi's Longest Civil War. Chapel Hill, NC, 2001.

Calhoun, Charles W. *Conceiving a New Republic: The Republican Party and the Southern Question, 1869–1900.* Lawrence, KS, 2006.

Campbell, Jacqueline Glass. *When Sherman Marched North from the Sea: Resistance on the Confederate Home Front.* Chapel Hill, NC, 2003.

Catton, Bruce. *Never Call Retreat.* New York, 1965.

Chandler, Alfred D. *The Visible Hand: The Managerial Revolution in American Business.* Cambridge, MA, 1977.

Chang, David A. *The Color of Land: Race, Nation, and the Politics of Land Ownership in 1832–1929.* Chapel Hill, 2010.

Cimbala, Paul A. *Under the Guardianship of the Nation: The Freedmen's Bureau and the Reconstruction of Georgia, 1865–1870.* Athens, GA, 1997.

Cole, Arthur Charles. *The Irrepressible Conflict, 1850–1865.* New York, 1934.

Cott, Nancy F. *The Bonds of Womanhood: "Women's Sphere" in New England, 1780–1835.* New Haven, CT, 1977.

 Public Vows: A History of Marriage and the Nation. Cambridge, MA, 2000.

Coulter, E. Merton. *The Confederate States of America, 1861–1865.* Baton Rouge, LA, 1950.

Cox, Coy F. *Justin Smith Morrill: Father of the Land-Grant Colleges.* East Lansing, MI, 1999.

Cox, LaWanda. *Lincoln and Black Freedom: A Study in Presidential leadership.* Columbia, SC, 1981.

Cox, LaWanda and John H. Cox. *Politics, Principle, and Prejudice, 1865–1866: Dilemma of Reconstruction America.* New York, 1963.

Craven, Avery. *The Repressible Conflict 1830–1861.* Baton Rouge, LA, 1939.

Crofts, Daniel W. *Reluctant Confederates: Upper South Unionists in the Secession Crisis.* Chapel Hill, NC, 1989.

Davis, Hugh. *"We Will Be Satisfied with Nothing Less": The African American Struggle for Equal Rights in the North during Reconstruction.* Ithaca, NY, 2011.

Davis, William C. *Jefferson Davis: A Man and His Hour.* New York, 1991.

DeRosa, Marshall L. *The Confederate Constitution of 1861: An Inquiry into American Constitutionalism.* Columbia, MO, 1991.

Douglas, Davison M. *Jim Crow Moves North: The Battle over Northern School Segregation, 1865–1954.* New York, 2005.

Douglass, Frederick. *The Life and Writings of Frederick Douglass, 4 Vols.* Edited by Philip Foner. New York, 1950–75.

Downs, Gregory P. *Declarations of Dependence: The Long Reconstruction of Popular Politics in the South, 1861–1908.* Chapel Hill, NC, 2011.

"The Ends of War: Fighting the Civil War after Appomattox." Unpublished manuscript.

DuBois, Ellen Carol. *Feminism and Suffrage: The Emergence of an Independent Women's Movement in America, 1848–1869.* Ithaca, NY, 1978.

DuBois, W. E. B. *Black Reconstruction: An Essay toward a History of the Part Which Black Folk Played in the Attempt to Reconstruct Democracy in America, 1860–1880.* New York, 1935.

Dudden, Faye E. *Fighting Chance: The Struggle over Woman Suffrage and Black Suffrage in Reconstruction America.* New York, 2011.

Dunning, William Archibald. *Essays on the Civil War and Reconstruction and Related Topics.* New York, 1898.

Reconstruction, Political and Economic, 1865–1877. New York, 1907.

Durden, Robert Franklin. *The Gray and the Black: The Confederate Debate on Emancipation.* Baton Rouge, LA, 1972.

Durrill, Wayne K. *War of Another Kind: A Southern Community in the Great Rebellion.* New York, 1990.

Eaton, Clement. *Jefferson Davis.* New York, 1977.

Edwards, Laura F. "Sexual Violence, Gender, Reconstruction, and the Extension of Patriarchy in Granville County, North Carolina." *North Carolina Historical Review* 68 (1991): 237–60.

"'The Marriage Covenant Is at the Foundation of All Our Rights': The Politics of Slave Marriages in North Carolina after Emancipation." *Law and History Review* 14 (1996): 81–124.

Gendered Strife and Confusion: The Political Culture of Reconstruction. Urbana, IL, 1997.

"The Problem of Dependency: African Americans, Labor Relations, and the Law in the Nineteenth-Century South." *Agricultural History* 72 (1998): 313–40.

Scarlett Doesn't Live Here Anymore: Southern Women and the Civil War Era. Urbana, IL, 2000.

"Status without Rights: African Americans and the Tangled History of Law and Governance in the Nineteenth-Century U.S. South." *American Historical Review* 112 (2007): 365–93.

The People and Their Peace: Legal Culture and the Transformation of Inequality in the Post-Revolutionary South. Chapel Hill, NC, 2009.

Escott, Paul D. "Poverty and Governmental Aid for the Poor in Confederate North Carolina." *North Carolina Historical Review* 61 (1984): 462–80.

Many Excellent People: Power and Privilege in North Carolina, 1850–1900. Chapel Hill, NC, 1985.

Military Necessity: Civil-Military Relations in the Confederacy. Westport, CT, 2006.

The Confederacy: The Slaveholders' Failed Venture. Santa Barbara, CA, 2010.

Faulkner, Carol. *Women's Radical Reconstruction: The Freedmen's Aid Movement.* Philadelphia, 2003.

Faust, Drew Gilpin. *The Creation of Confederate Nationalism: Ideology and Identity in the Civil War South.* Baton Rouge, LA, 1990.

Mothers of Invention: Women of the Slaveholding South in the American Civil War. Chapel Hill, NC, 2004.

Feimster, Crystal. *Southern Horrors: Women and the Politics of Rape and Lynching in the American South.* Cambridge, MA, 2009.

Fellman, Michael. *Inside War: The Guerilla Conflict in Missouri during the American Civil War.* New York, 1989.

Fehrenbacher, Don E. *The Dred Scott Case: Its Significance in American Law and Politics.* New York, 1978.

The Slaveholding Republic: An Account of the United States Government's Relationship to Slavery. New York, 2001.

Fields, Barbara J. *Slavery and Freedom on the Middle Ground: Maryland during the Nineteenth Century.* New Haven, CT, 1985.

"Slavery, Race and Ideology in the United States of America." *New Left Review* 181 (1990): 95–118.

Finkelman, Paul. *An Imperfect Union: Slavery, Federalism, and Comity.* Chapel Hill, NC, 1981.

Foner, Eric. *Free Soil, Free Labor, Free Men: The Ideology of the Republican Party before the Civil War.* New York, 1970.

Nothing but Freedom: Emancipation and Its Legacy. Baton Rouge, LA, 1983.

Reconstruction: America's Unfinished Revolution. New York, 1988.

The Fiery Trial: Abraham Lincoln and American Slavery. New York, 2010.

Forbath, William E. "The Ambiguities of Free Labor: Labor and the Law in the Gilded Age." *Wisconsin Law Review* 4 (1985): 767–817.

Frankel, Noralee. *Freedom's Women: Black Women and Families in Civil War Era Mississippi.* Bloomington, IN, 1999.

Freehling, William W. *The Road to Disunion,* 2 Vols. New York, 1990–2007.

The South versus The South: How Anti-Confederate Southerners Shaped the Course of the Civil War. New York, 2001.

Gallagher, Gary W. *Confederate War: How Popular Will, Nationalism, and Military Strategy Could Not Stave Off Defeat.* Cambridge, MA, 1997.

Garrison, Tim Alan. *The Legal Ideology of Removal: The Southern Judiciary and the Sovereignty of Native American Nations.* Athens, GA, 2002.

Genovese, Eugene D. *The Political Economy of Slavery: Studies in the Economy and Society of the Old South.* New York, 1965.

Gerteis, Louis. *From Contraband to Freedman: Federal Policy toward Southern Blacks, 1861–1865.* Westport, CT, 1973.

Glymph, Thavolia. *Out of the House of Bondage: The Transformation of the Plantation Household.* New York, 2008.

Goldman, Robert. *A Free Ballot and a Fair Count: The Department of Justice and the Enforcement of the Voting Rights Act in the South, 1877–1893.* New York, 2001a.

  Reconstruction and Black Suffrage: Losing the Vote in Reese and Cruikshank. Lawrence, KS, 2001b.

Goodrich, Thomas. *Black Flag: Guerilla Warfare on the Western Border, 1861–1865.* Bloomington, IN, 1995.

Graber, Mark. *Dred Scott and the Problem of Constitutional Evil.* New York, 2006.

Greenwald, Emily. *Reconfiguring the Reservation: The Nez Perces, Jicarilla Apaches, and the Dawes Act.* Albuquerque, NM, 2002.

Gross, Ariela J. *Double Character: Slavery and Mastery in the Antebellum Southern Courtroom.* Princeton, NJ, 2000.

  What Blood Won't Tell: A History of Race on Trial in America. Cambridge, MA, 2008.

Grossberg, Michael. *Governing the Hearth: Law and the Family in Nineteenth-Century America.* Chapel Hill, NC, 1985.

  A Judgment for Solomon: The d'Hauteville Case and Legal Experience in Antebellum America. New York, 1996.

Hahamovitch, Cindy. *The Fruits of Their Labor: Atlantic Coast Farmworkers and the Making of Migrant Poverty, 1870–1945.* Chapel Hill, NC, 1997.

Hahn, Steven. *The Roots of Southern Populism: Yeoman Farmers and the Transformation of the Georgia Upcountry, 1850–1890.* New York, 1983.

  A Nation under Our Feet: Black Political Struggles in the Rural South from Slavery to the Great Migration. Cambridge, MA, 2003.

Hahn, Steven, Steven F. Miller, Susan E. O'Donovan, John C. Rodrigue, and Leslie S. Rowland, eds. *Freedom: A Documentary History of Emancipation, 1861–1867.* Series 3, Vol. 1: *Land and Labor, 1865.* Chapel Hill, NC, 2008.

Hall, Catherine. *White, Male, and Middle-Class: Explorations in Feminism and History.* New York, 1992.

Hall, Jacquelyn Dowd. *Revolt against Chivalry: Jessie Daniel Ames and the Women's Campaign against Lynching.* New York, 1979.

Hamburger, Phillip. "Privileges or Immunities." *Northwestern University Law Review* 105 (2011): 61–148.

Hamilton, Daniel W. *The Limits of Sovereignty: Property Confiscation in the Union and the Confederacy during the Civil War.* Chicago, 2007.

Harring, Sidney I. *Crow Dog's Case: American Indian Sovereignty, Tribal Law, and United States Law in the Nineteenth Century.* New York, 1994.

Harris, Cheryl I. "Whiteness as Property." *Harvard Law Review* 106 (1993): 1923–2015.

Harris, Leslie M. *In the Shadow of Slavery: African Americans in New York City, 1626–1863.* Chicago, 2003.

Harris, William C. *With Charity for All: Lincoln and the Restoration of the Union.* Lexington, KY, 1997.

Hartog, Hendrik. *Man and Wife in America: A History.* Cambridge, MA, 2000.

Hewitt, Nancy A. *Women's Activism and Social Change: Rochester, New York, 1822–1872.* Ithaca, NY, 1984.

Hoff, Joan. *Law, Gender, and Injustice: A Legal History of U.S. Women.* New York, 1991.

Holt, Thomas C. "'An Empire over the Mind': Emancipation, Race, and Ideology in the British West Indies and the American South." In *Region, Race, and Reconstruction: Essays in Honor of C. Vann Woodward,* edited by J. Morgan Kousser and James McPherson, 283–331. New York, 1982.

  The Problem of Freedom: Race, Labor, and Politics in Jamaica and Britain. Baltimore, MD, 1992.

Hoxie, Frederick E. *A Final Promise: The Campaign to Assimilate the Indians, 1880–1920.* Lincoln, NE, 1984.

Hyman, Harold M. *A More Perfect Union: The Impact of the Civil War and Reconstruction on the Constitution.* New York, 1973.

Hyman, Harold M. and William M. Wiecek. *Equal Justice under Law: Constitutional Development, 1835–1875.* New York, 1982.

Isenberg, Nancy. *Sex and Citizenship in Antebellum America.* Chapel Hill, NC, 1998.

Jaynes, Gerald David. *Branches without Roots: Genesis of the Black Working Class in the American South, 1862–1882.* New York, 1986.

Jeffrey, Julie Roy. *The Great Silent Army of Abolition: Ordinary Women and the Anti-Slavery Movement.* Chapel Hill, NC, 1998.

Johnson, Suzanne Stone and Robert Allison Johnson, eds. *Bitter Freedom: William Stone's Record of Service in the Freedmen's Bureau.* Columbia, SC, 2008.

Jones, Martha S. "Time, Space, and Jurisdiction in Atlantic World Slavery: The Volunbrun Household in Gradual Emancipation New York." *Law and History Review* 29 (2011): 1031–60.

"*Hughes v. Jackson*: Race and Rights beyond Dred Scott." *North Carolina Law Review* 91 (2013): 1757–83.

Josephy, Alvin M. *The Civil War in the American West*. New York, 1991.

Kaczorowski, Robert J. "Searching for the Intent of the Framers of the Fourteenth Amendment." *Connecticut Law Review* 5 (1972–3): 368–98.

The Politics of Judicial Interpretation: The Federal Courts, Department of Justice, and Civil Rights, 1866–1876. New York, 1985.

Kammen, Michael. *A Machine That Would Go of Itself: The Constitution in American Culture*. New York, 1986.

Keith, Leanna. *The Colfax Massacre: The Untold Story of Black Power, White Terror, and the Death of Reconstruction*. New York, 2008.

Kerber, Linda K. *No Constitutional Right to Be Ladies: Women and the Obligations of Citizenship*. New York, 1998.

Kessler-Harris, Alice. *In Pursuit of Equity: Women, Men, and the Quest for Economic Citizenship in 20th-Century America*. New York, 2001.

Kettner, James H. *The Development of American Citizenship, 1608–1870*. Chapel Hill, NC, 1978.

Kyvig, David E. *Explicit and Authentic Acts: Amending the U.S. Constitution, 1776–1995*. Lawrence, KS, 1996.

Labbé, Ronald M. and Jonathan Lurie. *The Slaughterhouse Cases: Regulation, Reconstruction, and the Fourteenth Amendment*. Lawrence, KS, 2003.

Lane, Charles. *The Day Freedom Died: The Colfax Massacre, the Supreme Court, and the Betrayal of Reconstruction*. New York, 2008.

Lash, Kurt T. "The Origins of the Privileges and Immunities Clause, Part 1: 'Privileges and Immunities' as an Antebellum Term of Art." *Georgetown Law Journal* 98 (2010): 1241–1302.

"The Origins of the Privileges and Immunities Clause, Part II: John Bingham and the Second Draft of the Fourteenth Amendment." *Georgetown Law Journal* 99 (2011): 329–433.

Lee, Charles Robert. *The Confederate Constitutions*. Chapel Hill, NC, 1963.

Levine, Bruce C. *Confederate Emancipation: Southern Plans to Free and Arm Slaves during the Civil War*. New York, 2006.

The Fall of the House of Dixie: The Civil War and the Social Revolution That Transformed the South. New York, 2013.

Levy, Leonard W. *The Law of the Commonwealth and Chief Justice Shaw*. Cambridge, MA, 1957.

Lichtenstein, Alex. *Twice the Work of Free Labor: The Political Economy of Convict Labor in the New South*. New York, 1996.

Litwack, Leon F. *Been in the Storm So Long: The Aftermath of Slavery*. New York, 1979.

Livesay, Harold C. *Andrew Carnegie and the Rise of Big Business*. Boston, 1975.

Lonn, Ella. *Desertion during the Civil War*. New York, 1928.

Manning, Chandra. *What This Cruel War Was Over: Soldiers, Slavery, and the Civil War*. New York, 2007.

Masur, Kate. "'A Rare Phenomenon of Philological Vegetation': The Word 'Contraband' and the Meanings of Emancipation in the United States." *Journal of American History* 93 (2007): 1050–84.

  An Example for All the Land: Emancipation and the Struggle over Equality in Washington, D.C. Chapel Hill, NC, 2010.

McCrary, Peyton. *Abraham Lincoln and Reconstruction: The Louisiana Experiment*. Princeton, NJ, 1978.

McCurry, Stephanie. *Masters of Small Worlds: Yeoman Households, Gender Relations, and the Political Culture of the Antebellum South Carolina Low Country*. New York, 1995.

  Confederate Reckonings: Power and Politics in the Civil War South. Cambridge, MA, 2010.

McPherson, James M. *Battle Cry of Freedom: The Civil War Era*. New York, 1998.

Melish, Joanne Pope. *Disowning Slavery: Gradual Emancipation and "Race" in New England, 1780–1860*. Ithaca, NY, 1998.

Mettler, Suzanne. *Dividing Citizens: Gender and Federalism in New Deal Public Policy*. Ithaca, NY, 1998.

Mihm, Stephen. *A Nation of Counterfeiters: Capitalists, Con Men, and the Making of the United States*. Cambridge, MA, 2007.

Montgomery, David. *Beyond Equality: Labor and the Radical Republicans, 1862–1872*. New York, 1967.

  Workers' Control in America: Studies in the History of Work, Technology, and Labor Struggles. New York, 1979.

Montoya, Maria. *Translating Property: The Maxwell Land Grant and the Conflict over Land in the American West, 1840–1900*. Berkeley, CA, 2002.

Moore, Albert Burton. *Conscription and Conflict in the Confederacy*. New York, 1924.

Nedelsky, Jennifer. *Private Property and the Limits of American Constitutionalism*. Chicago, 1990.

Nelson, William E. *The Fourteenth Amendment: From Political Principle to Judicial Doctrine*. Cambridge, MA, 1988.

Neely, Mark E., Jr. *The Last Best Hope of Earth: Abraham Lincoln and the Promise of America*. Cambridge, MA, 1983.

  The Fate of Liberty: Abraham Lincoln and Civil Liberties. New York, 1991.

Southern Rights: Political Prisoners and the Myth of Confederate Constitutionalism. Charlottesville, VA, 1999.

Lincoln and the Triumph of the Nation: Constitutional Conflict in the American Civil War. Chapel Hill, NC, 2011.

Newman, Louise. *White Women's Rights: The Racial Origins of Feminism in the United States.* New York, 1999.

Nicolay, John G. and John Hay, eds. *Abraham Lincoln: Complete Works, Comprising His Speeches, State Papers, and Miscellaneous Writings,* Vol. 1. New York, 1920.

Nieman, Donald G. *To Set the Law in Motion: The Freedmen's Bureau and the Legal Rights of Blacks, 1865–1868.* Millwood, NY, 1979.

Oakes, James. *Freedom National: The Destruction of Slavery in the United States.* New York, 2013.

O'Donovan, Susan E. *Becoming Free in the Cotton South.* Cambridge, MA, 2007.

Owsley, Frank L. *State Rights in the Confederacy.* Chicago, 1925.

Paludan, Phillip Shaw. *A Covenant with Death: The Constitution, Law, and Equality in the Civil War Era.* Urbana, IL, 1975.

A People's Contest: The Union and the Civil War, 1861–1865. Lawrence, KS, 1996.

Pateman, Carole. *The Sexual Contract.* Stanford, CA, 1988.

Peck, Gunther. *Reinventing Free Labor: Padrones and Immigrant Workers in the North American West, 1880–1930.* New York, 2000.

Penningroth, Dylan C. *The Claims of Kinfolk: African American Property and Community in the Nineteenth-Century South.* Chapel Hill, NC, 2003.

Potter, David M. *The Impending Crisis 1848–1861.* New York, 1976.

Quarles, Benjamin. *The Negro in the Civil War.* Boston, 1953.

Quigley, Paul. *Shifting Grounds: Nationalism and the American South, 1848–1865.* New York, 2012.

Rabinowitz, Howard N. *Race Relations in the Urban South, 1865–1890.* New York, 1978.

Rable, George C. *But There Was No Peace: The Role of Violence in the Politics of Reconstruction.* Athens, GA, 1984.

Civil Wars: Women and the Crisis of Southern Nationalism. Urbana, IL, 1989.

The Confederate Republic: A Revolution against Politics. Chapel Hill, NC, 1994.

Ramsdell, Charles W. "The Confederate Government and the Railroads." *American Historical Review* 22 (1917): 794–810.

"The Control of Manufacturing by the Confederate Government." *Mississippi Valley Historical Review* 8 (1921): 231–49.

Randall, James G. *Constitutional Problems under Lincoln.* New York, 1926.

Lincoln the President, 4 Vols. New York, 1945–55.

Ransom, Roger L. and Richard Sutch. *One Kind of Freedom: The Economic Consequences of Emancipation*. New York, 1977.

Reidy, Joseph P. *From Slavery to Agrarian Capitalism in the Cotton Plantation South: Central Georgia, 1800–1880*. Chapel Hill, NC, 1992.

Rhodes, James Ford. *History of the United States from the Compromise of 1850 to the Final Restoration of Home Rule at the South in 1877*, 7 Vols. New York, 1893–1906.

Richardson, Heather Cox. *The Greatest Nation of the Earth: Republican Economic Policies during the Civil War*. Cambridge, MA, 1997.

The Death of Reconstruction: Race, Labor, and Politics in the Post-Civil War North. Cambridge, MA, 2001.

West from Appomattox: The Reconstruction of America after the Civil War. New Haven, CT, 2007.

Ringold, May Spencer. *The Role of State Legislatures in the Confederacy*. Athens, GA, 1966.

Ritter, Gretchen. *Goldbugs and Greenbacks: The Antimonopoly Tradition and the Politics of Finance in America*. New York, 1997.

Robertson, Lindsay G. *Conquest by Law: How the Discovery of America Dispossessed Indigenous Peoples of Their Lands*. New York, 2005.

Robinson, Armstead. "Beyond the Realm of Social Consensus: New Meanings of Reconstruction for American History." *Journal of American History* 68 (1981): 276–97.

Rodrigue, John C. *Reconstruction in the Cane Fields: From Slavery to Free Labor in Louisiana's Sugar Parishes, 1862–1880*. Baton Rouge, LA, 2001.

Rose, Willie Lee. *Rehearsal for Reconstruction: The Port Royal Experiment*. New York, 1964.

Rosen, Hannah. *Terror in the Heart of Freedom: Citizenship, Sexual Violence, and the Meaning of Race in the Postemancipation South*. Chapel Hill, NC, 2009.

Ross, Michael A. "Justice Miller's Reconstruction: The Slaughter House Cases, Health Codes, and Civil Rights in New Orleans, 1861–1873." *Journal of Southern History* 64 (1998): 649–76.

Justice of Shattered Dreams: Samuel Miller Freeman and the Supreme Court during the Civil War Era. Baton Rouge, LA, 2003a.

"Obstructing Reconstruction: John Archibald Campbell and the Legal Campaign against Louisiana's Republican Government, 1868–1873." *Civil War History* 49 (2003b): 235–53.

Rubin, Anne S. *A Shattered Nation: The Rise and Fall of the Confederacy, 1861–1868*. Chapel Hill, NC, 2005.

Ryan, Mary P. *Cradle of the Middle Class: The Family in Oneida County, New York, 1790–1865*. New York, 1981.

Civic Wars: Democracy and Public Life in the American City during the Nineteenth Century. Berkeley, CA, 1997.

Samito, Christian G. *Becoming American under Fire: Irish Americans, African Americans, and the Politics of Citizenship during the Civil War Era.* Ithaca, NY, 2009.

Samito, Christian G., ed. *Changes in Law and Society during the Civil War and Reconstruction: A Legal History Documentary Reader.* Carbondale, IL, 2009.

Saville, Julie. *The Work of Reconstruction: From Slave to Wage Laborer in South Carolina, 1860–1870.* New York, 1994.

Schwalm, Leslie A. *A Hard Fight for We: Women's Transition from Slavery to Freedom in South Carolina.* Urbana, IL, 1997.

  Emancipation's Diaspora: Race and Reconstruction in the Upper Midwest. Chapel Hill, NC, 2009.

Sidali, Silvana. *From Property to Person: Slavery and the Confiscation Acts, 1861–1862.* Baton Rouge, LA, 2005.

Smith, Stacey L. *Freedom's Frontier: California and the Struggle over Unfree Labor, Emancipation, and Reconstruction.* Chapel Hill, NC, 2013.

Sommerville, Diane Miller. *Rape and Race in the Nineteenth-Century South.* Chapel Hill, NC, 2004.

Spruill, Marjorie Julian. *New Women of the New South: The Leaders of the Woman Suffrage Movement in the Southern States.* New York, 1993.

Stampp, Kenneth M. *The Era of Reconstruction, 1865–1877.* New York, 1965.

Stanley, Amy Dru. *From Bondage to Contract: Wage Labor, Marriage, and the Market in the Age of Slave Emancipation.* New York, 1998.

Steinfeld, Robert J. *The Invention of Free Labor: The Employment Relation in English and American Law and Culture, 1350–1870.* Chapel Hill, NC, 1991.

  Coercion, Contract, and Free Labor in the Nineteenth Century. New York, 2001.

Stone (Holmes), Sarah Katherine. *Brokenburn: The Journal of Kate Stone, 1861–1868,* edited by John Q. Anderson. Baton Rouge, LA, 1955.

Sutherland, Daniel. *A Savage Conflict: The Decisive Role of Guerrillas in the American Civil War.* Chapel Hill, NC, 2009.

Syrett, David. *The Civil War Confiscation Acts: Failing to Reconstruct the South.* New York, 2005.

Thomas, Emory M. *The Confederacy as a Revolutionary Experience.* Englewood Cliffs, NJ, 1970.

  The Confederate State of Richmond: A Biography of the Capital. Austin, TX, 1971.

  The Confederate Nation, 1861–1865. New York, 1979.

Tomlins, Christopher L. *Law, Labor, and Ideology in the Early American Republic.* New York, 1993.

  Freedom Bound: Law, Labor, and Civic Identity in Colonizing English America, 1580–1865. New York, 2010.

Trefousse, Hans L. *The Radical Republicans: Lincoln's Vanguard for Racial Justice.* New York, 1969.

Trelease, Allen W. *White Terror: The Ku Klux Klan Conspiracy and Southern Reconstruction.* New York, 1971.

Turner, Frederick Jackson. *The Frontier in American History.* New York, 1920.

The United States, 1830–1860: The Nation and Its Sections. New York, 1935.

Vandiver, Frank Everson. *Jefferson Davis and the Confederate State: An Inaugural Lecture Delivered before the University of Oxford on 26 February 1964.* Oxford, 1964.

Van Riper, Paul P. and Harry N. Scheiber. "The Confederate Civil Service." *Journal of Southern History* 25 (1959): 448–70.

Vorenberg, Michael. *Final Freedom: The Civil War, the Abolition of Slavery, and the Thirteenth Amendment.* New York, 2001.

Wang, Xi. *The Trial of Democracy: Black Suffrage and Northern Republicans, 1860–1910.* Athens, GA, 1997.

Wald, Priscilla. *Constituting Americans: Cultural Anxiety and Narrative Form.* Durham, NC, 1995.

Waldrep, Christopher. *Roots of Disorder: Race and Criminal Justice in the American South, 1817–80.* Urbana, IL, 1998.

Weiner, Jonathan. "AHR Forum: Class Structure and Economic Development in the American South, 1865–1955." *American Historical Review* 84 (1979): 970–1006.

Weitz, Mark A. *More Damning Than Slaughter: Desertion in the Confederate Army.* Lincoln, NE, 2005.

Welke, Barbara Young. *Recasting American Liberty: Gender, Race, Law, and the Railroad Revolution, 1865–1920.* New York, 2001.

Law and the Borders of Belonging in the Long Nineteenth Century United States. New York, 2010.

Wesley, Charles. *The Collapse of the Confederacy.* Washington, DC, 1937.

West, Elliott. *The Last Indian War: The Nez Perce Story.* New York, 2009.

White, G. Edward. "The Origins of Civil Rights in America" (April 15, 2013). *Case Western Reserve Law Review,* Forthcoming; Virginia Public Law and Legal Theory Research Paper No. 2013–03. Available at SSRN: http://ssrn.com/abstract=2251425.

White, Jonathan W. *Abraham Lincoln and Treason in the Civil War: The Trials of John Merryman.* Baton Rouge, LA, 2011.

White, Richard. *Railroaded: The Transcontinentals and the Making of Modern America.* New York, 2011.

Wiecek, William M. *The Guarantee Clause of the U.S. Constitution.* Ithaca, NY, 1972.

The Sources of Anti-Slavery Constitutionalism in America, 1760–1848. Ithaca, NY, 1977.

Williams, Heather. *Self–Taught: African American Education in Slavery and Freedom*. Chapel Hill, NC, 2005.

Williams, Lou Falkner. *The Great South Carolina Ku Klux Klan Trials, 1871–1872*. Athens, GA, 2004.

Wong, Eldie L. *Neither Fugitive nor Free: Atlantic Slavery, Freedom Suits, and the Legal Culture of Travel*. New York, 2009.

Woodman, Harold D. *New South, New Law: The Legal Foundations of Credit and Labor Relations in the Postbellum Agricultural South*. Baton Rouge, LA, 1995.

Woodward, C. Vann. *Origins of the New South, 1877–1913*. Baton Rouge, LA, 1951.

The Strange Career of Jim Crow. New York, 1955.

Yearns, Wilfred Buck. *The Confederate Congress*. Athens, GA, 1960.

Zackin, Emily. *Looking for Rights in All the Wrong Places: Why State Constitutions Contain America's Positive Rights*. Princeton, NJ, 2014.

Zagarri, Rosemary. *Revolutionary Backlash: Women and Politics in the Early American Republic*. Philadelphia, 2007.

Index

CPSIA information can be obtained
at www.ICGtesting.com
Printed in the USA
LVHW050008150120
643606LV00017B/625

9 781107 401341